InfoPath 2010 Cookbook

101 Codeless Recipes for Beginners

S.Y.M. Wong-A-Ton

InfoPath 2010 Cookbook – 101 Codeless Recipes for Beginners

Copyright © 2011 by S.Y.M. Wong-A-Ton

Cover photo by S.Y.M. Wong-A-Ton: Snow and hoar frost in Central Otago, South Island, New Zealand

For Mom

I miss you

For Mom

I miss you

Table of Contents

Introduction

What is InfoPath?

InfoPath 2010 is a desktop application that comes with the Microsoft Office Professional Plus 2010 suite of applications. When you install InfoPath 2010, two applications are installed: InfoPath Designer 2010 and InfoPath Filler 2010. InfoPath Designer 2010 is used to design InfoPath form templates, while InfoPath Filler 2010 can be used to fill out InfoPath forms.

InfoPath can be used to create electronic forms. A few examples of electronic forms are: Leave request forms, travel expense forms, purchase order forms, etc. All forms are then stored on a computer instead of in a file cabinet as would be the case with paper-based forms.

InfoPath forms are meant to replace their paper-based counterparts, and like paper-based forms:

- InfoPath forms can be stored in a repository such as for example a database or SharePoint document library instead of a file cabinet.

- InfoPath forms can go from person to person via email instead of snail mail.

- InfoPath forms can go from system to system (for example from an HR system to a storage system), and can forego manual entry or data transfer as would be the case with paper-based forms that must be entered into a system.

The main benefits of using InfoPath are:

1. Reduction of human errors. Data validation can be built into InfoPath forms, so that there is a smaller chance on human errors when forms are being filled out. In addition, if the data from forms need to be entered into a system, they need not be manually entered, which significantly reduces typos and other errors.

2. Increase in productivity. A search system can be built around electronic forms to be able to find information quicker than when using paper-based forms.

3. Easy extraction of information. InfoPath forms are XML files, which are text files, and from which data can be easily extracted and read.

4. Easy passing and sharing of data between systems. InfoPath forms are XML files for which a structure can be defined and then used as a contract between systems. Systems can then pass these XML files between each other for data processing and automation.

If you are reading this book, I assume you have already installed InfoPath and have an idea what InfoPath could potentially do for your business, so want to learn how to best use it and do not need to be convinced of its benefits.

Who should read this book?

This book was written for Microsoft Office users who want to learn to use Microsoft InfoPath Designer 2010 without first going through countless pages of reference material about InfoPath before being able to design their first InfoPath form template. While this book was written for beginners who have no prior knowledge of InfoPath, it assumes that you are familiar with one or more other Microsoft Office products (such as Word or Excel) and that you are not a complete beginner using a computer and software products.

This book was also written specifically for beginners who are not necessarily programmers. While this book contains mathematical formulas, it does not contain any code instructions.

This book follows a practical approach. Almost each chapter presents you first with a short amount of theory explaining a few key concepts and then slowly builds your InfoPath design skills with step-by-step recipes (tutorials) that follow a logical sequence and increase in complexity as you progress through the book.

Almost every recipe has a discussion section that expands on the steps outlined in the recipe, offers additional information on what you learned, or builds your knowledge and experience through additional exercises.

You will not find everything you can do with InfoPath explained in this book, because this book is not meant to be used as reference material. You must see this book as a short course; a course that will quickly get you up and running with InfoPath 2010 and teach you how to design form templates using the most often used controls in InfoPath. Its goal is to get you as a beginning InfoPath 2010 user comfortable enough to design InfoPath 2010 form templates while getting invaluable tips and tricks along the way as you learn, and enable you to explore InfoPath 2010 further on your own.

How to use this book

This book has been set up in a cookbook style with 101 recipes. Each recipe consists of 3 parts: A description of the problem, a step-by-step outline of the recipe (solution), and further discussion highlighting important parts of the recipe or expanding on what you have learned.

Chapters 1 through 4 are meant to give you a foundation for designing basic InfoPath 2010 form templates. They explain how to design form templates, work with views and formulas, and add controls and rules to controls in InfoPath. You should not skip these chapters if you are an absolute beginner with InfoPath.

Chapters 5 and 6 are required if you want to design InfoPath form templates that get data from external data sources and if you want to set up forms to be submitted to a particular destination instead of just saving forms locally on disk.

Chapters 7, 8, and 9 present over 50 step-by-step recipes for working with several of the most popular controls in InfoPath. These chapters also uncover some valuable tips and tricks, hidden secrets, and solutions you may have thought not to be possible in InfoPath without writing code.

About the author

My name is S.Y.M. Wong-A-Ton and I have been a software developer since the start of my IT career back in 1997. The first Microsoft products I used as a developer were Visual Basic 4 and SQL Server 6.5. During my IT career I have developed as well as maintained and supported all types of applications ranging from desktop applications to web sites and web services. I have been a Microsoft Certified Professional since 1998 and have held the title of Microsoft Certified Solution Developer for almost as long as I have been in IT.

I was originally trained as a Geophysicist and co-wrote (as the main author) a scientific article while I was still a scientist. This article was published in 1997 in the Geophysical Research Letters of the American Geophysical Union.

I started exploring the first version of InfoPath in 2005 in my spare time and was hooked on it from day one. What I liked most about InfoPath was the simplicity with which I was able to quickly create electronic forms that were in reality small applications on their own; all this without writing a single line of code!

While exploring InfoPath, I started actively helping other InfoPath users, who were asking questions on the Internet, to come up with innovative solutions. And because the same questions were being asked frequently, I decided to start writing tutorials and articles about InfoPath on my web site "Enterprise Solutions", which evolved into what is known today as "Biz Support Online" and can be visited at http://www.bizsupportonline.net.

Shortly after starting to share my knowledge about InfoPath with others, I received recognition from Microsoft in the form of the Microsoft Most Valuable Professional (MVP) award, and have received this award every year after then, which as of writing has been 5 years in a row.

I hope you enjoy reading this book as much as I enjoyed writing it for you. In this book, I do not hold back anything I know about InfoPath and share several tips, tricks, and secrets with you I have never shared anywhere before – not even on my own web site - so I do hope you take away a lot from this book and that it achieves its purpose of getting you up and running with InfoPath 2010.

Support

Every effort has been made to ensure the accuracy of this book. Corrections for this book are provided at http://www.bizsupportonline.com.

If you have comments, questions, suggestions, improvements, or ideas about this book, please send them to bizsupportonline@gmail.com with "InfoPath 2010 Cookbook" in the subject line.

Chapter 1: Form Template Design Basics

Form vs. form template

The terms **form** and **form template** are used interchangeably when talking about InfoPath, but there is a difference between the two that you should understand.

An InfoPath form template forms the basis for an InfoPath form. This means that an InfoPath form cannot exist without first having an InfoPath form template. You use InfoPath Designer 2010 to create InfoPath form templates.

You can see an InfoPath form template as a blueprint to create one or more InfoPath forms. Let us take building a house as an analogy. Before you can build a house, you need a blueprint and all of the materials such as blocks, cement, wood, etc. before you can start building. And once you have created a blueprint, you can build several of the same types of houses using that blueprint. And last but not least, you can put furniture in the houses, and that furniture can differ per house.

In the world of InfoPath, the form template is the blueprint which consists of building materials such as views, layout tables, controls, rules, data sources, etc. The InfoPath form is the house, and you can create several of the same types of forms (houses) using the same form template (blueprint). The data you fill out each InfoPath form with can be seen as the furniture you put in the house. InfoPath forms can be filled out using either InfoPath Filler 2010 or a browser, depending on the type of form template you create.

InfoPath form templates are published to a particular location, and once published, can be used to create InfoPath forms. InfoPath form templates have an .XSN file extension, while InfoPath forms are saved as .XML files. InfoPath forms are always internally linked to the corresponding form template from which they were created. This also means that if you publish an InfoPath form template, use it to create InfoPath forms, and then delete or move it, you will not be able to open those InfoPath forms that are based on it anymore using InfoPath or a browser, because the forms will not be able to find their corresponding form template.

Tip:

An InfoPath form cannot exist without an InfoPath form template. So never ever delete an InfoPath form template or move it once it has been published, because you will be unable to open any InfoPath forms that are based on that InfoPath form template.

When you use InfoPath Designer 2010, you use it to design InfoPath form templates and can also preview InfoPath forms with it. In preview mode InfoPath Designer 2010 becomes InfoPath Filler 2010, which is only used to fill out InfoPath forms.

The 4 most basic steps to design an InfoPath form template are:

1. Create a new form template.

2. Add views, page layouts, and layout tables to the form template.

3. Add controls to the form template.

4. Publish the form template.

In the recipes in this chapter you will explore each one of these steps.

1. Create a new form template

Problem

You have installed InfoPath Designer 2010 and want to create an InfoPath form template.

Solution

You can use one of the several default form templates provided by InfoPath 2010 to create and design an InfoPath form template.

To create a new **Blank Form** template in InfoPath 2010:

1. Open InfoPath Designer 2010.

2. Click **File ➤ New ➤ Blank Form**, and then click **Design Form**, or double-click **Blank Form**.

InfoPath creates a new form template and switches to the **Home** tab.

Discussion

When you open InfoPath Designer 2010, the first screen you are presented with is the **New** tab on the **File** tab. The **File** tab is also known as the **Backstage**.

The type of form template you choose to create depends largely on what the InfoPath form is going to be used for, where you are going to publish the InfoPath form template, and how users are going to access and fill it out.

Where filling out a form is concerned, you can create either a form that will be filled out using InfoPath Filler 2010, also known as an InfoPath Filler Form, or you can create a form that will be filled out through a browser, also known as a Web Browser Form. You must have access to a SharePoint Server for the latter type of forms.

InfoPath Filler Forms can be filled out only through InfoPath Filler 2010, while Web Browser Forms can be filled out using either a browser or InfoPath Filler 2010. If you are creating an InfoPath form template and are unsure which form template type to choose and have a SharePoint Server at your disposal, choosing a Web Browser Form will offer you more flexibility where filling out forms are concerned. The downside is that Web Browser Forms offer much less functionality than InfoPath Filler Forms, so you must assess whether you will be losing access to critical functionality (such as a few controls that are only available in InfoPath Filler Forms) before making your final decision. In any case, if you decide to first create a Web Browser Form and then later want to change this to an InfoPath Filler Form, you can always make the switch.

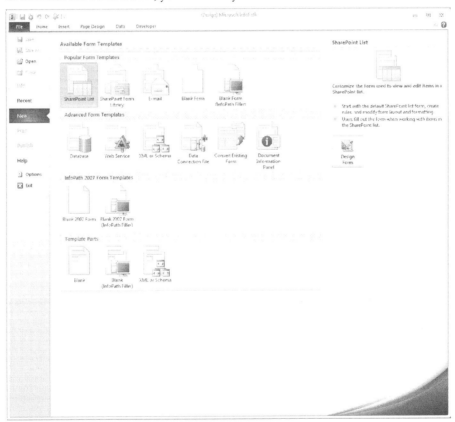

Figure 1. The File tab - also known as the Backstage - in InfoPath Designer 2010.

Throughout this book, you will be using mostly the **Blank Form** template to create form templates. The **Blank Form** template allows you to create an InfoPath form template that can be published to a SharePoint Server and create InfoPath forms that can be filled out either through a browser or Microsoft InfoPath Filler, so it results in a Web Browser Form being created.

To view the type of form template you have created, click **File ➤ Info ➤ Form Options**, and then on the **Form Options** dialog box, click **Compatibility** and look at what has been selected in the **Form type** drop-down list box.

You will see one of five values in the **Form type** drop-down list box:

1. Web Browser Form
2. InfoPath Filler Form
3. Web Browser Form (InfoPath 2007)
4. InfoPath 2007 Filler Form
5. InfoPath 2003 Filler Form

The 2003 and 2007 versions of form template types are provided so that you can create form templates that are compatible with InfoPath 2003, InfoPath 2007, and SharePoint 2007.

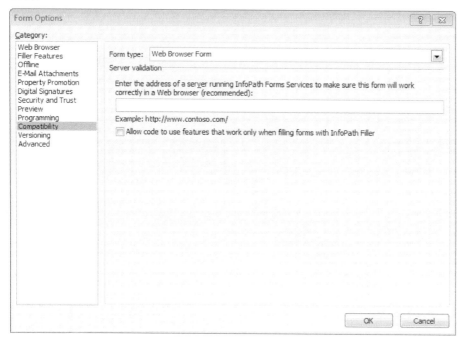

Figure 2. Compatibility category on the Form Options dialog box in InfoPath 2010.

When you click **Blank Form** under **Popular Form Templates**, you will see a brief description for the form template appear at the right-hand side of the screen and below that a **Design Form** button.

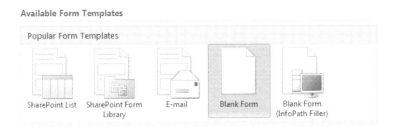

Figure 3. Blank Form template selected on the New tab in the Backstage in InfoPath Designer 2010.

The description provides guidance as to what type of form template you are about to create.

For example, the description of the **E-mail** form template says:

Design a form that can be distributed and submitted through e-mail

- *Start with a built-in layout, add controls, create rules, and apply formatting.*
- *Users will fill out and submit the form in Microsoft Outlook.*

Figure 4. Description of the Blank Form template in InfoPath 2010.

So the description tells you what the form template can be used for (Design a form that can be distributed and submitted through e-mail), how you can go about customizing it (Start with a built-in layout, add controls, create rules, and apply formatting.), and how users can access and fill out the form (Users will fill out and submit the form in Microsoft Outlook.).

Exercise

Click on each one of the available form templates on the **File ➤ New** tab and read their corresponding descriptions to familiarize yourself with the types of form templates you can create using InfoPath Designer 2010.

2. Preview an InfoPath form

Problem

You designed an InfoPath form template and want to see what forms based on this form template would look like and how they would function when you open them in InfoPath.

Solution

To see what an InfoPath form looks like at runtime and how it will work, you can preview it from within InfoPath Designer 2010.

To preview an InfoPath form:

1. In InfoPath, create a new **Blank Form** template.
2. Click **Home ➤ Preview** or press **Ctrl+Shift+B** to preview the form.

Discussion

You can also save the InfoPath form template (.XSN file) to disk and then double-click on the form template to fill out an InfoPath form (.XML file) that uses that form template.

Whether you preview a form from within InfoPath Designer 2010 or double-click a form template to open and fill out a form, in both cases, InfoPath Filler 2010 is opened and used to preview, test, or fill out the form.

If you have previously saved an InfoPath form template to disk and want to open it from disk, right-click the .XSN file, and then select **Design** from the context menu that appears. Selecting **Design** will open the form template in InfoPath Designer 2010, while selecting **Open** will open a form that is based on the form template in InfoPath Filler 2010.

Figure 5. Opening an InfoPath form template that has been saved on disk.

Exercise

When previewing a form in InfoPath Filler 2010, click on the save button and save the form locally on disk. When saving the form, you will see that you will be prompted to save the form as an **InfoPath Form (.xml)** file. Then open Notepad, select **File ➤ Open**, and browse to and open the form you just saved. Remember to select **All Files (*.*)** as the file type to open in Notepad. What you will see in Notepad is a bunch of text, which is called XML.

This proves that InfoPath forms are just XML files that contain text. You can use this technique to verify the data that is stored in your InfoPath forms.

Page layouts and layout tables

When you create a new form template in InfoPath, InfoPath automatically creates the first view, which is called the **default view**, for you and adds a standard page layout to it. To see the view InfoPath created for you, select **Page Design ➤ Views ➤ View**.

Figure 6. View drop-down list box showing default view created by InfoPath.

A view is a canvas on which you can place layout tables, text, and controls. You use views as the basis for designing your InfoPath form template.

If you do not like the standard page layout InfoPath adds when you create a **Blank Form** template, you can select it (by first clicking anywhere in the page layout table and then clicking on the small square in the upper left-hand corner of the page layout table), press **Delete** to delete it, and then add your own page layout.

Figure 7. Small square in the top left-hand corner of a page layout table in InfoPath 2010.

To add your own page layout, click **Page Design ➤ Page Layouts ➤ Page Layout Templates**, and then select one of the available page layouts from the drop-down menu.

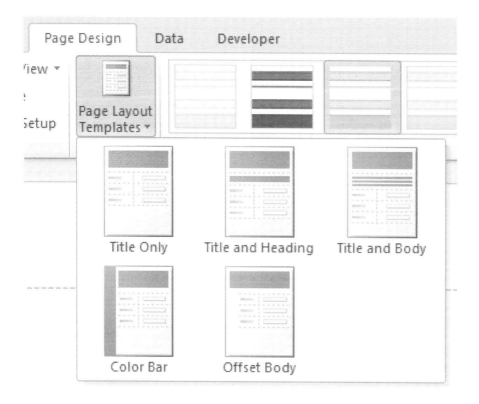

Figure 8. Page Layout Templates in InfoPath 2010.

Once you have a page layout on your view, you can refine the position of labels and controls by using layout tables. You can add a layout table with any number of rows and columns to it to layout elements on a form.

For layout tables you can choose from either predefined layout tables or custom tables.

To use one of the predefined layout tables, click on any of the layout tables on the **Insert** tab under the **Tables** group to add it to your form template.

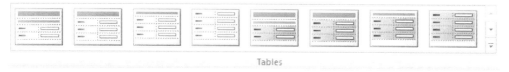

Figure 9. Predefined layout tables in InfoPath 2010.

You can expand the list of layout tables by clicking on the drop-down arrow in the bottom right-hand corner of the list.

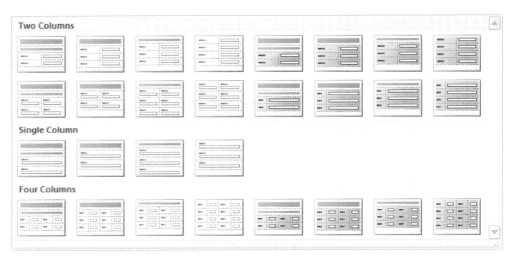

Figure 10. Expanded predefined layout tables group in InfoPath 2010.

To create a custom table you can use the **Custom Table** button on the **Insert** tab under the **Tables** group.

Figure 11. Custom Table button on the Insert tab under the Tables group.

You can add extra rows and columns to either a predefined layout table or a custom table by right-clicking in a table cell, selecting **Insert**, and then **Columns to the Left**, **Columns to the Right**, **Rows Above**, or **Rows Below** from the context menu that appears.

Themes are sets of predefined colors and fonts you can use on layout tables on your form. **Themes** are applied on a per view basis meaning that you can have two different themes applied to two different views, but all page layouts and layout tables on the same view get the same theme applied to them.

Note: Themes are not applied to custom layout tables, so if you want to make use of themes when designing an InfoPath form template, you must use the predefined layout tables and then apply the theme of your choice.

Tip:

> To take advantage of themes in InfoPath you must use the predefined layout tables that are available on the **Insert** tab under the **Tables** group.

> While the **Custom Table** option on the **Insert** tab under the **Tables** group offers flexibility when creating layout tables, it is not associated with any theme that is available on the **Page Design** tab under the **Themes** group.

The following figure shows the relationship between views, page layouts, and layout tables in InfoPath.

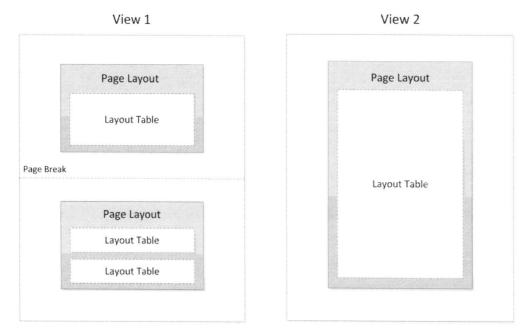

Figure 12. Relationship between Views, Page Layouts, and Layout Tables.

An InfoPath form can consist of more than one view. In the example above, the form consists of two views: View 1 and View 2.

You can place multiple page layouts on a view and a page layout can contain one or more layout tables. In the example above, View 1 consists of two page layouts, while View 2 only has one.

You can place controls and text directly on a view, within a page layout, or within a layout table.

When printing a form, a view can span multiple pages when you add page breaks between the page layouts on the view. View 1 in the example above has a page break between its two page layouts.

You can also add page breaks between views when creating views for printing purposes and for printing multiple views. You will learn more about print views later in *15 Add a print view*.

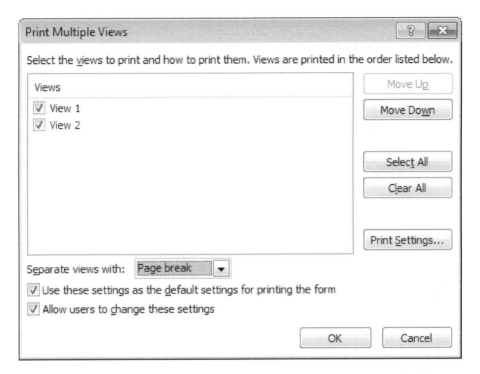

Figure 13. Separating views with page breaks when printing multiple views in InfoPath.

Note that page breaks are used only when printing forms and not when filling out forms. If you want to separate controls on multiple pages when filling out a form (either in the InfoPath Filler 2010 or a browser), you must use multiple views to do so.

Tip:

> To see what a form would look like if you printed it, you can use the **Print Preview** option, which is available via **File ➤ Print ➤ Print Preview**.

You will learn more about views in Chapter 2.

3. Align labels and controls

Problem

You have several labels and controls on an InfoPath form template and you want to align these labels and controls with each other.

Solution

You can use **Layout Tables** to organize and align labels and controls in rows and columns of tables on an InfoPath form template.

To align labels and controls:

1. Create a new **Blank Form** template. InfoPath creates a default view with a standard page layout for you.

Figure 14. Default page layout added to a new Blank Form template in InfoPath 2010.

2. You can add layout tables inside the page layout. To do this, place the cursor inside the page layout, and then on the **Insert** tab under the **Tables** group, click any of the layout tables to add one inside the standard page layout table.

3. To add extra rows and columns to the layout table, right-click in the table cell to which you want to add a neighboring column or row, select **Insert** from the context menu that appears, and then select **Columns to the Left**, **Columns to the Right**, **Rows Above**, or **Rows Below** from the context menu that appears.

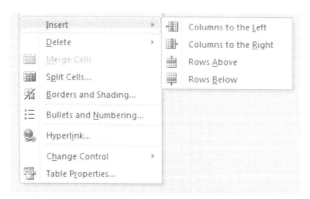

Figure 15. Insert table columns and rows context menu.

4. If you want to merge cells, select the cells you want to merge by highlighting them, right-click on the selection, and select **Merge Cells** from the context menu that appears. If you want to split a cell in columns and rows, select **Split Cells** from the context menu.

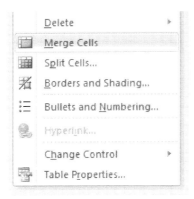

Figure 16. Merge Cells context menu item in InfoPath 2010.

5. To apply a theme to the layout table, on the **Page Design** tab under the **Themes** group, click on one of the available themes. Note: Themes cannot be applied to custom tables; only to predefined layout tables.

6. To further position content within a cell, right-click in the cell, and select **Table Properties** from the context menu that appears.

7. On the **Table Properties** dialog box, use the **Table**, **Row**, **Column**, and **Cell** tabs to further configure the layout table as you wish.

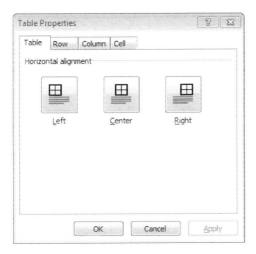

Figure 17. Table Properties dialog box in InfoPath 2010.

8. To design your form template, place controls or type text in the cells of the layout table.

Discussion

The steps outlined in the recipe above gave you a brief overview of laying out a form. For a step-by-step and concrete example of laying out controls on a form template, see *16 Print data on a print view.*

Tip:

> To quickly add a row below the last row in a layout table, you can place the cursor in the right-most cell of the last row in the table, and then press **Tab** on your keyboard to add a new row below the last row.

Controls

Controls are visual elements that allow you to interact with and enter data on an InfoPath form. InfoPath comes with three categories of controls:

1. Input controls
2. Objects
3. Containers

Input controls allow you to enter data on a form, objects allow you to interact with a form or add objects to it such as files, and containers are controls that can contain other controls.

You can open the **Controls** task pane to see the entire collection of controls that is available to you. To open the **Controls** task pane, click on the small arrow in the bottom right-hand corner of the **Controls** group on the **Home** tab.

Figure 18. Arrow in the bottom right-hand corner of Controls group to open the Controls task pane.

You can also expand the controls section on the **Home** tab by clicking on the drop-down arrow in the bottom right-hand corner of the controls list box under the **Controls** group on the **Home** tab.

The amount and type of controls you have available to you for designing your InfoPath form template depends on the type of form you are designing.

If you are designing an InfoPath form that will be filled out only through the InfoPath Filler application, then you will have more controls available to you for use than if you are designing a form that will be filled out through a browser. The reason for this is that browser forms do not support the full set of controls that is available in InfoPath.

In the following recipe, you are going to add the simplest of input controls to a form template, a text box control, and then continue to explore how to use controls in InfoPath.

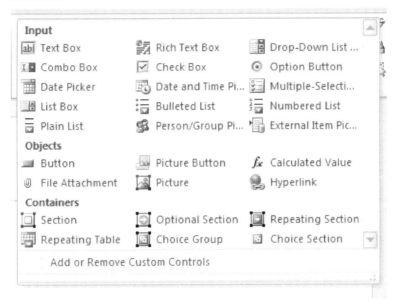

Figure 19. Expanded Controls group on the Home tab in InfoPath 2010.

4. Add a text box – method 1

Problem

You want to allow users to enter text on an InfoPath form.

Solution

You can use a text box or a rich text box control in InfoPath to allow users to enter text on an InfoPath form.

To add a text box control to an InfoPath form template:

1. Create a new **Blank Form** template.

2. Click anywhere on the form template, but preferably within a layout table or page layout, to place the cursor.

3. On the **Home** tab under the **Controls** group or on the **Controls** task pane, click **Text Box** to add a text box control to the form template.

A text box should now appear wherever you last placed the cursor on the view.

Discussion

A text box control allows users to enter a text string into a field. It is one of the most basic controls you can add to an InfoPath form template.

There are two ways you can add any control to a form template:

1. By selecting the control from the **Controls** group on the **Home** tab on the ribbon or from the **Controls** task pane. This action automatically creates a corresponding field for the control in the Main data source of the InfoPath form.

2. By first creating a field in the Main data source of a form template and then binding this field to a control on the InfoPath form.

We will get to what the *Main data source of an InfoPath form* is shortly.

A second way for adding a text box (or any other control) to an InfoPath form template is discussed in *5 Add a text box – method 2*.

The terms **fields** and **controls** are terms that are used interchangeably when talking about InfoPath, but they represent two different things.

The fact that they represent two different things becomes clear when you select a control and then look at the **Properties** group on the **Properties** tab. There you will see two buttons: **Field Properties** and **Control Properties**.

Name:	Data Type:
field1	Text (string) ▾

📝 Field Properties   📄 Control Properties

Properties

Figure 20. Field Properties and Control Properties on the Properties tab in InfoPath 2010.

An InfoPath form in its most primitive form is an XML file that contains data, and this data is stored in XML elements. The XML elements in an InfoPath form are represented by fields and groups on the **Fields** task pane in InfoPath Designer 2010.

Fields and groups define the entire structure of an InfoPath form template, and allow data to be stored within an InfoPath form according to what is called an XML schema definition.

This brings us to the definition of the Main data source of an InfoPath form: The Main data source of an InfoPath form is the collection of fields and groups that define the structure of the form and in which data for the InfoPath form is stored.

You can see what the structure of the Main data source of an InfoPath form template looks like by looking at the **Fields** task pane in InfoPath Designer 2010. If the **Fields** task pane is not already open in InfoPath, you can open it via **Data ➤ Form Data ➤ Show Fields**.

In Figure 21, the Main data source of the InfoPath form consists of one group named **myFields** and a field named **field1**. The **myFields** group is a standard root group that InfoPath automatically creates for you when you do not base your form template on a custom XML schema. **field1** exists because of the text box you previously added to the form template; more on this later.

Figure 21. Fields task pane in InfoPath Designer 2010.

Figure 22. The Show Fields button under the Form Data group on the Data tab in InfoPath 2010.

Without fields or groups in the Main data source of an InfoPath form, you cannot have data entry controls on a form, because fields allow data to be stored within an InfoPath form.

Controls, on the other hand, are visual elements that expose data that is stored in fields and groups of an InfoPath form. So controls have to be linked to fields or groups in the Main data source of a form to allow data to be stored within the form and/or to expose data that is stored within a form. The linking of a control with a field or group is called "binding". Buttons are an exception to this rule, because they do not contain any data, so you do not have to bind them to a field in the data source.

When you click on and select a control on an InfoPath form, you will see the field or group that control is bound to automatically highlight on the **Fields** task pane.

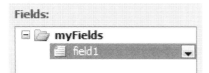

Figure 23. Highlighted field on the Fields task pane when the control is selected.

You can also see which field or group a control is bound to by looking at the binding information shown on the right-hand side of a control when you click on it to select it.

Figure 24. A Text Box control that is bound to field1.

Not every field in the Main data source needs to be bound to a control on the form. Fields can exist in the Main data source without being exposed through controls on a form. Such fields are present in the Main data source but remain hidden from users and are therefore called "hidden fields" (also see *10 Add a hidden field*). While users are unable to access hidden fields when filling out a form, such fields remain accessible through rules or code.

Technically speaking, you do not have to bind a control to a field, but practically speaking, if you do not bind a control to a field, you will not be able to store data for it in the InfoPath form. Always remember that controls function as a "gateway" to store data in the Main data source of an InfoPath form.

5. Add a text box – method 2

Problem

You want to allow users to enter text on an InfoPath form.

Solution

You can use a text box or a rich text box control in InfoPath to allow users to enter text on an InfoPath form.

To add a text box control to an InfoPath form template:

1. Create a new **Blank Form** template.

2. If the **Fields** task pane is not open, click **Data ➤ Form Data ➤ Show Fields**. This will open the **Fields** task pane.

3. On the **Fields** task pane, click the down arrow on the right-hand side of the **myFields** node and select **Add** from the drop-down menu that appears.

4. On the **Add Field or Group** dialog box, type a name for the field (for example **firstName**) in the **Name** text box, leave **Field (element)** selected in the **Type** drop-down list box, leave **Text (string)** selected in the **Data type** drop-down list box, and click **OK**.

5. Drag the field you just created from the **Fields** task pane and drop it onto the form template. InfoPath will automatically bind it to a **Text Box** control.

Discussion

As you saw in the recipe above, a field has a name, a type, and a data type. To create a text box control, you created a field that had the data type **Text (string)** and then bound it to a **Text Box** control.

It is a best practice to give fields meaningful names, such as for example, **firstName** for a text field in which a person's first name will be entered, or **isSubmitted** for a true/false (boolean) field that represents a flag that indicates whether the form has been submitted or not. Always give fields names that describe the data that is being stored in them.

You can give a field a name on one of 3 ways:

1. Via the **Fields** task pane by double-clicking on the field and then entering a name on the **Field or Group Properties** dialog box.

Figure 25. Name text box on the Field or Group Properties dialog box of a field.

2. By right-clicking the control on the form template, opening its **Properties** dialog box, and then entering a field name there.

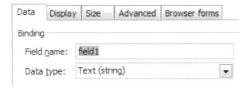

Figure 26. Field name text box on the Properties dialog box of a control.

3. By changing the **Name** field on the **Properties** tab under the **Properties** group on the ribbon after you have selected the control on the form template.

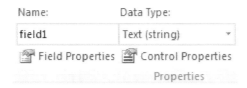

Figure 27. Name text box under the Properties group on the Properties.

The **Field (element)** field type is suitable for most fields you create unless you want to create attributes on the XML elements contained in an InfoPath form, in which case you must select the **Field (attribute)** field type.

Other field and group types that are available in InfoPath are:

- Group

- Group (choice)

- Complete XML schema or XML document

A group does not directly contain any data, but rather other groups and/or fields. Therefore, you can see a group as a container.

Note that you can make a group or field (element) repeating by selecting the **Repeating** check box on the **Add Field or Group** dialog box.

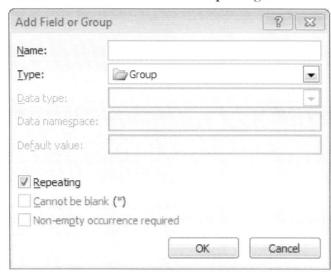

Figure 28. Repeating group settings on the Add Field or Group dialog box.

Repeating groups are used for binding to **Repeating Tables** and **Repeating Sections**. A repeating field can be used for binding to a **Multiple-Selection List Box**.

You can recognize a repeating group or field on the **Fields** task pane by the blue square with a white downwards pointing arrow that appears on the group or field.

Figure 29. Icon for a repeating group in InfoPath.

Figure 30. Icon for a repeating field in InfoPath.

Exercise

Try adding a group named **table** under the **myFields** node and then a repeating group named **row** under the **table** group, and then a text field named **column1** under the **row** repeating group. Then drag-and-drop the **row** repeating group onto the form template, and see what happens. If you have done it correctly, you would have been able to bind the **row** repeating group to a **Repeating Table**, **Repeating Section with Controls**, or **Repeating Section** control.

You can bind controls other than a **Text Box** control to a field that has the **Text (string)** data type. For example, had you right-clicked (instead of left-clicked) the **firstName** field in the **Fields** task pane and then dragged and dropped it onto the form template, InfoPath would have presented you with a context menu to choose a control from.

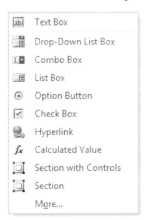

Figure 31. Control selection context menu for a Text (string) field.

You could have selected any of the controls listed in this context menu and bound that control to the **firstName** text field. As you can see, the top-most menu item is **Text Box**, which means that this is the default control that InfoPath will use to bind to the field if you do not specifically choose a control as is the case when you left-click a field on the **Fields** task pane and then drag and drop it on a form template.

Exercise

Add a second field named **lastName** under the **myFields** group. When you are on the **Add Field or Group** dialog box, take note of the rest of data types that are available in InfoPath to define fields.

The data types list consists of:

- Text (string)
- Whole Number (integer)
- Decimal (double)
- True/False (boolean)
- Hyperlink (anyURI)
- Date (date)
- Time (time)
- Date and Time (dateTime)
- Picture or File Attachment (base64)
- Rich Text (XHTML)

Exercise

Add any type of control to the form template by using the method described in *4 Add a text box – method 1*. Once added, click on the control to select it, and then look at the data type InfoPath assigned to the field in the **Data Type** drop-down list box under the **Properties** group on the **Properties** tab. Do this with as many controls as you can to familiarize yourself with the data type that can be used for each type of control.

When you dragged and dropped the field onto the InfoPath form template, a label may have automatically been added for the control. InfoPath comes preconfigured to do this.

You can turn this feature off as follows:

1. Click **File ➤ Options**.
2. On the **InfoPath Options** dialog box on the **General** tab, click **More Options**.

3. On the **Options** dialog box, click the **Design** tab.

4. On the **Design** tab, deselect the **Create labels for controls automatically** check box.

If you prefer InfoPath to automatically create labels for you every time you add a field to a form template, you can leave this feature turned on, of course.

Exercise

Click around on the **Options** dialog box to see what other options you can configure in InfoPath.

You may have also noticed that when you add any control to the form template, InfoPath automatically creates a corresponding field or group for it on the **Fields** task pane.

You can turn this feature off as follows:

1. Open the **Controls** task pane (see Figure 18).

2. At the bottom of the **Controls** task pane, deselect the **Automatically create data source** check box.

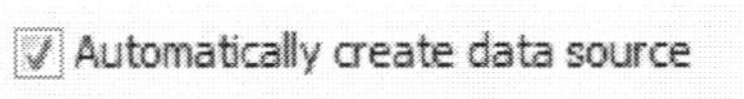

Figure 32. Check box on the Controls task pane to automatically create fields for controls.

I recommend that you leave this option turned on until you are a bit more advanced and know what type of field or group is required in the Main data source for binding to a particular type of control.

6. Delete a control

Problem

You have a text box control on an InfoPath form and want to delete it.

Solution

You can delete the control by selecting it and pressing the **Delete** key on your keyboard. Deleting a control from an InfoPath form template does not automatically also delete the field that it is bound to in the Main data source.

To delete the field that is bound to a control:

1. On the **Fields** task pane, select the field you want to delete, click the down arrow on the right-hand side of the field, and select **Delete** from the drop-down menu that appears.

2. On the **Delete Field or Group** message box, click **Yes** to confirm the deletion of the field.

3. If you have not already deleted the control that is bound to the field, select it on the InfoPath form template, and press the **Delete** key on your keyboard, otherwise the control will remain unbound.

Discussion

As mentioned in the recipe above, deleting a control from an InfoPath form template does not automatically also delete the field bound to the control. This is also why you can delete a control (the visual part of data storage) in InfoPath, and still be able to save data in the Main data source of the form, because the field is still present in the Main data source of the InfoPath form.

Remember, fields are the most basic components of an InfoPath form template. They contain all of the form's data. Controls are just visual elements that expose the data stored in fields.

Tip:

> When cleaning up an InfoPath form template and you are deleting controls from it, always remember to also delete the field that the control is bound to if you do not need the field anymore, otherwise the field will remain present in the Main data source of the form and unnecessarily take up space or if you have added rules to it, cause unexpected or unwanted behavior in your form.

7. Bind a control to a different field

Problem

You have deleted a field that was previously bound to a text box control on an InfoPath form. This action left the text box control unbound, so you want to bind the text box control to another field in the Main data source of the form.

Solution

You can use the **Change Binding** option to change the binding of a control.

To unbind a control from a field:

1. In InfoPath, create a new **Blank Form** template.

2. Add a **Text Box** control to the form template. This action will automatically create a field named **field1** on the **Fields** task pane if you did not turn off the **Automatically create data source** option on the **Controls** task pane (see *5 Add a text box – method 2*).

3. On the **Fields** task pane, click the down arrow at the right-hand side of the field (**field1**), and select **Delete** from the drop-down menu that appears.

4. Hover over the text box control on the form to verify that it is an unbound control. The text "Unbound (control cannot store data)" should appear.

To bind a control to a different field:

1. On the **Fields** task pane, click the down arrow on the **myFields** node and select **Add** from the drop-down menu.

2. On the **Add Field or Group** dialog box, type a name for the field (for example **firstName**) in the **Name** text box, leave **Field (element)** selected in the **Type** drop-down list box, leave **Text (string)** selected in the **Data type** drop-down list box, and click **OK**.

3. Click the unbound text box control to select it, and then click **Properties ➤ Properties ➤ Change Binding**.

4. On the **Text Box Binding** dialog box, ensure **Main** is selected in the **Data source** drop-down list box, select the **firstName** field, and click **OK**.

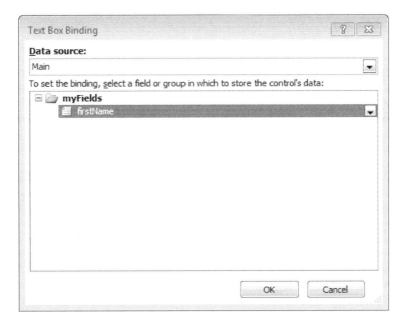

Figure 33. Text Box Binding dialog box in InfoPath 2010.

5. When you select the text box, the **firstName** field should now appear as the field the text box is bound to.

Figure 34. Text Box control bound to the firstName field.

Discussion

When a control on an InfoPath form is unbound, you will see the info text "Unbound (Control cannot store data)" appear when you hover over the control.

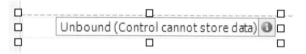

Figure 35. Info text for a control that is not bound to a field in the data source.

An unbound control exists on an InfoPath form, but is unable to store data in the Main data source of the form. You can see an unbound control as a "dummy" control, that is, it does not do anything.

Setting control and field properties

Once you have added controls to a form template, you can set the values of properties on the controls to control how they behave. For example, you can change a text box from accepting only one line of text to accepting multiple lines of text.

Not all controls support the same types of properties. The supported properties on controls may differ between the types of controls.

8. Make a text box multi-line

Problem

You have a text box on an InfoPath form and want the text box to be able to accept multiple lines of text.

Solution

You can set the **Multi-line** property on the text box to make it accept multiple lines of text.

To make a text box accept multiple lines of text:

1. In InfoPath, create a new **Blank Form** template.

2. Add a **Text Box** control to the form template.

3. Right-click the **Text Box** control, and select **Text Box Properties** from the context menu that appears.

4. On the **Text Box Properties** dialog box, click the **Display** tab.

5. On the **Text Box Properties** dialog box on the **Display** tab under **Options**, select the **Multi-line** check box, and click **OK**.

6. Preview the form

When the form opens, type a text string in the text box and press **ENTER** to add a new line. You should be able to type multiple lines of text in the text box.

Discussion

You can set properties on all controls in InfoPath. You can access the **Properties** dialog box of a control in one of two ways:

1. Via the **Properties** tab under the **Control Tools** tab. These tabs appear when you select a control on the form template. Click **Properties** ➤ **Properties** ➤ **Control Properties** to access the **Properties** dialog box for the selected control.

Figure 36. Properties tab in InfoPath Designer 2010.

2. Via the context menu of a control. This menu appears when you right-click a control. You can then select the **Properties** menu item to open the **Properties** dialog box for the selected control.

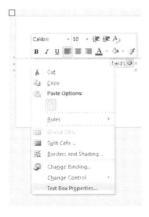

Figure 37. Context menu on a Text Box control in InfoPath 2010.

27

The settings that are available on the **Properties** dialog box differ per control. For example, while a text box control might have a **Read-only** property, a drop-down list box control does not have one.

In addition, the tabs that are available on the **Properties** dialog box also differ per control. For example, while the **Properties** dialog box of a text box control might have a **Display** tab, the **Properties** dialog box of a drop-down list box control does not have one.

Exercise

Take a moment to add a few controls to the form template, open up the **Properties** dialog box for each control, and study which settings are available on the tab pages of the **Properties** dialog box for each control.

9. Make a field required

Problem

You have a text box control on an InfoPath form, which you want to force users to always fill out.

Solution

If you require a user to always enter data in a particular control, you can make the field that is bound to the control required.

To make a field required:

1. In InfoPath, create a new **Blank Form** template.

2. Add a **Text Box** or any other type of control that can contain data to the form template.

3. On the **Properties** tab under the **Modify** group, click the **Cannot Be Blank** check box. Alternatively, you can click **Properties ➤ Properties ➤ Field Properties** or **Properties ➤ Properties ➤ Control Properties**, and select the **Cannot be blank** check box on the **Data** tab of the control or field **Properties** dialog box.

4. Preview the form.

When you open the form, you will see a red asterisk on the control that requires data to be entered, and when you hover over the control the tooltip "Cannot be blank" will appear.

Discussion

When you select the **Cannot be blank** check box, you will see a red asterisk appear behind the field name on the **Fields** task pane as an indication that the field must be filled out.

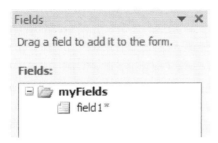

Figure 38. Red asterisk behind a required field on the Fields task pane in InfoPath 2010.

The method described in the recipe above should be your preferred method for making fields required in InfoPath, unless you need to make a field required only when a certain condition is met, in which case you can use a data validation rule (see *28 Make a field required based on a condition*).

Tip:

> If you are suddenly getting validation errors on an InfoPath form template you or someone else designed, always check the **Fields** task pane for the red asterisks that indicate required fields. Because hidden fields (see *10 Add a hidden field*) can be made required, this may result in unexpected validation errors.

10. Add a hidden field

Problem

You have a field on an InfoPath form which you want to hide from users.

Solution

You can add a field to the Main data source of an InfoPath form without binding the field to a control. This will make the field hidden.

A second way of making a field hidden is by adding a control to a form template – this step will automatically create a corresponding field in the Main data source of the form, and then delete the control from the form template. The latter will not delete the field from the Main data source, so the field will effectively be hidden.

Method 1: To create a hidden field in InfoPath:

1. In InfoPath, create a new **Blank Form** template.

2. On the **Fields** task pane, right-click the **myFields** group, and select **Add** from the drop-down menu.

3. On the **Add Field or Group** dialog box, enter a name for the field, select the desired **Data type**, enter a **Default value** if necessary, and then click **OK**.

Method 2: To create a hidden field in InfoPath:

1. In InfoPath, create a new **Blank Form** template.

2. Add a **Text Box** control or any other type of control that has the data type you want the hidden field to have, to the form template. This step will automatically add a field to the Main data source of the InfoPath form if you did not turn off the **Automatically create data source** option on the **Controls** task pane (see *5 Add a text box – method 2*).

3. Delete the control you just added from the form template. This action will delete the control, but not the field bound to the control from the Main data source, so will make the field hidden.

Discussion

Hidden fields are useful for storing data you do not want a user to see, but that you want to use to be able to manipulate the behavior of a form.

For example, if you want a user to be able to fill out a text box when she first opens the form, but not be able to modify the text anymore once she has submitted the form, you could add a hidden field to the form template to keep track of when the form has been submitted and then use the value of the hidden field to conditionally disable the text box when the user opens the submitted form (see for example *41 Switch to read-only view when form opens after submit*).

Tip:

> Never make a hidden field required. Because a user cannot access a hidden field through InfoPath Filler 2010 or a browser, she will not be able to set the value of a required hidden field unless you create a rule that sets the value of this field for her.

Saving and publishing

Technically speaking, once you have designed a form template and saved it on disk, it is ready to be used to create forms from it, that is, if you are the only one who is going to be using it from your own computer. This is called saving a form template.

If you want to allow other users to access and use your form template so that they too can create forms based on it, you must publish the form template to a publicly accessible location. This is called publishing a form template.

When you publish a form template to a particular location, the published location is saved in all InfoPath forms (at the top of the file in what is called an XML Processing Instruction) that are based on that form template. You can find this publish location by opening a saved InfoPath form (XML file) in Notepad and looking at the text at the top of the file. The text for the XML Processing Instruction might look something like the following:

```
<?mso-infoPathSolution solutionVersion="1.0.0.6" productVersion="14.0.0"
PIVersion="1.0.0.0"
href="file:///C:\InfoPath\Published\PublishedFormTemplate.xsn"
name="urn:schemas-microsoft-com:office:infopath:PublishedFormTemplate:-myXSD-
2010-12-08T19-48-59" ?>
```

Every time a user opens a previously saved InfoPath form that is based on the published form template, the form will look for its corresponding form template at the published location it has stored in its XML Processing Instruction. The **href** attribute in the XML Processing Instruction shown above points to the location where the InfoPath form will be looking for the form template that was used to create it.

If the form template has been moved or deleted from the published location, the form will not be able to find the form template, so will not be able to be opened using InfoPath Filler 2010 or a browser. However, you can still open the InfoPath form in Notepad as described in the exercise in *2 Preview an InfoPath form*.

InfoPath Designer 2010 offers several locations you can publish a form template to, so that it can be shared among users. Two of the most popular locations are network location and SharePoint Server. The following recipe explains how to publish a form template to a network location.

11. Publish an InfoPath form template

Problem

You have designed an InfoPath form template and want to publish the form template so that other users on your network can use it to create forms.

Solution

To publish an InfoPath form template to a network location:

1. In InfoPath, create a new **Blank Form** template or use an already designed form template.

2. Click **File ➤ Publish ➤ Network Location**.

3. If you have not already saved the form template, InfoPath will prompt you to save it. When a message box to save the form template appears, click **OK**, and then on the **Save As** dialog box, browse to a location, enter a name for the form template, and click **Save**. The **Publishing Wizard** should then appear in InfoPath.

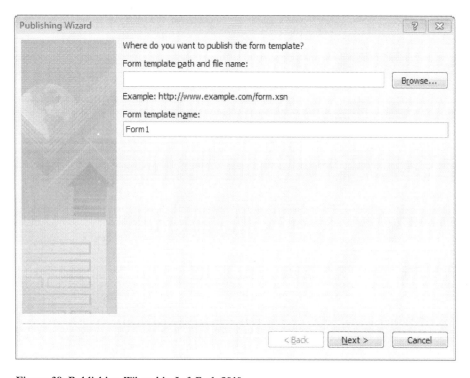

Figure 39. Publishing Wizard in InfoPath 2010.

4. On the **Publishing Wizard**, browse to and select a network location where you want to publish the form template, type in a new name for the form template in the **Form template name** text box if you wish, and click **Next**.

5. On the **Publishing Wizard**, you have the option to alter the location you entered in the previous step if all users who intend to fill out InfoPath forms are unable to access the location you specified. You have the option to specify a public URL or full network path. Specify a network path you have full access to, and then click **Next**.

6. On the **Publishing Wizard**, click **Publish**.

7. On the **Publishing Wizard**, you can select the **Send the form to e-mail recipients** or **Open this form template from the published location** check boxes if you wish before you click **Close**. The first option will send the form in

an email to a list of email addresses you specify, and the second option will open the form in InfoPath Filler 2010.

Users should now be able to go to the network location where you published the form template and double-click on it to fill out an InfoPath form using InfoPath Filler 2010.

Discussion

If you do not have access to a SharePoint Server, but still want users in your organization to be able to share and fill out forms, you can publish your InfoPath form template to a location on the network or file share that is accessible by all users who need to fill out forms.

While publishing to a network location allows for sharing, users will have to have InfoPath Filler 2010 installed on their computers to be able to fill out forms. Filling out forms through a browser is only possible if you have a SharePoint Server with InfoPath Forms Services installed on it available.

InfoPath 2010 remembers where a previously published form template was published. Therefore, if you change a previously published form template and want to republish it, you can click **File ➤ Publish ➤ Quick Publish**, press **Ctrl+Shift+Q** on your keyboard, or click the small **Quick Publish** button on the Quick Access toolbar in InfoPath Designer 2010.

Figure 40. Quick Publish button in InfoPath Designer 2010.

If you want to change a previously saved publish location to a new publish location, click **File ➤ Publish ➤ Network Location**, and republish the form template using the new publish location. The next time you use the **Quick Publish** button, InfoPath will publish the form template to the new publish location you specified.

Exercise

Explore and read the descriptions of the publishing options that are available to you on the **Publish** tab in the **Backstage** to familiarize yourself with them.

Chapter 2: Working with Views

What are views?

A view is a canvas on which you can place layout tables, text, and controls. You use views as the basis for designing an InfoPath form.

An InfoPath form can have one or more views. A default view in InfoPath is the first view that is shown when a form opens; the startup view. When you create a new form template, at least one view is added to it, and this view is automatically made the default view.

There can only be one default view at a time in an InfoPath form, but if you have multiple views in a form template, you can make another view the default view (see *13 Make a view the default view*). You can see which view is the default view by the additional piece of text **(default)** that is placed behind its name in the **View** drop-down under the **Views** group on the **Page Design** tab.

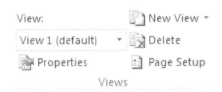

Figure 41. Default view as shown on the Page Design tab in InfoPath 2010.

When you create a new form template in InfoPath, InfoPath automatically creates the first view (default view) for you. Because a form template must always have at least one view, InfoPath will automatically create a new (default) view for you if you delete the last view in the form template.

12.   Add a second view to a form template

Problem

You have a form template that has one view and you want to add a second view to the form template.

Solution

You can use the **Page Design** tab to add a second view to an InfoPath form template.

To add a second view to a form template:

1. In InfoPath, create a new **Blank Form** template. InfoPath automatically creates a view named **View 1** and makes it the default view.

2. Click **Page Design ➤ Views ➤ New View** to open the **Add View** dialog box to add a second view to the form template.

3. On the **Add View** dialog box in the **New view name** text box, type a name for the view (for example **View 2**), and click **OK**.

View 2 should now appear as the current view in the **View** drop-down list box under the **Views** group on the **Page Design** tab.

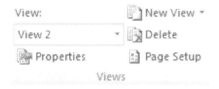

Figure 42. A second view (View 2) as the currently selected view on the Page Design tab in InfoPath.

To switch back to View 1 and make it the current view, select **Page Design ➤ Views ➤ View ➤ View 1 (default)**.

Discussion

Being able to add additional views to an InfoPath form template is an important action, because multiple views allow you to represent the same data in a form in different ways.

Remember we talked about the fact that the data of an InfoPath form resides in fields in the Main data source and that you use controls to visually expose this data? You can add to this that you can not only use controls to visually expose the data, but also place controls on different views to create different representations of the same data. Basically, you can have multiple controls pointing to the same field in the Main data source of a form to visually display the data in different ways.

For example, you can have a default view where a user can enter data, and when the user clicks a button, you switch to a second view and present the user with a read-only summary of the data she just entered. The second view would be called a read-only view (see *14 Add a read-only view*).

You can also use multiple views to split very large forms into smaller, more palatable chunks of data to make the form easier for users to fill out. And with this concept, you can even use views to create wizard-like forms if you wish.

And finally, you can add additional views to a form template to create views that can be used specifically for printing a form (see *15 Add a print view*). Here again you would be "creating a different representation of the same data" in a form.

In the recipe above, you saw how to use the **View** drop-down list box on the **Page Design** tab to switch between views at design time; so when you are designing an InfoPath form template in InfoPath Designer 2010. You also have the ability to switch between views during runtime; so when you are filling out a form either in InfoPath Filler 2010 or a browser.

If you preview a form that has two views as in the recipe above, you can use the **Current View** drop-down on the **Home** tab under the **Page Views** group to switch between **View 1** and **View 2**.

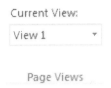

Figure 43. Current View drop-down list box on the Home tab in InfoPath Filler 2010.

If you do not want users to be able to use the **Current View** drop-down list box to switch between views, you can remove this option through the properties of the view.

To remove a view from the **Current View** drop-down list box in InfoPath Filler 2010 or a browser:

1.   In InfoPath Designer 2010, select the name of the view you want to remove in the **Page Design ➤ Views ➤ Current View** drop-down list box.

2.   Click **Page Design ➤ Views ➤ Properties**.

3.   On the **View Properties** dialog box on the **General** tab, deselect the **Show on the View menu when filling out this form** check box, and click **OK**.

Note: If your form template has two views and you remove one of them from the view menu, the **Current View** drop-down list box will not be shown. The **Current View** drop-down list box only appears if there is more than one view available to switch between in an InfoPath form.

You can delete a view in InfoPath Designer 2010 by first selecting the view from the **View** drop-down list box on the **Page Design** tab, and then clicking **Page Design ➤ Views ➤ Delete**.

13.   Make a view the default view

Problem

You have an InfoPath form template that has two views, View 1 and View 2, where View 1 is the default view. You want to make View 2 the default view.

Solution

If you have multiple views in an InfoPath form, you can change the properties of one of the non-default views to make it the default view.

To make a non-default view the default view:

1. In InfoPath, create a new **Blank Form** template.

2. Add a view named **View 2** to the form template (see *12 Add a second view to a form template*).

3. Select **Page Design ➤ Views ➤ View ➤ View 2**. Note: A view automatically becomes the currently selected view immediately after you add it to the form template.

4. Click **Page Design ➤ Views ➤ Properties** to open the **View Properties** dialog box.

5. On the **View Properties** dialog box on the **General** tab, select the **Set as default view** check box, and click **OK**. The text **(default)** should now appear behind the **View 2** item in the **View** drop-down list box on the **Page Design** tab under the **Views** group, and should be gone from behind the **View 1** item in the **View** drop-down list box.

6. Preview the form.

The form should open with **View 2** as the first view being displayed.

Note: When previewing a form in InfoPath Designer 2010, InfoPath always starts up with the view that was last selected in the **View** drop-down list box on the **Page Design** tab under the **Views** group in design mode. So if you last selected **View 1** and then preview the form, **View 1** will be shown as the startup view and not **View 2**, even if **View 2** is the default view.

To properly test the InfoPath form, save the form template to disk, and then open a new form by double-clicking the XSN file. This will open InfoPath Filler 2010 and display the correct default view you previously set.

Exercise

Open the **View Properties** dialog box of any view and on the **General** tab explore what you can configure on a view.

Read-only views

Read-only views are views that make all of the controls, except for button controls, you place on the view, read-only. If you want to disable a button on a read-only view, you must either not put the button on the view (because it is not going to be used anyway) or use conditional formatting to disable it (see *26 Disable a button on a read-only view*).

A read-only view is appropriate to use when you want to make all of the controls on a view read-only and also when controls do not offer a way to make them read-only.

If you want to have a mixture of read-only and non-read-only controls on a view, it is best not to make a view read-only, but to make the controls themselves read-only on an individual basis, unless you have a large amount of controls, in which case you may want to split the controls up and place a few on read-only and others on non-read-only views.

14.   Add a read-only view

Problem

You have an InfoPath form with a default view that is not read-only, and you want to create a second view to place fields on to make all of those fields read-only.

Solution

You can create a read-only view by setting the **Read-only** property on the view to true.

To add a read-only view to an InfoPath form:

1.   In InfoPath, create a new **Blank Form** template.

2.   Add any controls of your choice to the default view (**View 1**).

3.   Click **Page Design ➤ Views ➤ New View**.

4.   On the **Add View** dialog box, type a name in the text box (for example, **Read-Only View**), and click **OK**. InfoPath creates the view and switches to it. You can see which view is currently being displayed on the canvas in InfoPath by looking at the **View** drop-down list box under the **Views** group on the **Page Design** tab.

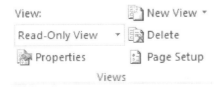

Figure 44. Views group on the Page Design tab in InfoPath 2010.

5. Click **Page Design** ➤ **Views** ➤ **Properties** to open the **View Properties** dialog box.

6. On the **View Properties** dialog box on the **General** tab under **View settings**, select the **Read-only** check box, and click **OK**.

7. Drag-and-drop existing fields (fields that you already placed on **View 1**) from the **Fields** task pane to the read-only view to create read-only controls.

8. Preview the form.

Now when you open the InfoPath form, if View 1 is not the view that comes up first (this depends on which view you had selected last in InfoPath Designer 2010), use the **Current View** drop-down list box on the **Home** tab to switch to View 1. Enter data into the controls on View 1, and then use the **Current View** drop-down list box to switch to the read-only view. On the read-only view, verify that the controls you placed on it have indeed been made read-only, that is, ensure that you cannot enter or change data that has been entered via View 1 in the fields bound to those controls.

Tip:

> If you want to have two views that look the same, but one is read-only and the other one is not, you can add a read-only view, then go to the non-read-only view, select all of the controls on the view by pressing **Ctrl+A**, press **Ctrl+C** to copy all of the controls, switch back to the read-only view, and then press **Ctrl+V** to paste the controls on the read-only view.

Print views

A print view is a view that allows you to create a visual design that can be used specifically for printing data stored in a form.

You can create a print view and designate it as the print view for one or more views that are used for filling out the form. If you do this, the print view will replace the non-print views when you print the form.

For example, if you have two views in a form, View 1 and View 2, and you have designated View 2 to be the print view for View 1, then View 1 will be replaced by View 2 when you print the form. So while users will have access to View 1 when they are filling out the form, they will only see View 2 when they print the form.

15.   Add a print view

Problem

You have several fields on an InfoPath form, but only want a selected few of those fields to appear on a separate view that you can use to print the form.

Solution

You can create a print view for the data in fields that you want to have printed on a form.

To add a print view to an InfoPath form template:

1. In InfoPath, create a new **Blank Form** template.

2. Click **Page Design** ➤ **Views** ➤ **New View**.

3. On the **Add View** dialog box, type a name in the text box (for example, **Print View**), and click **OK**.

4. Typically, a print view is not meant to be selected by a user, so you may want to remove it from the **View** menu. To do this, click **Page Design** ➤ **Views** ➤ **Properties**, and then on the **View Properties** dialog box, deselect the **Show on the View menu when filling out this form** check box.

5. Add any fields for which you want to print their data on the print view.

6. Select **Page Design** ➤ **Views** ➤ **View** ➤ **View 1 (default)**.

7. Click **Page Design** ➤ **Views** ➤ **Properties**.

8. On the **View Properties** dialog box, click the **Print Settings** tab.

9. On the **View Properties** dialog box on the **Print Settings** tab under the **Designate print view** section, select the print view you just created from the drop-down list box.

10. Repeat steps 6 through 9 for all of the views for which you want the print view to be used as the view for printing that view.

11. Ensure that **View 1 (default)** has been selected as the current view in the **Page Design** ➤ **Views** ➤ **View** drop-down list box and then preview the form.

When the form opens, click **File** ➤ **Print** ➤ **Print Preview**. The view that appears should be the print view you created.

Discussion

InfoPath allows you to print more than one view when printing a form. You can set up which views should be printed by clicking the **Print Multiple Views** button on the **Print Settings** tab on the **View Properties** dialog box, and then selecting and configuring the views to print.

Figure 45. Print Multiple Views button on the Print Settings tab on the View Properties dialog box.

Figure 46. Print Multiple Views dialog box in InfoPath 2010.

Tip:

When creating a print view, you can bind text fields to **Calculated Value** controls instead of **Text Box** controls or **Drop-Down List Box** controls or any other type of controls that has a border and stores just one value. Using a **Calculated Value** control will prevent an unwanted border from appearing around the data stored in the field bound to the control. You could also remove borders from a control through the **Borders and Shading** option on a control.

Take a moment to experiment with different settings on the **Print Settings** tab of the **View Properties** dialog box and on the **Print Multiple Views** dialog box, and then use the **Print Preview** option to see how the form would be printed.

16. Print data on a print view by overlaying text on an image

Problem

You have an InfoPath form with a text box and date picker control on it, and you want to be able to print out the name and date on a "Certificate of Completion" image when you print the form.

Solution

You can create a print view for the form that has an image of the "Certificate of Completion" as its background, and then use page layout and layout tables to position controls that are bound to the same fields as the controls on the default view.

To print data on a print view by overlaying text on an image:

1. In InfoPath, create a new **Blank Form** template.

2. Add a **Text Box** and **Date Picker** control to the form template. Name the text box **fullName** and the date picker **completionDate**.

3. Add a print view to the form template (see *15 Add a print view*), name it **Print View**, and set it as the print view for the default view (**View 1**). Remember to deselect the **Show on the View menu when filling out this form** check box on the **View Properties** dialog box, because you don't want the user to have access to this view unless she is printing the form.

4. Select **Page Design ➤ Views ➤ View ➤ Print View**, and then click **Page Design ➤ Views ➤ Properties**.

5. On the **View Properties** dialog box on the **General** tab under the **Background** section, click **Browse** to browse to and select the image that you want to use as the background image for the view.

6. On the **View Properties** dialog box on the **General** tab under the **Background** section, select **Upper Left** from the **Position** drop-down list box, and click **OK**. This will place the image in the upper left-hand corner of the view. The form template will now resemble the following figure.

Figure 47. Page layout on top of background image on the print view.

From the image above, you can see that the page layout table is centered on the design canvas for the view, so you must change its position to align it with the background image and also make the background of the page layout transparent.

7. Click anywhere inside the page layout, then right-click the small square in the upper left-hand corner of the page layout table and select **Borders and Shading** from the context menu.

8. On the **Borders and Shading** dialog box on the **Borders** tab, click **None** under the **Presets** section to remove all borders.

Figure 48. Presets section on the Border tab on the Borders and Shading dialog box.

9. On the **Borders and Shading** dialog box, click the **Shading** tab, select **No color**, and click **OK**.

10. Click anywhere inside the page layout, then right-click the small square in the upper left-hand corner of the page layout table and select **Table Properties** from the context menu.

11. On the **Table Properties** dialog box on the **Table** tab under the **Horizontal alignment** section, click **Left,** and then click **OK**.

Figure 49. Horizontal alignment section on the Table Properties dialog box.

12. Resize the page layout table so that it covers the background image by hovering over either the right or bottom border, clicking and holding the mouse button down when the resize arrows appear, and then moving the mouse to make the table larger or smaller. The results are shown in the following figure. Please note that the borders of the table have been made visible for clarity.

Figure 50. Transparent and resized page layout table on background image of print view.

13. Now you must divide the bottom cell of the layout table to be able to perfectly align the controls you will place later on the form template. To split the bottom cell of the page layout table in 4 rows and 2 columns, right-click inside the bottom cell, select **Split Cells** from the context menu, and then on the **Split Cells** dialog box, type **2** for **Number of columns** and **4** for **Number of rows**, and click **OK**.

14. Resize the rows and columns you just added. The results are shown in the following figure. Please note that the borders of the table have been made visible for clarity.

Figure 51. Page layout table with split cells.

15. Right-click the **fullName** field in the **Fields** task pane, drag it to the form template, drop it in row number 2 and column number 2 of the page layout table, and select **Calculated Value** from the context menu when you drop it.

    A calculated value control does not have borders by default, so it is ideal to be used to display labels or text that does not need to be edited (read-only text), but just printed as is the case with print views.

16. Select **Home ➤ Format Text ➤ Arial Narrow** (or any other font you want to use) as the font and select **Home ➤ Format Text ➤ 18** as the font size.

17. Right-click the calculated value control you just added and select **Calculated Value Properties** from the context menu.

18. On the **Calculated Value Properties** dialog box, click the **Size** tab, and type **0** for the **Top, Bottom, Left**, and **Right** paddings, type **20** for the **Top** and **Left** margins, type **0** for the **Bottom** and **Right** margins, and click **OK**.

    If you look closely at the canvas, the layout table does not start in the top left corner of the canvas in InfoPath Designer 2010 while there are no margins or paddings set on the page layout table. This is a visual design error that you must correct when printing. The background image however is placed nicely in the top left corner.

The page layout table has an offset of approximately 20 pixels from the top and left border of the canvas. When you print the form, this offset must be maintained for perfect alignment with the background image, which is why you must set this offset on the top and left margins of the controls.

19. Repeat steps 15 through 18 for the **completionDate** field, but place the field in row number 4 and column number 2, and make the font size **16** instead of **18**. The completed form should resemble the following figure. Please note that the borders of the table have been made visible for clarity.

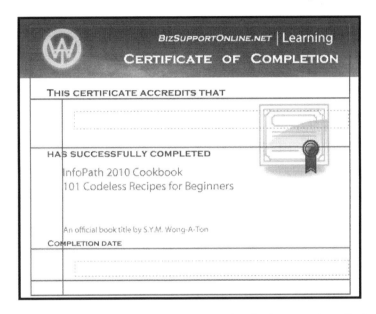

Figure 52. Completed print view with calculated value controls to display data.

20. Right-click the **completionDate** calculated value control and select **Calculated Value Properties** from the context menu.

21. On the **Calculated Value Properties** dialog box on the **General** tab under the **Result** section, click **Format**.

22. On the **Date Format** dialog box, select your preferred date format (for example **14 March 2001**), and click **OK**.

23. On the **Calculated Value Properties** dialog box, click **OK**.

24. Ensure that **View 1 (default)** is the currently selected view in the **View** drop-down list box on the **Page Design** tab, and then preview the form.

When the form opens, fill out the **fullName** and **completionDate** fields, and then press **Alt+F, V** to display the print preview dialog box or click **File ➤ Print ➤ Print Preview**.

InfoPath should automatically use the print view you created for printing View 1 (because you set it to do this in step 3), and the print preview dialog box should resemble the following figure.

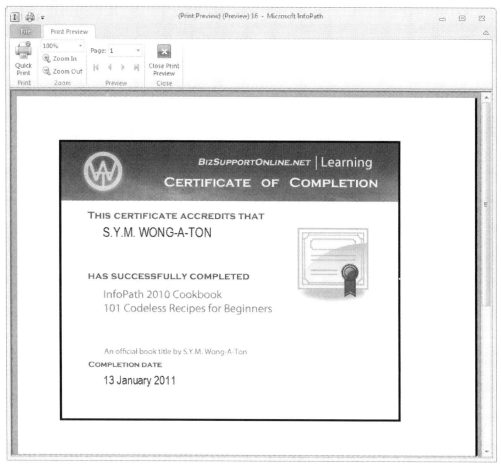

Figure 53. Print preview displaying print view of InfoPath form.

Had you made the layout table's borders visible, you would have seen that the layout table moved up to the top left corner in the print view in print preview mode as shown in the following figure, which is why the correction of 20 pixels at the top and to the left of each calculated value control was necessary.

Figure 54. Completed InfoPath form with visible borders in the Print Preview window.

Discussion

Background images are set to print by default, but this setting can also be disabled. If it has been disabled, you can enable printing background images by clicking **File ➤ Options ➤ More Options**, and then on the **Options** dialog box on the **General** tab, selecting the **Print background colors and pictures** check box.

When creating a print view you generally want to use existing fields from the Main data source to add controls on the print view and design the view. Therefore, you must drag-and-drop existing fields from the **Fields** task pane onto the print view and not add new controls via **Home ➤ Controls** or the **Controls** task pane.

Tip:

> If you want to use a text box instead of a calculated value control to print text without getting the borders around the control, you can remove the borders through the **Borders and Shading** dialog box of the text box control, and then make the text box read-only through the **Text Box Properties** dialog box.

Chapter 3: Formulas

A formula in InfoPath is a calculation or expression that can be used to calculate or construct the value of a field.

A formula can contain the values of fields, functions, or plain text. You can construct a formula for a field in InfoPath everywhere where you see the formula button

Figure 55. Button to open the Insert Formula dialog box in InfoPath.

The formula button opens the **Insert Formula** dialog box where you can construct a formula.

Figure 56. Insert Formula dialog box in InfoPath 2010.

On the **Insert Formula** dialog box, you can use the **Insert Field or Group** button to add the XPath expression for a field or group to a formula, you can use the **Insert Function** button to add a function to a formula, and you can type text into the **Formula** text box.

Note: XPath is used to navigate an XML document using paths to XML nodes. While you do not need to know XPath to be able to work with InfoPath on a basic level, it helps to know a little bit about it to be able to manually modify XPath expressions that InfoPath creates for you or just to understand what exactly is going on.

Once you are done constructing a formula, it is always recommended that you click the **Verify Formula** button to check whether your constructed formula contains any errors, and if it does, try to fix those errors.

On the **Insert Formula** dialog box, you will also see an **Edit XPath (advanced)** check box. InfoPath does not display the complete XPath expressions for fields by default, because XPath expressions can get very long and verbose. But if you want to see the full XPath expression of a field, you can select the **Edit XPath (advanced)** check box.

For example, if you add a text box named **field1** to your InfoPath form template and then click the **Insert Field or Group** button on the **Insert Formula** dialog box to select **field1**, you will see that InfoPath will show the field as

field1

in the **Formula** text box on the **Insert Formula** dialog box. And depending on which control or object you are adding the formula to, when you select the **Edit XPath (advanced)** check box, **field1** might appear as

my:field1

instead of

field1

When you get proficient at writing or manually modifying formulas and XPath expressions, you may want to use the **Edit XPath (advanced)** check box. A good example is when you want to manually add a filter to the XPath expression.

Tip:

When adding a function to a formula through the **Insert Function** dialog box, when you click on the name of a function in the **Functions** list to select it, you will see a short description appear under the **Functions** list. Always use this description as guidance for how to use a particular function until you get familiar and comfortable using all available functions in InfoPath.

You will have ample opportunity to work with the **Insert Formula** dialog box as you progress through this book. This chapter only serves as a brief introduction on how to use the dialog box to insert formulas.

The following three recipes will demonstrate the use of functions, fields, and text in formulas.

17.   Capitalize text in a text box

Problem

You have a text box on an InfoPath form and want any text that is typed into this text box to be converted to uppercase letters (capitals) whenever the cursor moves off the text box.

Solution

You can use the **translate** function to convert lowercase letters into uppercase letters.

To capitalize text that is typed into a text box:

1.   In InfoPath, create a new **Blank Form** template.

2.   Add a **Text Box** control to the form template.

3.   Right-click the text box control and select **Text Box Properties** from the context menu to open the **Text Box Properties** dialog box.

4.   On the **Text Box Properties** dialog box on the **Data** tab under **Default Value**, click the formula button behind the **Value** text box.

5.   On the **Insert Formula** dialog box, click **Insert Function**.

6.   On the **Insert Function** dialog box, select **Text** in the **Categories** list, select **translate** in the **Functions** list, and click **OK**.

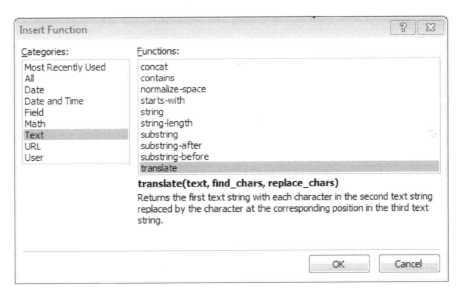

Figure 57. Insert Function dialog box in InfoPath 2010.

7. On the **Insert Formula** dialog box, double-click the first argument (the first text within the **translate** function that says "double-click to insert field"). This will open the **Select a Field or Group** dialog box.

Figure 58. Select a Field or Group dialog box in InfoPath 2010.

8. On the **Select a Field or Group** dialog box, select the field bound to the text box (**field1**), and click **OK**.

9. On the **Insert Formula** dialog box, replace the second argument by "abcdefghijklmnopqrstuvwxyz", and the third argument by "ABCDEFGHIJKLMNOPQRSTUVWXYZ". The final formula should look like the following:

```
translate(., "abcdefghijklmnopqrstuvwxyz", "ABCDEFGHIJKLMNOPQRSTUVWXYZ")
```

10. Click **Verify Formula** to check whether the formula contains any errors, and fix them if necessary or click **OK** on the message box if there are no errors.

11. On the **Insert Formula** dialog box, click **OK**.

12. On the **Text Box Properties** dialog box, click **OK**.

13. Preview the form.

When the form opens, type a text string in the text box, and then press **Tab** to move off the text box. The text within the text box should be converted to capital letters.

Discussion

The **translate** function takes 3 arguments and returns the first text string with each character in the second text string replaced by the character at the corresponding position in the third text string.

In the recipe above, the characters being replaced are contained in the text string you type into the text box, and then all lowercase letters are replaced by corresponding uppercase letters.

For example, the letter "c" is located on the third position in the text string containing the characters to replace. This letter would be replaced by a "C", because "C" is the letter located on the third position in the text string containing the characters to use for replacement.

Exercise

Open the **Insert Function** dialog box via the **Insert Formula** dialog box, click on **All** in the **Categories** list, and then in the **Functions** list, sequentially go through each function and read its description below the **Functions** list box to familiarize yourself with the functions that are available in InfoPath.

18. Join text strings from two text boxes together

Problem

You have three text box controls on an InfoPath form. You want to enter text in the first two text box controls and have those two pieces of text joined together, be separated by a space, and placed into the third text box.

For example: Text box 1 contains the text "John", text box 2 contains the text "Doe", and you want the text "John Doe" to appear in text box 3.

Solution

You can use the **concat** function in InfoPath to join two or more strings together.

To join text strings from two text boxes together:

1. In InfoPath, create a new **Blank Form** template.
2. Add 3 **Text Box** controls to the form template. The text box controls will have the names **field1**, **field2**, and **field3** by default.

3. Click the third text box to select it, and then on the ribbon click **Properties ➤ Properties ➤ Default Value**.

    Note that you can set the default value on either the control itself or the field that the control is bound to. In this case, you are setting the default value on the field, not the control.

    Tip: Look at the title of the **Properties** dialog box (which says: "Field or Group Properties") and you will see that you are modifying properties of the field itself, not of the text box control. In *17 Capitalize text in a text box*, you set the default value on the control, not on the field. Remember: If you set properties on a control, you are defining visual behavior of the form. If you set properties on a field, you are defining settings on the data source itself. Where the **Default Value** property is concerned, there is no difference between whether you set it on the control or on the field it is bound to.

4. On the **Field or Group Properties** dialog box on the **Data** tab under the **Default Value** section, click the formula button behind the **Value** text box.

5. On the **Insert Formula** dialog box, click **Insert Function**.

6. On the **Insert Function** dialog box, select **All** in the **Categories** list, then select **concat** in the **Functions** list, and click **OK**.

7. On the **Insert Formula** dialog box, double-click the first argument in the **concat** function where it says "double click to insert field".

8. On the **Select a Field or Group** dialog box, select **field1**, and click **OK**.

9. On the **Insert Formula** dialog box, replace the second argument in the **concat** function where it says "double click to insert field" with a space " ".

10. On the **Insert Formula** dialog box, double-click the third argument in the **concat** function where it says "double click to insert field".

11. On the **Select a Field or Group** dialog box, select **field2**, and click **OK**.

12. On the **Insert Formula** dialog box, the formula should now say:

    ```
    concat(field1, " ", field2)
    ```

    Click **OK**.

13. On the **Field or Group Properties** dialog box, ensure the **Refresh value when formula is recalculated** check box is selected, and then click **OK**. Selecting this check box ensures that the value of **field3** is recalculated whenever the value of either **field1** or **field2** changes.

14. Preview the form.

When the form opens, type text strings in the first and second text boxes, and then look at how the text in the third text box appears or changes.

Discussion

The **concat** function combines two or more fields or text strings into one text string, and is defined as follows:

```
concat(text1, text2, ...)
```

You must pass at least two fields or text strings as arguments to the **concat** function, otherwise InfoPath will raise an error.

Be aware that the **concat** function accepts either static text strings or InfoPath fields as its arguments. For example, if you want to join the static text string "Name: " with the value of **field1**, you could use a formula such as:

```
concat("Name: ", field1)
```

The **concat** function can be used by itself or you can use its results as input for another function as demonstrated in *19 Join two text strings and remove spaces if either text string is empty*.

19. Join two text strings and remove spaces if either text string is empty

Problem

You have three text box controls on an InfoPath form. One for a first name, a second one for a last name, and a third for a full name, which is composed by joining first and last names with a space between them.

If the first or second text boxes do not contain any text, you want the resulting text in the third text box not to be separated by a space.

For example: Text box 1 contains the text "John", text box 2 contains the text "Doe", and you want the text "John Doe" to appear in text box 3. But if text box 2 is empty and text box 1 contains the text "John", you want text box 3 to contain the text "John" instead of "John " (did you notice the extra space behind the name?).

Solution

You can use the **concat** and **normalize-space** functions to join strings together and remove unwanted spaces from the resulting text string.

To join two text strings together and remove empty spaces if either text string is blank:

1. In InfoPath, create a new **Blank Form** template.

2. Add 3 **Text Box** controls to the form template and name them **firstName**, **lastName**, and **fullName**.

3. Use the steps you learned in *18 Join text strings from two text boxes together* to set the **Default Value** of **fullName** to the following formula:

    ```
    normalize-space(concat(firstName, " ", lastName))
    ```

    or

    ```
    normalize-space(concat(../my:firstName, " ", ../my:lastName))
    ```

    if you have the **Edit XPath (advanced)** check box selected on the **Insert Formula** dialog box.

4. Click **OK** to close all open dialog boxes.

5. Preview the form.

When the form opens, type a first and last name into the corresponding text boxes and see what name appears in the full name text box. Then empty the last name text box and check whether there is an empty space behind the first name in the full name text box.

To see the difference in behavior if you do not use the **normalize-space** function, you should change the formula to the following formula:

```
concat(firstName, " ", lastName)
```

or use the form template you created for recipe *18 Join text strings from two text boxes together* to test the difference in behavior between the two recipes.

Discussion

The **normalize-space** function removes whitespace from a text string. You can use it to trim spaces from around a text string.

Exercise

Try to figure out what the **substring** function does and how you can use it. If you cannot figure it out, do not worry, because you will be using it in several recipes throughout the book.

Chapter 4: Adding Rules

What are rules?

A rule in InfoPath is declarative logic that is executed in response to certain events and conditions. An example of a rule is the following: If a text box does not contain any text, so is blank, change its background color to red.

Types of rules

There are four types of rules in InfoPath:

1. Action
2. Formatting
3. Validation
4. Default Value

Action rules perform actions, such as for example setting the value of a field (see *21 Set the value of a field*) or switching views (see *23 Switch to a read-only view when a button is clicked*).

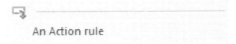

An Action rule

Figure 59. Icon and text for an Action rule on the Rules task pane in InfoPath 2010.

Formatting rules apply formatting to controls, such as for example when hiding a control or setting the background color on a control as demonstrated in *20 Change the background color of a text box to red if blank*.

A Formatting rule

Figure 60. Icon and text for a Formatting rule on the Rules task pane in InfoPath 2010.

Validation rules validate whether the data entered in a field is what is expected, such as for example when checking whether a number is entered into a text box that should only accept numbers (see *29 Check whether a number was entered*).

A Validation rule

Figure 61. Icon and text for a Validation rule on the Rules task pane in InfoPath 2010.

Default Value, while not officially called a "rule" in InfoPath, is similar to a "Set a field's value" action rule, but then without any conditions. And unlike a "Set a field's value" action where the value of a field is set by an action taking place elsewhere on the form, a default value is set by the field itself based on a formula that uses either its own value or the value of other fields on the form.

20. Change the background color of a text box to red if blank

Problem

You have a text box control on an InfoPath form and want its background color to change to red whenever there is no text in the text box.

Solution

You can use the **Add Rule** button in InfoPath to quickly add a rule with a condition to a control.

To change the background color of a text box to red if it is blank:

1. In InfoPath, create a new **Blank Form** template.

2. Add a **Text Box** control to the form template.

3. Click the text box to select it, and then select **Home ➤ Rules ➤ Add Rule ➤ Is Blank ➤ Bad**. The **Rules** task pane automatically opens and InfoPath creates a **Formatting** rule as displayed in the following figure.

Figure 62. Rule details on the Rules task pane in InfoPath 2010.

4. Preview the form.

When you open the form, the background color of the text box should be red. As you type text in the text box, the text will also be red, because according to InfoPath, no change has taken place yet. Once you leave the text box, this will signal a change to InfoPath and any rules you have set on the text box will then run. So when you are done typing, click or tab away from the text box. The background and foreground colors of the text box should return to their normal colors (black text on a white background).

Discussion

You can add a rule to an InfoPath form or control by clicking **Add Rule** or **Manage Rules** under the **Rules** group on the **Home** tab.

Add Manage
Rule ▾ Rules
Rules

Figure 63. Add Rule and Manage Rules under the Rules group on the Home tab.

Add Rule allows you to quickly add rules with conditions, but does not allow you to add all types of rules. If you need to add a rule that is not available through the **Add Rule** option, you must use the **Manage Rules** button to open the **Rules** task pane and then add a rule from there.

On the **Rules** task pane, you will see a couple of things:

1. The name of the field or group you have added or are going to add a rule to is displayed just below the title bar of the task pane. Always use this name to double-check whether you selected the correct group or field to add a rule to.

2. Rules that have been added to a field or group are listed below the name of the field or group on the **Rules** task pane. You can click on any rule listed here and select **Delete** from the drop-down menu to delete it.

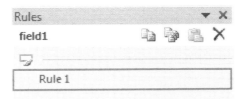

Figure 64. Rules task pane displaying a field's name with the field's rules beneath it.

3. There is a **New** button on the **Rules** task pane with which you can add one of three types of rules (**Validation**, **Formatting**, or **Action**) to a field or group.

Figure 65. New button on the Rules task pane to add a rule.

4. There is a rule details section where you can change the name of the rule, add one or more conditions to the rule, change the rule type (if you initially added the wrong type of rule), and depending on the rule type you selected, a section where you can add actions or define formatting.

You can get a quick overview of which rules have been defined in a form template by using the **Rule Inspector**, which you can open by clicking **Data ➤ Rules ➤ Rule Inspector**.

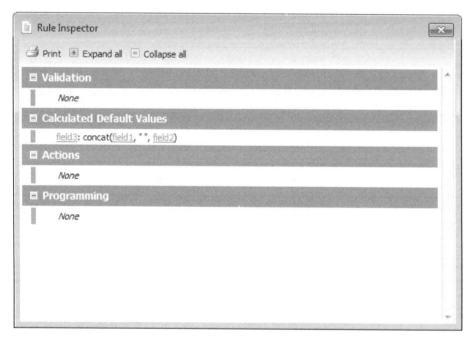

Figure 66. Rule Inspector in InfoPath 2010.

The **Rule Inspector** becomes a very useful tool to use when you are trying to debug a very complex form template which contains many rules that may be causing unexpected behavior.

Note that **Formatting** rules are not displayed on the **Rule Inspector**. Only rules that contain actions (**Action** rules, **Validation** rules, and **Default Values** containing calculations) can be found on the **Rule Inspector**.

Action rules

Action rules perform actions, such as for example setting the value of a field (see *21 Set the value of a field*) or switching views (see *23 Switch to a read-only view when a button is clicked*).

Action rules can be defined when:

- Buttons are clicked
- Values of fields change
- A form is opened (**Form Load**)
- A form is submitted (**Form Submit**)

You can set one or more conditions that determine when an **Action** rule should run.

An **Action** rule can contain one or more actions, but you can also create several **Action** rules with one action each. So when do you create one rule that contains multiple actions? And when do you create multiple rules that have one action each?

If you want to run a batch of actions under the same condition, then you should place all of the actions in one rule if possible, and add the condition to that rule. If you have several conditions under which actions should run, you must create several rules with the desired conditions and then add actions that should run under the condition for each rule.

Action rules run from top to bottom, one after the other. For example, if you have two **Action** rules (Rule 1 and Rule 2) on a control without any conditions set on any of the rules, Rule1 will run first and then Rule 2 will run next. If both rules do the same thing, for example, set the value of a field, the result of Rule 2 will override that of Rule 1.

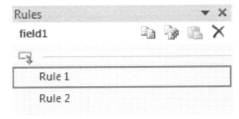

Figure 67. Two rules set on one field.

Once a rule has run, you can prevent any other **Action** rules that have been added to a control from running by selecting the **Don't run remaining rules if the condition of this rule is met** check box on the **Rules** task pane. Selecting this check box will prevent any rules further down the chain from running.

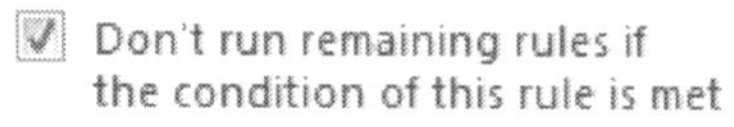

☑ Don't run remaining rules if
the condition of this rule is met

Figure 68. Check box on a rule to prevent running other rules further down the chain.

A common question many who are new to InfoPath ask is: "To which control do I add the rule?" If there is one golden tip I can give you for **Action** rules, it is the following one.

Tip:

> You must always add **Action** rules to the source of the action. The source is defined as the control that drives the action (e.g. a button being clicked). The source determines what happens to the target, which receives the result of the action (e.g. the value of a field being set).

The following figure visually explains the statement above.

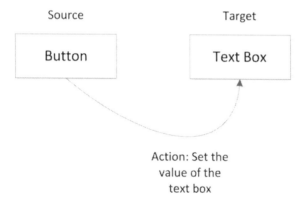

Figure 69. Action rule on a button setting the value of a text box.

In the figure above, the **Action** rule should go on the button and not the text box.

While not officially called a rule in InfoPath, the simplest type of **Action** rule you can define in InfoPath is by setting the **Default Value** of a field or control to a formula. A **Default Value** calculation runs when the form opens or when the value of a field changes, and every time the formula is recalculated if you have selected that option.

A **Default Value** works slightly different than an **Action** rule. Because you cannot set conditions on a **Default Value**, it always runs. In addition, with **Action** rules you set the rule on the source, while with a **Default Value**, the target sets its own value which can be based on the value of another field (the source).

It is good to know what kind of things you can do with each type of rule, so that if you are given the task to "disable a button" you know that you must add a **Formatting** rule to the button control and not an **Action** rule.

InfoPath offers the following actions you can use with **Action** rules:

- Set a field's value
- Switch views
- Query for data
- Submit data
- Close the form
- Send data to Web Part
- Change REST URL

Do not worry if you cannot memorize this list. As you continue to work with InfoPath, you will remember the types of rules you can add, and as you work through this book you will become familiar with several of the actions listed above.

21.   Set the value of a field

Problem

You want to click a button on an InfoPath form and then have the text in a text box be set to "Hello InfoPath".

Solution

You can use an **Action** rule to set the value of a field.

To set the value of a field:

1. In InfoPath, create a new **Blank Form** template.
2. Add a **Text Box** and **Button** control to the form template.
3. Click the button control to select it, and then select **Home ➤ Rules ➤ Add Rule ➤ When This Button Is Clicked ➤ Set a Field's Value**. This will open the **Rule Details** dialog box.

Figure 70. Rule Details dialog box in InfoPath 2010.

4. On the **Rule Details** dialog box, click the button behind the **Field** text box. This will open the **Select a Field or Group** dialog box where you can select a field for which the value must be set.

5. On the **Select a Field or Group** dialog box, select **field1** (which is bound to the text box control on the form), and click **OK**.

6. On the **Rule Details** dialog box, type the text **Hello InfoPath** in the **Value** text box, and click **OK**. The **Rules** task pane should automatically open if it was not already open.

7. If the **Rules** task pane is not open in InfoPath, click **Home ➤ Rules ➤ Manage Rules** to open it, and then select the button on the form template to display any rules that have been set on the button on the **Rules** task pane.

The details for the rule on the **Rules** task pane should resemble the following figure.

Figure 71. Rules task pane with a rule on a button to set the value of a field.

8. Preview the form.

When the form opens, click the button. The text string "Hello InfoPath" should appear in the text box.

Discussion

Let us dissect the logic for adding the rule in the recipe above.

The requirement for the recipe said: You want to click a button on an InfoPath form and then have the text in a text box be set to "Hello InfoPath".

The first question you should ask yourself when adding a rule is: What type of rule should I add? A default value, action, formatting, or validation rule?

From reading the requirement above you know you want to take an action (click a button), which means that you have to add an **Action** rule; not a **Formatting** or **Validation** rule. This narrows the field down to an **Action** rule or **Default Value**. Because you want to click a button to execute an action, and a button does not have a **Default Value** property, you must add an **Action** rule.

Once you know you must add an **Action** rule, you must figure out what the source and what the target is.

From reading the requirement above you know that clicking the button is driving the action of setting the value of the text box, which means that the button is the source and the text box is the target.

Once you have identified the rule type to create (**Action**), the source (button), and the target (text box), you can go ahead and add the rule to the control, which in this case is the button.

In the recipe above, you used the **Add Rule** button on the **Home** tab to add an **Action** rule to the button. A second way of adding an **Action** rule to a button is to open the **Rules** task pane via **Home ➤ Rules ➤ Manage Rules**, and then on the **Rules** task pane click **New ➤ Action**.

22. Close a form when a button is clicked

Problem

You have a button on an InfoPath form and you want to be able to click the button to close the form.

Solution

You can add an **Action** rule with a **Close the form** action on the button to close the form when a user clicks the button.

To add a button with a rule that closes a form:

1. Create a new **Blank Form** template.

2. Add a **Button** control to the form template.

3. Click the button to select it, and then select **Home ➤ Rules ➤ Manage Rules**.

4. On the **Rules** task pane, click **New ➤ Action**.

5. On the **Rules** task pane behind **Run these actions**, click **Add ➤ Close the form**.

6. On the **Rule Details** dialog box, click **OK**.

7. Preview the form.

When the form opens, click the button. The form should close.

Discussion

Let us dissect the logic for adding the rule in the recipe above.

You want to close a form by clicking a button. Because closing a form is an action in InfoPath, you know you must add an **Action** rule.

You want to close a form by clicking a button. From this you know that clicking the button should take place first, so the button is the source for the action. Then you must close the form. This makes the form the target.

Having gone through the thought process above, you know you must create an **Action** rule on the button (the source) with an action to close the form (the target).

23. Switch to a read-only view when a button is clicked

Problem

You added a read-only view to an InfoPath form template. Now you want to have the form switch to the read-only view when a button is clicked.

Solution

From the discussion in two previous recipes, you should now know that when someone says: "I want to be able to switch to another view when a button is clicked", you must add a **Switch views** action to a rule on a button.

Before you continue, review these questions and answers:

1. What is the action the user wants to perform? Answer: The user wants to switch to another view, so I must add an action rule that switches views.

2. I must add an action rule, so what is the source? Answer: The button, because that drives switching views. So I must add the rule to the button.

3. Does this rule depend on the value of another field? Is there a condition that must be met before this rule can run? Answer: No, so I must add an action that is unrestricted, so there are no conditions that have to be set on the rule.

Can you follow this train of thoughts? This is the kind of thought process you must try to develop whenever you want to have something happen on an InfoPath form.

Now let us walk through the steps for making this recipe work.

To switch to a read-only view when a button is clicked:

1. In InfoPath, create a new **Blank Form** template.

2. Add a read-only view to the form template (see *14 Add a read-only view*).

3. Switch back to the default view, and add a **Button** control to it.

4. Click the button to select it, and then select **Home ➤ Rules ➤ Add Rule ➤ When This Button Is Clicked ➤ Switch Views**.

5. On the **Rule Details** dialog box, select the read-only view from the **View** drop-down list box, and then click **OK**.

6. Preview the form.

When the form opens, click the button on the default view. The read-only view should be displayed.

Discussion

Typically when you add a **Switch Views** button to an InfoPath form, you may not want the user to be able to select a view from the **View** drop-down list box.

You can prevent users from switching views by removing a view from the menu via the **View** drop-down list box as you saw in *12 Add a second view to a form template*.

Switching views does not have to be restricted to button controls. You can also add a **Switch views** action to a rule that runs when the form opens. You could use this technique for example with a condition to check whether the form has already been submitted, and if it has been, switch to the read-only view when the form is opened after it has been submitted (see *41 Switch to read-only view when form opens after submit*).

Another example would be to submit a form using rules, and then add a rule to switch to the read-only view immediately after the form has been submitted without closing the form (see *40 Switch to read-only view on submit*).

Formatting rules

Formatting rules apply formatting to controls, such as for example when hiding a control or setting the background color on a control as demonstrated in *20 Change the background color of a text box to red if blank*.

Formatting rules can be applied to controls, but not to form events (load and submit).

InfoPath offers the following formatting options you can use with **Formatting** rules:

- Hide this control

- Disable this control

- Don't allow users to insert or delete this control

- Change the style or color of a font on this control

- Change the background color of this control

You can set one or more conditions that determine when a formatting rule should run.

The difference between **Action** and **Formatting** rules is that you are forced to set a condition on a **Formatting** rule, while this is not the case for **Action** rules. So a **Formatting** rule always runs under a specified condition.

Another difference is that unlike **Action** rules, a **Formatting** rule can only apply one type of formatting to a control at a time. In the case of **Action** rules, all of the rules run from top to bottom unless you stop them by selecting a check box. This is not the case for **Formatting** rules.

So while you can add multiple **Formatting** rules that have the same condition and different or the same type of formatting to a control, if the condition of the first **Formatting** rule defined on the control is met, its formatting will be applied to the control and all other **Formatting** rules further down the chain will be ignored.

So you should always add only one **Formatting** rule to a control or if you want to add multiple **Formatting** rules ensure that the conditions of all of the **Formatting** rules on the control are mutually exclusive.

To answer the question "To which control do I add the **Formatting** rule?" I can give you the following tip.

Tip:

You must always set **Formatting** rules on the target. The target is defined as the control that receives the results (e.g. setting the color of the font for the control) based on a condition (e.g. if the field is blank). Conditions can be based on the value of the target itself, value of another field, a static value, or a formula.

The following figure visually explains the statement above.

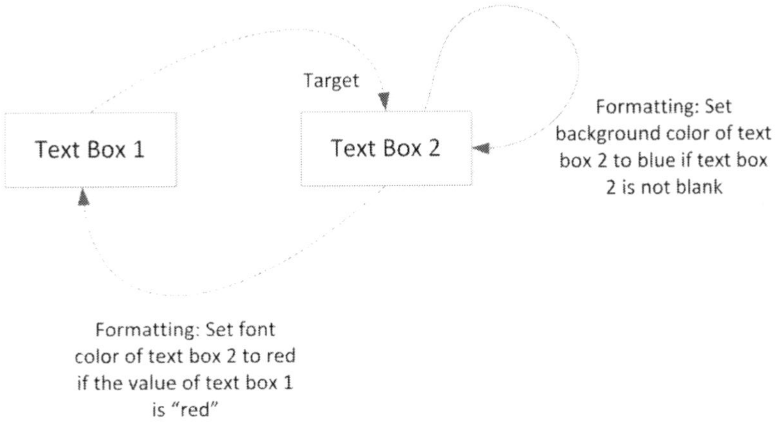

Target

Text Box 1

Text Box 2

Formatting: Set
background color of text
box 2 to blue if text box
2 is not blank

Formatting: Set font
color of text box 2 to red
if the value of text box 1
is "red"

Figure 72. Formatting rules on text box 2 setting its font and background color based on conditions.

In the example in Figure 72, you want to add two formatting rules to text box 2.

The first formatting rule depends on the value of text box 1. This formatting rule says that the font color of text box 2 should be set to red if "red' is typed into text box 1. So text box 1 is driving the action of setting the font color of text box 2. This makes text box 1 the source and text box 2 the target. Setting the font color falls under formatting, so you must add a formatting rule to the target (text box 2), with a condition that is based on the value of the source (text box 1).

The second formatting rule depends on the value of text box 2 itself. This formatting rule says that the background color of text box 2 should be set to blue if text box 2 is not blank. So text box 2 is driving the action of setting its own background color. This makes text box 2 both the source and the target. Setting the background color falls under formatting, so you must add a formatting rule to the target (text box 2) with a condition that is based on the value of the source (text box 2).

Because you want to set two formatting rules on the same control (text box 2), you must make sure that the conditions of the two rules are mutually exclusive. And if you map out the logic, you will see that you must add 4 formatting rules instead of 2 to make the rules mutually exclusive as listed in the following table.

Rule	Conditions	Formatting to Apply
1	Text box 1 = "red" and Text box 2 is not blank	Font Color = Red Background Color = Blue
2	Text box 1 = "red" and Text box 2 is blank	Font Color = Red Background Color = White
3	Text box 1 ≠ "red" and	Font Color = Black

	Text box 2 is not blank	Background Color = Blue
4	Text box 1 ≠ "red" and Text box 2 is blank	Font Color = Black Background Color = White

Table 1. Creating mutually exclusive Formatting rules in InfoPath.

You will learn more about conditions in the recipes to come.

24. Show a repeating table when check box is selected

Problem

You have a check box on an InfoPath form and want to show a repeating table whenever the check box is selected.

Solution

You can use conditional formatting (a **Formatting** rule with conditions) on the repeating table to show or hide the repeating table when the check box is selected or deselected.

To show or hide a repeating table when a check box is selected:

1. In InfoPath, create a new **Blank Form** template.

2. Add a **Check Box** control to the form template and name it **showTable**.

3. Add a **Section** control to the form template, then click anywhere within the **Section** control, and add a **Repeating Table** control in the **Section** control.

4. Click on the **Section** control to select it, and then click **Home** ➤ **Rules** ➤ **Manage Rules**.

5. On the **Rules** task pane, ensure that **group1** (which is bound to the section control) is listed at the top of the task pane, and then click **New** ➤ **Formatting**.

6. On the **Rules** task pane under **Formatting**, select the **Hide this control** check box. This will hide the section with the repeating table in it.

7. On the **Rules** task pane under **Condition**, click the text **None** to add a condition.

8. On the **Condition** dialog box, select **showTable** from the first drop-down list box, leave **is equal to** selected in the second drop-down list box, select **FALSE** from the third drop-down list box, and click **OK**. This condition will allow the section containing the repeating table to be hidden when the value of **showTable** is equal to **FALSE**, so when the check box has not been selected. The following condition should now appear on the **Rules** task pane

```
showTable = FALSE
```

9. Preview the form.

When the form opens, the repeating table should be invisible. Select the check box. The repeating table should appear.

Discussion

Let us dissect the logic for adding the rule in the recipe above.

You want to show a repeating table. Because showing and hiding falls under formatting in InfoPath, you know you must create a formatting rule.

You want to show a repeating table by selecting a check box. From this you know that the value of the check box will drive visibility of the repeating table. So the check box is the source and the repeating table is the target.

But because you can only hide fields or rows in a repeating table and not the entire repeating table itself, and you want to show or hide the entire table, you must create a container for the repeating table.

Section controls are ideal containers to use, because when they are invisible, they give up their space. So for example, if you had a text box right below the section and you made the section control hidden, the text box would automatically move up to take in the space of the section control.

You can place any type of control within a section control. In this case, you want to place the repeating table within the section control, and then make the section control become the target for formatting instead of the repeating table.

Having gone through the thought process above, you now know that you must create a formatting rule on the section control (the target) with a formatting of "hide this control" and a condition that checks whether the value of the check box (the source) is equal to FALSE (value of the check box when it is deselected).

In other words, the section control should be shown when the check box is selected. If you reverse this logic it means that the section control should be hidden when the check box is deselected. You use the latter logic to set up the formatting rule.

25.   Make a control read-only based on a condition

Problem

You have a date picker and button on an InfoPath form and want to make the date picker read-only when the button is clicked.

Solution

You can use a **Formatting** rule to make a control read-only and then add a condition to the rule to apply the formatting only when the condition is met.

To make a control read-only based on a condition:

1. In InfoPath, create a new **Blank Form** template.

2. Add a **Date Picker** and **Button** control to the form template.

3. Add a hidden field named **isReadOnly** to the Main data source of the form (see *10 Add a hidden field*). You will use this hidden field to make the date picker read-only. If the hidden field has a value of "lock" then the date picker should be read-only, otherwise you should be able to select a date. The button will be used to set the value of the hidden field.

4. Click the button to select it, and then select **Home** ➤ **Rules** ➤ **Add Rule** ➤ **When This Button Is Clicked** ➤ **Set a Field's Value**.

5. On the **Rule Details** dialog box, click the button behind the **Field** text box.

6. On the **Select a Field or Group** dialog box, select **isReadOnly**, and click **OK**.

7. On the **Rule Details** dialog box, type the text **lock** (without any double quotes) in the **Value** text box, and click **OK**. The action on the **Rules** task pane for the button should now say:

   ```
   Set a field's value: isReadOnly = "lock"
   ```

8. Click the date picker to select it, and click **Home** ➤ **Rules** ➤ **Manage Rules**.

9. On the **Rules** task pane, click **New** ➤ **Formatting**.

10. On the **Rules** task pane under **Condition**, click the text **None**.

11. On the **Condition** dialog box, select **isReadOnly** from the first drop-down list box, leave **is equal to** selected in the second drop-down list box, select **Type text** in the third drop-down list box (this will change the drop-down list box into a text box), type **lock** (without any double quotes) in the text box, and click **OK**. The condition on the **Rules** task pane should now say:

    ```
    isReadOnly = "lock"
    ```

    This condition restricts the formatting rule to run only when the value of the **isReadOnly** hidden field has been set to the text **lock**.

12. On the **Rules** task pane under **Formatting**, select the **Disable this control** check box. This will make the date picker read-only if the condition has been met.

13. Preview the form.

When the form opens, enter a date in the date picker and then click the button. After clicking the button, try to change the date in the date picker by either typing a date or clicking on the calendar button on the date picker to select a date. You should not be able to modify the date in the date picker anymore.

Discussion

In the recipe above you had to use a formatting rule to make a date picker control read-only. Unlike a text box control which has a **Read-Only** property you can set at design time, many controls in InfoPath do not have such a property, and the date picker is one of those controls.

So to make controls that do not have a **Read-Only** property read-only, you must use a formatting rule with a formatting of **Disable this control**.

Another situation in which you may want to use such a formatting rule is if you want to make a control read-only based on a condition. The **Read-Only** property of the text box is not accessible at runtime through rules, so if you want to make a text box control read-only just like you did with the date picker control, you would have to use a formatting rule to achieve this.

And finally, there are controls on which you cannot set conditional formatting (for example file attachment controls on web browser forms). In such cases you will have to get creative or change your form design in such a way to achieve the results you are after. For two examples of how you could make a file attachment control read-only, see *79 Make an attachment read-only – method 1* and *80 Make an attachment read-only – method 2*.

Exercise

Try making the date picker read-only when a check box is selected instead of when a button is clicked. Hint: The check box control should replace the hidden field.

26. Disable a button on a read-only view

Problem

You want to permanently display a button on a read-only view of an InfoPath form as disabled.

Solution

You can permanently disable a button by using a **Formatting** rule that has a condition that makes the rule always run.

To disable a button on a read-only view:

1.   In InfoPath, create a new **Blank Form** template.

2.   Add a read-only view to the form template (see *14 Add a read-only view*).

3.   Add a **Button** control to the read-only view.

4.   Click the button to select it, and then select **Home ➤ Rules ➤ Manage Rules**.

5.   On the **Rules** task pane, click **New ➤ Formatting**.

6.   On the **Rules** task pane under **Condition**, click the text **None**.

7.   On the **Condition** dialog box, select **The expression** from the first drop-down list box (a text box to enter an expression will appear), replace all of the text in the text box with **true()**, and click **OK**. This condition will always return TRUE, so will always be met, so the rule will always run.

8.   On the **Rules** task pane, select **Disable this control** under **Formatting**.

9.   Preview the form.

When the form opens, the button on the read-only view should be shown as dimmed, so disabled.

Discussion

If you require the button to only be disabled on the read-only view when the read-only view is displayed, you must implement a solution as described in *25 Make a control read-only based on a condition* to keep track of when the read-only view is displayed (for example by using a **Switch views** action) and then set a **Formatting** rule on the button based on the value of the field that is tracking the switch to the read-only view.

In the recipe above you made a formatting rule always run by adding a condition to it that said:

```
true()
```

While the function **true()** returns a value of TRUE in InfoPath, you could have used any expression that returns the value of TRUE. For example, the following expression could also be used to return a value of TRUE.

```
1 = 1
```

In the recipe above you also learned how to use an expression to return the value for a condition by selecting **The expression** on the **Condition** dialog box. Ordinarily, whenever you select **The expression** from the first drop-down list box on the **Condition** dialog box, you are forced to know the exact expression you want to type into the text box and do not get any help from InfoPath to construct it. So while I knew I had to type in **true()** to return a value of TRUE, you as a beginner would not know this. So in recipe *30 Set a maximum length on a text box* I will show you a way to cheat when constructing expressions for conditions in InfoPath.

Tip:

> Because buttons do not display data visually such as text boxes, it is recommended that you delete them from a read-only view rather than disable them, unless they have a useful function such as switching back to a non-read-only view or submitting the form.

27. Enable a control when a check box is selected

Problem

You have a date picker control on an InfoPath form that you want to enable whenever a check box is selected.

Solution

You can add a **Formatting** rule on the date picker to enable it based on a condition that the check box should be selected for the rule to be applied.

To enable a control when a check box is selected:

1. In InfoPath, create a new **Blank Form** template.

2. Add a **Check Box** and **Date Picker** control to the form template. Name the check box control **isEnabled**.

3. Add a **Formatting** rule on the date picker control with a condition that says:

   ```
   isEnabled = FALSE
   ```

   and with a formatting where the **Disable this control** check box is selected. This rule will disable the date picker when the **isEnabled** check box is deselected, so will enable the date picker when the check box is selected.

4. Preview the form.

When the form opens, the date picker should be disabled and you should not be able to enter or select any date. Select the check box. The date picker should now be enabled and you should be able to enter or select a date.

Discussion

You can use conditional formatting to enable or disable any input control. To see the list of input controls in InfoPath, open the **Controls** task pane by clicking on the arrow in the bottom right-hand corner of the **Controls** group on the **Home** tab.

Figure 73. Opening the Controls task pane in InfoPath 2010.

The controls are listed in categories on the **Controls** task pane, and the first category of controls listed is the **Input** group of controls.

From the controls that fall under the **Objects** category, you can enable or disable any control, except for the **File Attachment** and **Ink Picture** controls when placed on web browser forms. If you want to disable a file attachment control based on a condition, see *79 Make an attachment read-only – method 1* and *80 Make an attachment read-only – method 2*.

And finally, you cannot disable **Containers**, but you are able to hide and show them.

Validation rules

Validation rules validate whether the data entered in a field is what is expected, such as for example when checking whether a number is entered into a text box that should only accept numbers (see *29 Check whether a number was entered*).

Validation rules are only applied to controls and not to form events (load and submit).

Validation rules behave very much like **Formatting** rules with the only difference that you do not apply formatting to a control, but rather display a screen tip message for the control if its value is invalid.

You can have more than one **Validation** rule on a control and can set one or more conditions that determine when a **Validation** rule should be run, but like **Formatting** rules, if you add multiple **Validation** rules, you should always add rules that have mutually exclusive conditions.

To answer the question "To which control do I add the **Validation** rule?" I can give you the following tip.

Tip:

> You must always set **Validation** rules on the target. The target is defined as the control that should be validated (show an error message) based on a condition (e.g. if the field is blank). Conditions can be based on the value of the target itself, the value of another field, a static value, or a formula.

28. Make a field required based on a condition

Problem

You have a drop-down list box control on an InfoPath form and want to force users to select an item from it when they have typed a piece of text into a text box elsewhere on the form.

Solution

In *9 Make a field required* you learned about the preferred way for making fields required when there are no conditions for a field to be mandatory. However, you must use a **Validation** rule if you want a field to be required based on a condition.

In the example in this recipe, you can use a **Validation** rule with conditions to check whether the text box is not empty and if it is not, require the value of the drop-down list box not to be equal to an empty string.

To make a drop-down list box required if a text box contains text:

1. In InfoPath, create a new **Blank Form** template.

2. Add a **Drop-Down List Box** and **Text Box** control to the form template. Name the drop-down list box **title** and the text box **lastName**.

3. Right-click the drop-down list box and select **Drop-Down List Box Properties** from the context menu that appears.

4. On the **Drop-Down List Box Properties** dialog box on the **Data** tab under **List box choices**, ensure the **Enter choices manually** radio button is selected and click **Add**.

5. On the **Add Choice** dialog box, type the text **Mr** in both the **Value** and **Display name** text boxes, and click **OK**. With this you have added a static item to the drop-down list box.

6. Repeat the previous step to add the following items to the list box: **Mrs**, **Ms**, **Miss**, and **Sir**. Click **OK** to close the **Drop-Down List Box Properties** dialog box when you are done.

7. Click the **Drop-Down List Box** to select it, and then click **Home ➤ Manage Rules**.

8. On the **Rules** task pane, click **New ➤ Validation**.

9. On the **Rules** task pane under **Condition**, click the text **None**.

10. On the **Condition** dialog box, select **lastName** from the first drop-down list box, select **is not blank** from the second drop-down list box, and click **And**.

11. On the **Condition** dialog box, select **title** from the first drop-down list box, select **is blank** from the second drop-down list box, and click **OK**. The final conditions on the **Rules** task pane should now say:

    ```
    lastName is not blank
    and
    title is blank
    ```

    which means that if the **lastName** field (bound to the text box) contains text and the **title** field (bound to the drop-down list box) is empty (no item has been selected from the drop-down list box), then a message must be displayed to the user to select an item from the **title** drop-down list box.

12. On the **Rules** task pane under **ScreenTip**, enter a message such as for example "You must select a title."

13. Preview the form.

When the form opens, type text into the text box, and then move away from the text box by clicking elsewhere on the form. A red asterisk should appear in the drop-down list box. And if you hover over the drop-down list box, you should see the message you typed in earlier for the **ScreenTip**. Select a title from the drop-down list box. The red asterisk should disappear.

Discussion

Had you enabled submission of the form and clicked on the **Submit** button, the following message would have been shown and prevented you from submitting the form until you selected an item from the drop-down list box:

"InfoPath cannot submit the form, because it contains validation errors. Errors are marked with either a red asterisk (required fields) or a red, dashed border (invalid values)."

Exercise

Try making a text box required when a check box is selected.

29.   Check whether a number was entered

Problem

You have a text box on an InfoPath form in which users are allowed to enter numbers. You want to be able to check whether a number was entered into the text box when the user navigates away from the text box.

Solution

You can add a **Validation** rule that uses a regular expression on the text box to check whether a number was entered into the text box.

To check whether a number was entered into a text box control:

1. In InfoPath, create a new **Blank Form** template.
2. Add a **Text Box** control to the form template.
3. Click the text box to select it, and then click **Home ➤ Rules ➤ Manage Rules**.
4. On the **Rules** task pane, click **New ➤ Validation**.
5. On the **Rules** task pane under **Condition**, click the text **None**.
6. On the **Condition** dialog box, select **field1** from the first drop-down list box, select **does not match pattern** from the second drop-down list box, and select **Select a pattern** from the third drop-down list box.
7. On the **Data Entry Pattern** dialog box, type the following regular expression in the **Custom pattern** text box:

    `[\-\+]?[0-9]*\.?[0-9]+`

    and click **OK**.
8. On the **Condition** dialog box, click **OK**.
9. On the **Rules** task pane, type in a **ScreenTip** message for the validation rule, for example, "Invalid number".
10. Preview the form.

When the form opens, type a piece of text in the text box. A red dashed border should appear around the text box and when you hover over the text box, you should see the **ScreenTip** message you entered earlier. Now enter a valid number in the text box and move away or tab away from the text box. The red dashed border should disappear.

Discussion

If you have a field in which only numbers should be entered, it is recommended to set the **Data type** of the field to **Whole Number (integer)** or **Decimal (double)** instead of leaving the data type of the field set to **Text (string)** and then adding a validation rule to the control bound to the field.

By setting the data type of a field to a numeric data type, InfoPath will automatically validate any data entered into that field.

The added benefit of setting the data type to a numeric data type as a way of automatically validating data is that you can then use the **Format** option on the properties dialog box of the control bound to a field to set the appearance of the number, for example by setting the amount of decimal places that should be displayed, setting whether to use digit grouping or not, and how negative numbers should be displayed.

In the recipe above, you used a regular expression to validate data. While the explanation of how regular expressions work and are constructed is beyond the scope of this book, just be aware that you can use them in InfoPath as expressions for conditions on rules, and that you can use the Internet to find regular expression patterns for use in InfoPath.

30. Set a maximum length on a text box

Problem

You have a text box on an InfoPath form and want to prevent users from typing more than 10 characters into the text box.

Solution

You can use the **string-length** function in a **Validation** rule to check the length of a text string typed into a text box and then display an error message if the length exceeds the maximum allowable length.

To set a maximum text string length on a text box:

1. In InfoPath, create a **Blank Form** template.
2. Add a **Text Box** control to the form template.
3. With the text box control still selected, click **Home ➤ Rules ➤ Manage Rules**.
4. On the **Rules** task pane, click **New ➤ Validation**.
5. On the **Rules** task pane under **Condition**, click the text **None**.
6. On the **Condition** dialog box, select **Use a formula** from the third drop-down list box.
7. On the **Insert Formula** dialog box, type **string-length()** or select the function by clicking **Insert Function**, selecting **string-length** from the **Functions** list on the **Insert Function** dialog box, and then clicking **OK**.

8. Place the cursor between the brackets of the function and click **Insert Field or Group**.

9. On the **Select a Field or Group** dialog box, select **field1** (which is bound to the text box to evaluate), and click **OK**. The final formula should look like the following:

```
string-length(.)
```

This expression returns the amount of characters of the text string typed into the text box (field1).

10. On the **Insert Formula** dialog box, click **OK**.

11. On the **Condition** dialog box, select **The expression** from the first drop-down list box. The expression in the text box now looks like the following:

```
. = string-length(.)
```

12. On the **Condition** dialog box in the text box, delete everything in front of and including the equal sign (InfoPath added this to the expression when you selected **The expression** from the first drop-down list box), and add a comparison that checks whether the string length is greater than 10 as follows:

```
string-length(.) > 10
```

and click **OK**. This expression evaluates to TRUE when the amount of characters typed into the text box is greater than 10.

13. On the **Rules** task pane in the **ScreenTip** text box, type **Only 10 characters maximum allowed**.

14. Preview the form.

When the form opens, type a text string that has more than 10 characters in the text box. A red dashed border should appear around the text box when you tab away from the field, and when you hover over the text box you should see the error message appear.

Now delete a few of the characters until the text string is less than 10 characters long. The red dashed border should disappear.

Discussion

Text boxes do not have a maximum length property you can set, so you have to resort to data validation to check the length of a text string typed into a text box, and then display an error message.

You can use the **string-length** function to check the length of a text string. The **string-length** function accepts one argument (the text string to evaluate) and returns the number of characters in a text string.

In this recipe you also learned a trick to construct an expression for use with **The expression** option on the **Condition** dialog box. The **Use a formula** option in the third drop-down list box on the **Condition** dialog box is a handy feature to use when you want to construct a formula for use as an expression.

Had you selected **The expression** from the first drop-down list box immediately after you opened the **Condition** dialog box, you would have been forced to know the exact expression to type into the text box for the expression. By using the **Use a formula** option in the third drop-down list box (this option is available if a field has been selected in the first drop-down list box), you can cheat your way to constructing an expression that can be used with the **The expression** option on the **Condition** dialog box.

In step 12 of the recipe above, you used the "is greater than" comparison operator to complete the expression. There are several other comparison operators you can use in expressions in InfoPath. The following table lists comparison operators you can use in expressions in InfoPath along with their meaning.

Comparison Operator	Meaning
=	Is equal to
!=	Is not equal to
<	Is less than
>	Is greater than
<=	Is less than or equal to
>=	Is greater than or equal to

Table 2. Comparison operators that can be used in expressions in InfoPath.

Multiple conditions on rules

In previous recipes, you have already seen how to add a condition to a rule. All types of rules, except for default values, can have conditions added to them. Conditions are optional for **Action** rules and mandatory for **Formatting** and **Validation** rules.

In InfoPath, you can add only one condition to a rule. If you want to add multiple conditions to a rule, you must add multiple expressions to the condition for the rule, and join these expressions together using the "and" or "or" Boolean operators. The following recipe shows and explains how.

31. Show/hide sections based on a drop-down list box

Problem

You have one drop-down and two section controls on an InfoPath form and you want to show each section control depending on the item that is selected in the drop-down list box.

Solution

You can use multiple conditions on a **Formatting** rule to show or hide sections based on the selected item in a drop-down list box.

To show or hide sections based on the selected item in a drop-down list box:

1. In InfoPath, create a new **Blank Form** template.

2. Add a **Drop-Down List Box** and two **Section** controls to the form template. Ensure that the sections are placed one under the other and that there are no blank lines between them. Name the drop-down list box **selectColor**.

3. Right-click the drop-down list box and select **Drop-Down List Box Properties** from the context menu that appears.

4. On the **Drop-Down List Box Properties** dialog box on the **Data** tab, leave the **Enter choices manually** radio button selected, and click **Add**.

5. On the **Add Choice** dialog box, type **1** in the **Value** text box, type **Red** in the **Display name** text box, and click **OK**. Repeat this step to add a second choice that has a value of **2** and a display name of **Blue**, and then click **OK**.

6. On the **Drop-Down List Box Properties** dialog box, click **OK**. With this you have added two static items to the drop-down list box.

7. Right-click the first section and select **Borders and Shading** from the drop-down menu.

8. On the **Borders and Shading** dialog box, select the **Shading** tab, select the **Color** radio button, select red, and click **OK**.

9. Right-click the second section and select **Borders and Shading** from the drop-down menu.

10. On the **Borders and Shading** dialog box, select the **Shading** tab, select the **Color** radio button, select blue, and click **OK**.

11. Click the first section to select it, and then click **Home ➤ Rules ➤ Manage Rules**.

12. On the **Rules** task pane, ensure **group1** is listed under the title bar. If it is not, click the title of the first section control again to select it.

13. On the **Rules** task pane, click **New ➤ Formatting**.

14. On the **Rules** task pane under **Formatting**, select the **Hide this control** check box.

15. On the **Rules** task pane under **Condition**, click the text **None**.

16. On the **Condition** dialog box, select **selectColor** from the first drop-down list box, leave **is equal to** selected in the second drop-down list box, select **Type text** from the third drop-down list box, and type **2** in the text box.

17. On the **Condition** dialog box, click **And** to add a second expression, and select **or** from the fourth drop-down list box.

18. On the **Condition** dialog box on the second row, select **selectColor** from the first drop-down list box, select **is blank** from the second drop-down list box, and click **OK**.

19. The condition on the **Rules** task pane should now say:

    ```
    selectColor = "2"
    or
    selectColor is blank
    ```

    What this condition does is hide the first section if the item **Blue**, which has a value of **2**, is selected from the **selectColor** drop-down list box (selectColor = "2") **or** if no item has been selected from the drop-down list box (selectColor is blank).

20. Repeat the steps 11 through 19 for the second section, but add two expressions that say:

    ```
    selectColor = "1"
    or
    selectColor is blank
    ```

    What this condition does is hide the second section if the item **Red**, which has a value of **1**, is selected from the **selectColor** drop-down list box (selectColor = "1") **or** if no item has been selected from the drop-down list box (selectColor is blank).

21. Preview the form.

When the form opens, the drop-down list box should not have an item selected in it, so both sections should be hidden (invisible). When you select Red from the drop-down list box, the red section should be shown. And when you select Blue from the drop-down list box, the blue section should be shown.

Discussion

As you can see from the recipe above, you can add multiple conditions on a rule by adding multiple expressions to the condition for the rule.

After adding the first expression, you can add a second expression by clicking the **And** button behind the third drop-down list box on the **Condition** dialog box. Once you click the **And** button, a drop-down list box will appear from which you can select either **and** or **or** to join the two expressions together.

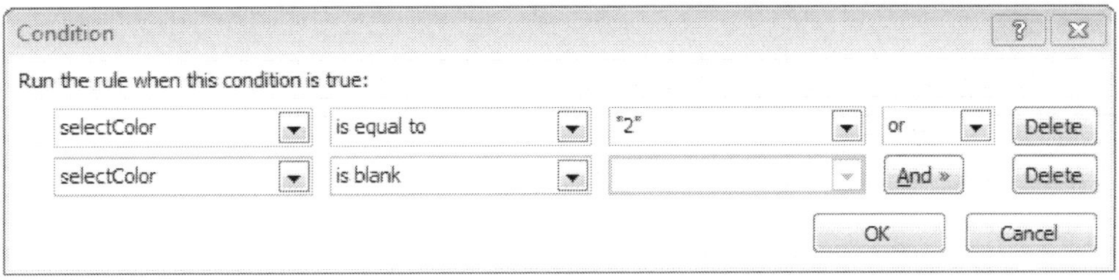

Condition			? ☒

Run the rule when this condition is true:

selectColor ▼	is equal to ▼	"2" ▼	or ▼	Delete
selectColor ▼	is blank ▼	▼	And »	Delete

OK   Cancel

Figure 74. Condition dialog box for a condition with multiple expressions.

To delete an expression for a condition you have previously added, click the **Delete** button on the **Condition** dialog box behind the expression you want to delete.

InfoPath allows you to add up to a maximum of five rows of expressions on the **Condition** dialog box. But if you require more than five expressions for a condition, you can add additional expressions as follows:

1. For an existing condition, for the first row of expressions, select **The expression** from the first drop-down list box. If we take the recipe above, the following expression for the condition on the first section would then appear:

   ```
   ../my:selectColor = "2"
   ```

2. For an existing condition, for the second row of expressions, select **The expression** from the first drop-down list box. If we take the recipe above, the following expression for the condition on the first section would then appear:

   ```
   ../my:selectColor = ""
   ```

3. Join the two previous expressions together with an "or" operator by copying the text for the second expression, typing **or** behind the text for the first expression, and then pasting the text for the second expression you copied in the text box for the first expression. The complete expression for the condition for the first section would then look as follows:

   ```
   ../my:selectColor = "2" or ../my:selectColor = ""
   ```

4. Delete the second row of expressions or use it to add another new expression to the condition.

5. Continue adding expressions until you hit the maximum of five or continue combining the text for expressions to fit your needs.

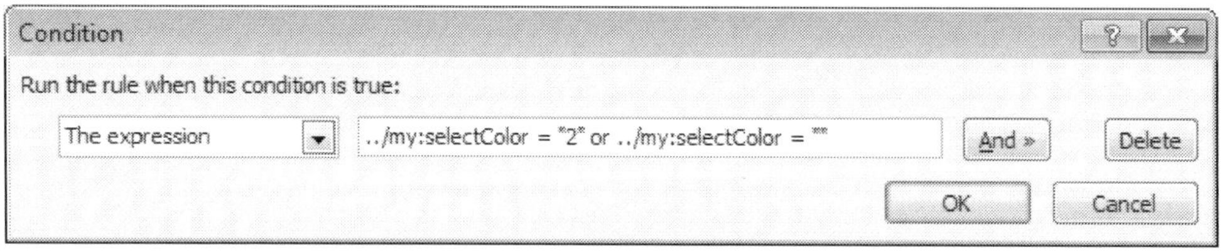

Figure 75. Condition dialog box for a condition where two expressions have been combined.

You can make use of any of the Boolean operators listed in the following table when using the **The expression** option on the **Condition** dialog box to join expressions together.

Boolean Operator	Function
and	Joins two expressions together by stating that both expressions must be true for the result of the combination of expressions to evaluate to true.
or	Joins two expressions together by stating that either one of the expressions can be true for the result of the combination of expressions to evaluate to true.
not	Negates the result of an expression, meaning that the opposite of the expression must be true for the final expression to evaluate to true.
( )	Groups expressions.

Table 3. Boolean operators that can be used in expressions for conditions in InfoPath.

Remember that the result of a condition must always evaluate to either TRUE or FALSE. Whether you use one or multiple expressions to construct a condition so that it evaluates to either TRUE or FALSE is irrelevant. The final result of the condition is what InfoPath uses to run an action, apply formatting, or validate a field.

Tip:

When joining expressions together using a combination of **or** and **and** operators, it is recommended to use brackets to group and separate **and**-expressions from **or**-expressions. For example, if you have the following expression:

```
a = "2" or a = "" and b = "1"
```

group the expressions as follows:

```
(a = "2" or a = "") and b = "1"
```

This will ensure that the Boolean logic is clear and that it does not result in unexpected behavior.

Chapter 5: Getting Data from External Sources

InfoPath allows you to connect to external data sources such as XML files, databases, and SharePoint lists and libraries to retrieve data. Once you have set up a connection to retrieve data from an external data source, this data source becomes what is called a Secondary data source in the InfoPath form.

InfoPath form templates may contain the structure (XML schema) for Secondary data sources, but data from Secondary data sources is never stored in the InfoPath form itself.

Important:

> If you want to permanently store data in an InfoPath form, always create fields in the Main data source of the InfoPath form to store this data in. Data in Secondary data sources of an InfoPath form is never stored in the form.

Secondary data sources can be used in InfoPath to populate drop-down list boxes, lookup data (for example, lookup the name of the manager of an employee), or used as a temporary storage location while a user is filling out a form.

32.   Get data from an XML file

Problem

You have an XML file that contains data you want to use in an InfoPath form.

Solution

You can add a receive data connection to the XML file to the form template to be able to read in data from that XML file and use it within the InfoPath form.

Suppose you have an XML file named **LineBreak** with the following contents:

```
<?xml version="1.0" encoding="UTF-8" ?>
<break>&#xD;</break>
```

To add a data connection to retrieve data from an XML file:

1.   In InfoPath, create a new **Blank Form** template.
2.   Select **Data ➤ Get External Data ➤ From Other Sources ➤ From XML File**.
3.   On the **Data Connection Wizard**, click **Browse** to browse to and select the XML file mentioned above, and then click **Next**.

4. On the **Data Connection Wizard**, click **Next**.

5. On the **Data Connection Wizard**, enter a name for the data connection (for example **LineBreak**), leave the **Automatically retrieve data when form is opened** check box selected, and click **Finish**.

With this you have added a Secondary data source to an XML file to the form template. If you look in the **Fields** drop-down list box on the **Fields** task pane, you will see **LineBreak (Secondary)** listed.

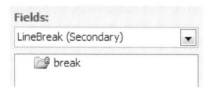

Figure 76. LineBreak Secondary data source selected on the Fields task pane in InfoPath.

Now you can use the XML data connection to get data from the XML file and use it in your InfoPath form for example to add a line break in the text on a button (see *76 Add line breaks to a button caption*).

Discussion

You can also add a data connection to an InfoPath form template via the **Data Connections** dialog box.

To open the **Data Connections** dialog box and add a receive data connection to an XML file:

1. Click **Data ➤ Get External Data ➤ Data Connections**.

2. On the **Data Connections** dialog box, click **Add**.

3. When the **Data Connection Wizard** opens, select **Receive data**, and click **Next**.

4. On the second screen of the **Data Connection Wizard**, select **XML document** and click **Next**. After this you will be on the same screen as in step 3 of the recipe described above, so can continue adding the connection by following the rest of the steps in the recipe.

In InfoPath you can create two types of data connections: **Receive** and **Submit** data connections. **Receive data** connections are used to retrieve data into InfoPath and **Submit data** connections are used to submit InfoPath data to a particular destination.

If you are adding an XML file as a Secondary data source to an InfoPath form, you can choose to **Include the data as a resource file in the form template**. This option is selected by default in InfoPath if you are adding an XML file to a Web browser form, because a Web browser form does not have access to the local computer or the network location where the original XML file might be located.

Once the XML file has been added as a resource file to the form template, you can find that XML file by opening up the **Resource Files** dialog box. To open the **Resource Files** dialog box, click **Data** ➤ **Form Data** ➤ **Resource Files**.

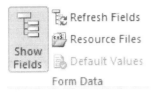

Figure 77. Form Data group on the Data tab containing the Resource Files button.

Resource files are files that exist in a form template (XSN file) and are useful when you require data to be available in the form template when a form has no connectivity (to the Internet or elsewhere). Because they are part of the form template itself, their availability is not negatively impacted when an InfoPath form is taken offline.

While you can add resource files to an InfoPath form through the **Resource Files** dialog box, they will not be of much use to you unless you connect them to a Secondary data source, because you cannot directly access resource files from within InfoPath.

In step 3 of the recipe above, you clicked **Browse** to add an XML file as a resource file to the form template. Had you already previously added a resource file to the form template via the **Resource Files** dialog box, then you could have clicked on the **Resource Files** button on the **Data Connection Wizard** in step 3 of the recipe to select that existing XML file, instead of browsing to and selecting a new XML file. This is how you can also add a **Receive data** connection to an XML file to be able to create a Secondary data source for an existing XML resource file.

Figure 78. Resource Files dialog box in InfoPath 2010.

In the recipe above you selected the **Automatically retrieve data when form is opened** check box when creating the data connection. Because the XML file contained very little data it was OK to select this check box in this case. On the other hand, if the XML file contained a very large amount of data and you selected this check box, the form would have taken a very long time to load.

So whenever Secondary data sources have a chance of containing large amounts of data, it is best not to select the check box to automatically retrieve data when the form is opened, but to:

1. Only retrieve the data when the user really needs it by using a **Query for data** action in a rule on a button; or

2. To filter the data before it is retrieved into InfoPath so that it only loads the data that is absolutely required by the user.

Taking the two aforementioned precautions will speed up the initial load time for InfoPath forms.

33.   Get data from a database table

Problem

You have an Access database table that contains data you want to use on an InfoPath form.

Solution

You can add a receive data connection to the Access database to the form template to be able to read data from a table within that database and use that data within the InfoPath form.

Suppose you have an Access database named **RunningShoes.accdb**, which has a table named **Brand** and another table named **Model**.

Brand has two columns:

1. BrandID (autonumber; primary key)

2. BrandName (text).

Model has three columns:

1. ModelID (autonumber; primary key)

2. ModelName (text)

3. BrandID (number; foreign key related to the BrandID column in Brand)

To get data from the **Brand** database table:

1. In InfoPath, create a new **Blank Form (InfoPath Filler)** template.

2. Click **Data ➤ From Other Sources ➤ From Database**.

3. On the **Data Connection Wizard**, click **Select Database** and browse to and select the **RunningShoes.accdb** database file. After you have selected the Access database, the **Select Table** dialog box will pop up.

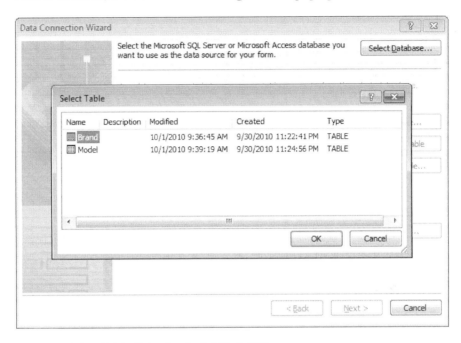

Figure 79. Select Table dialog box in InfoPath 2010.

4. On the **Select Table** dialog box, select **Brand**, and click **OK**.

5. On the **Data Connection Wizard**, click **Next**.

6. On the **Data Connection Wizard**, click **Next** again. Note: If you want to store the data from the database in the form template for offline use, you can select the **Store a copy of the data in the form template** check box, before clicking **Next**. It is not recommended to select this check box if the database contains sensitive information.

7. On the **Data Connection Wizard**, name the data connection **Brand**, leave the **Automatically retrieve data when form is opened** check box selected, and click **Finish**. See the discussion of *32 Get data from an XML file* for when to and when not to select the **Automatically retrieve data when form is opened** check box.

With this you have added a Secondary data source to an Access database table to the form template. If you look in the **Fields** drop-down list box on the **Fields** task pane, you will see **Brand (Secondary)** listed.

Discussion

You can also use the technique described in the recipe above to retrieve data from a SQL Server database. In this recipe you started out creating an **InfoPath Filler Form** template, because you cannot connect a **Web Browser Form** template to an Access database. You will see the following message appear if the InfoPath form template you are adding the database data connection to is a Web Browser Form template, so if you chose to create a new **Blank Form** template instead of a new **Blank Form (InfoPath Filler)** template.

Figure 80. Message box to alert you that you cannot use Access database connections in Web browser forms.

Tip:

You can see what kind of form template you have open in InfoPath Designer 2010 by going to **File ➤ Form Options ➤ Compatibility**, and then checking the currently selected form type in the **Form type** drop-down list box.

34.   Get data from a SharePoint List

Problem

You have a SharePoint List that contains data you want to display on an InfoPath form.

Solution

You can add a receive data connection to the SharePoint List to the form template to be able to read data from that SharePoint List and display it on the InfoPath form.

Suppose you have a SharePoint list named **OfficeApplications** that contains the following data:

Title	Color
Word	Blue
Excel	Green
Access	Red

PowerPoint	Orange
OneNote	Purple
InfoPath	Purple
Publisher	Blue

To get data from a SharePoint List:

1. In InfoPath, create a new **Blank Form** template.

2. Click **Data ➤ Get External Data ➤ From SharePoint List**.

3. On the **Data Connection Wizard**, type the URL to the SharePoint site where the SharePoint List you want to connect to is located, and click **Next**.

4. On the **Data Connection Wizard**, select the SharePoint list you want to connect to (**OfficeApplications** is this case) from the lists and libraries list box, and click **Next**.

5. On the **Data Connection Wizard**, select any fields (for example, **Title** and **Color**) from the SharePoint list that you want to display or use on the InfoPath form, and click **Next**.

6. On the **Data Connection Wizard**, click **Next**.

7. On the **Data Connection Wizard**, enter a name for the data connection, leave the **Automatically retrieve data when form is opened** check box selected, and click **Finish**. See the discussion of *32 Get data from an XML file* for when to and when not to select the **Automatically retrieve data when form is opened** check box.

Now you can use the data connection to the SharePoint list to get data from the SharePoint list and use it in your InfoPath form for example to populate a drop-down list box (see *48 Populate a drop-down list box from an XML file*).

Discussion

If you click **Data ➤ Get External Data ➤ Data Connections**, you should see the receive data connection listed on the **Data Connections** dialog box. At the bottom of the **Data Connections** dialog box you can see more details on the data connection, such as for example that its type is **Retrieve data**, that it is a **Secondary data source**, and that it connects to a SharePoint site.

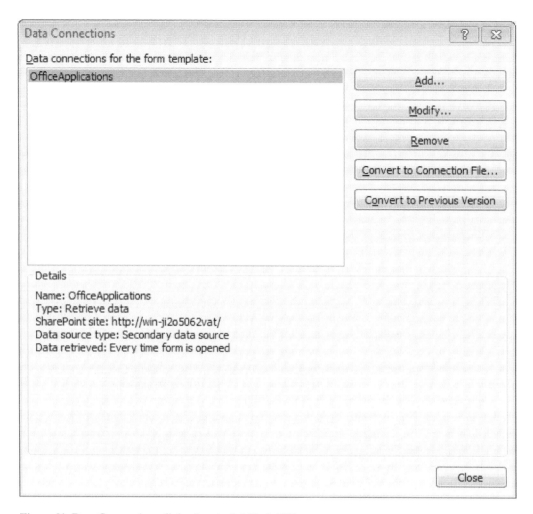

Figure 81. Data Connections dialog box in InfoPath 2010.

Chapter 6: Submitting Forms

Submitting a form means sending it to a particular destination for it to be stored or processed. You can submit an InfoPath form to one of five destinations:

1. To an email address or list of email addresses.

2. To a SharePoint Library.

3. To a Web Service.

4. To a SharePoint Server Connection.

5. To a hosting environment, such as an ASP.NET page or a hosting application.

All submit destinations have one thing in common: The InfoPath form is sent to someone or somewhere (to a person, to a SharePoint site, to a database, etc.) and stored there, and is not stored locally on disk.

35. Submit a form to a single destination using rules

Problem

You have an InfoPath form which you want to submit (send) to a list of people via e-mail.

Solution

You can enable submit on the InfoPath form and then create an e-mail submit data connection to submit the form to a list of e-mail addresses.

To submit an InfoPath form to a single destination (here: a list of e-mail addresses) using rules:

1. In InfoPath, create a new **Blank Form** template.

2. Add 4 **Text Box** controls to the form template. Name them **managerEmail**, **employeeEmail**, **subject**, and **notes**, respectively.

3. Click **Data ➤ Submit Form ➤ To E-mail**.

4. On the **Data Connection Wizard**, click the formula button behind the **To** text box.

5. On the **Insert Formula** dialog box, construct a formula similar to the following:

   ```
   concat(managerEmail, "; ", employeeEmail)
   ```

   and click **OK**. What this formula does is concatenate two e-mail addresses with a semi-colon separating them.

6. On the **Data Connection Wizard**, type an email address (e.g. someone@somewhere.com) in the **Cc** text box. As you can see, you can also type in a static e-mail address to send the form to.

7. On the **Data Connection Wizard**, click the formula button behind the **Subject** text box.

8. On the **Insert Formula** dialog box, click the **Insert Field or Group** button.

9. On the **Select a Field or Group** dialog box, select the **subject** field, and click **OK**. Here you are using the value of a form field as the subject for the e-mail. You could have also typed in a static piece of text in the **Subject** text box instead of using the value of a form field. The latter applies to all of the text boxes on the **Data Connection Wizard**.

10. On the **Insert Formula** dialog box, click **OK**.

11. On the **Data Connection Wizard**, click **Next**.

12. On the **Data Connection Wizard**, select **Send only the active view of the form and no attachment**. You could also opt to send the form as an attachment in the email and even attach the form template to the e-mail so that users are able open the form if you have not published the form template to a shared (network) location. By selecting the option to send only the active view, you must ensure that you publish the form template to a network location after you are done designing the form template. Read the descriptive text on the **Data Connection Wizard** and then click **Next**

13. On the **Data Connection Wizard**, accept the default data connection name of **Email Submit** and also to set the data connection as the default submit connection, and click **Finish**.

14. Now that you have created the submit data connection, you must enable the form to be submitted. Click **Data ➤ Submit Form ➤ Submit Options**.

15. On the **Submit Options** dialog box you will see that **Allow users to submit this form** has already been automatically selected for you and that the **Send form data to a single destination** has been set to **E-mail** with the **Email Submit** data connection you created in the previous steps. Had these options not been selected automatically for you, you could have selected and set them yourself. In addition, you could have also created the submit data connection via the **Submit Options** dialog box by clicking the **Add** button that is located behind the **Choose a data connection for submit** drop-down list box.

16. On the **Submit Options** dialog box, click **OK**.

17. Preview the form.

When the form opens, type e-mail addresses into the **managerEmail** and **employeeEmail** text boxes, a subject line into the **subject** text box, and some notes in the **note** field if you wish, and then click **Submit**.

InfoPath should open a **Message** dialog box.

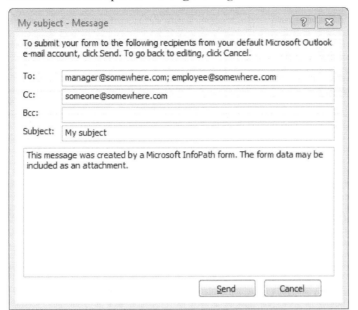

Figure 82. Message dialog box to submit an InfoPath form to a list of e-mail recipients.

Click **Send** to send the email. Once the message has been send, the e-mail in Outlook should contain the current view with the data you entered in InfoPath.

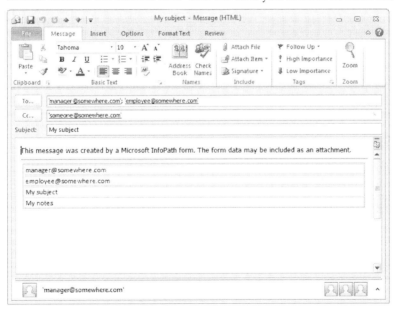

Figure 83. E-mail message in Outlook 2010 containing current view of InfoPath 2010 form.

Discussion

Submitting an InfoPath 2010 form to one or more e-mail addresses requires users to have Microsoft Outlook 2010 installed on their computers.

You cannot prevent the **Message** dialog box from appearing before sending an e-mail from InfoPath. The dialog box not only serves as a confirmation that you do indeed want to send the e-mail, but also to prevent e-mail messages from accidentally being sent or the e-mail functionality in InfoPath being abused to send spam e-mails.

Exercise

Open the **Submit Options** dialog box again, and explore the options present on it. For example, click on the **Advanced** button and explore what kind of things you can do if the form submissions fails or succeeds, and what you can do after submitting the form.

36. Submit a form to multiple destinations using rules

Problem

You have an InfoPath form which you want to submit to two different SharePoint form libraries.

Solution

You can use **Action** rules to submit an InfoPath form to more than one destination.

To submit an InfoPath form to multiple destinations (for example two SharePoint libraries) using rules:

1. In SharePoint, create two form libraries and name them **TwoLibs1** and **TwoLibs2**, respectively.

2. In InfoPath, create a new **Blank Form** template.

3. Click **Data ➤ Submit Form ➤ To SharePoint Library**.

4. On the **Data Connection Wizard**, type the URL to the **TwoLibs1** SharePoint Form library you created earlier, for example

   ```
   http://servername/TwoLibs1/
   ```

5. On the **Data Connection Wizard**, click the formula button behind the **File name** text box.

6. On the **Insert Formula** dialog box, construct a formula similar to the following:

```
concat("TwoLibs1_", now())
```

This formula generates a unique name for the InfoPath form by appending the date and time to the text "TwoLibs1_". Note: You must do this to prevent error messages from appearing when you try to submit a form that has a name that already exists in the SharePoint Form Library. The chances of two people submitting a form at exactly the same time are small. However, you could select the **Allow overwrite if file exists** check box to prevent such error messages from taking place, but I recommend not doing this just in case two people do happen to submit a form at exactly the same time. It is best to have the submission fail rather than to overwrite someone else's form. Another option is to include the user name in the form name by using a formula such as:

```
concat("TwoLibs1_", userName(), "_", now())
```

because a combination of user name and date/time should be guaranteed to be unique.

7. On the **Data Connection Wizard**, click **Next**.

8. On the **Data Connection Wizard**, type **TwoLibs1 SharePoint Library Submit** as the name for the data connection, deselect the **Set as the default submit connection** check box, and click **Finish**.

9. Click **Data ➤ Submit Form ➤ To SharePoint Library**, and repeat steps 4 through 8 for creating a data connection to submit the form to the **TwoLibs2** SharePoint Form library.

10. Click **Data ➤ Submit Form ➤ Submit Options**.

11. On the **Submit Options** dialog box, select **Allow users to submit this form**, select **Perform custom action using Rules**, and click **OK**. This will open the **Rules** task pane to define actions for the **Form Submit** event.

12. On the **Rules** task pane, InfoPath already added a submit action to the first data connection (**TwoLibs1 SharePoint Library Submit**) you created, so click **New ➤ Action** to add a rule for the **TwoLibs2** data connection.

13. On the **Rules** task pane with **Rule2** selected, click **Add ➤ Submit data**.

14. On the **Rule Details** dialog box, select **TwoLibs2 SharePoint Library Submit** from the **Data connection** drop-down list box, and click **OK**.

15. Save the form template to a location on disk.

16. Click **File ➤ Publish ➤ SharePoint Server** to start publishing the form template to SharePoint.

17. On the **Publishing Wizard**, type the URL to the SharePoint site where the two form libraries are located, and click **Next**.

18. On the **Publishing Wizard**, leave **Enable this form to be filled out by using a browser** selected, leave **Form Library** selected, and click **Next**.

19. On the **Publishing Wizard**, select **Update the form template in an existing form library**, select **TwoLibs1** from the **Form library to update** list, and click **Next**.

20. On the **Publishing Wizard**, click **Next**.

21. On the **Publishing Wizard**, click **Publish**.

22. On the **Publishing Wizard**, click **Close**.

23. Go to the **TwoLibs1** Form Library in SharePoint, and click **Add document** to test the form.

When the form opens, click **Submit** to submit the form. A new form named "TwoLibs1_[datetimevalue]" should have been created in the **TwoLibs1** SharePoint Form library.

Go to the **TwoLibs2** SharePoint Form Library. A new form named "TwoLibs2_[datetimevalue]" should have also been created in the **TwoLibs2** SharePoint Form Library. Note that the datetime value should be the same as on the form in the **TwoLibs1** SharePoint Form library and that the contents of the two forms in the two libraries should also be the same, because it is the one and same form that has been submitted to two different SharePoint form libraries.

Discussion

This recipe is not limited to submitting to two data connections, neither to only SharePoint Form Libraries. You can add any number of data connections to submit a form to as well as mix up the type of submit destinations.

If you do not have a SharePoint Server available to you, you could try creating two e-mail submit connections (see *35 Submit a form to a single destination using rules*) instead of two SharePoint form library submit connections, and configure the form to be submitted through rules using those two e-mail submit data connections.

Note that for this recipe in particular, the forms created will always be linked to the form template you published to the **TwoLibs1** SharePoint Form Library, even though forms will also be stored in the **TwoLibs2** SharePoint Form Library.

37. Prevent form submit if a check box has not been selected

Problem

You have an InfoPath form with an "I have read and understood these terms and conditions" check box. You want to prevent users from submitting the form if they have not selected the terms and conditions check box.

Solution

In this recipe, you want to prevent submission of a form. The action is to submit the form. This is an action that must go on a rule on a source, which in this case is the submit button on the toolbar or any other button or control you want to use to submit the form.

Then there is a check box that has a value that determines whether the form should be submitted or not, so this check should become a condition on the submit rule, that is, if the check box is selected submission is allowed, if the check box is not selected submission is not allowed to take place.

And finally, to let the user know why the form cannot be submitted, you should display a message. In this recipe, a message is shown to the user using text on a section control, which is hidden when the form opens, but appears as soon as the user tries to submit the form and the check box is not selected.

Showing/hiding is a formatting action, so you must create a formatting rule on a target. The section is being hidden, so the section is the target. The formatting of the target should be driven by the value of a field that is set when the form is submitted and the check box is not checked. The latter indicates that you should create a hidden field and a second action rule on the submit button that sets the value of this hidden field based on a condition that the check box is selected or not selected.

Do you see the thought process? Don't worry if you don't; at the end of this recipe, we will go through it again. Just assume for now that you can configure an InfoPath form to be submitted using a rule and then add a condition on this rule to check whether the terms and conditions check box has been selected.

To allow a form to be submitted based on a check box selection:

1. In InfoPath, create a new **Blank Form** template.

2. Add a second view to the form template (see *12 Add a second view to a form template*) and name it **Submit View**.

3. Switch back to View 1 (the default view), and add a **Check Box** and **Section** control to the form template. Name the check box control **termsConditionsCheck**.

4. Type the text "You must accept the terms and conditions before submitting the form" on the section control.

5. On the **Fields** task pane under the **myFields** group, add a hidden field (see *10 Add a hidden field*) with the name **isSectionVisible**, the data type **Text(string)**, and a default value of **0**.

6. Click the **Section** control to select it, and then click **Home ➤ Rules ➤ Manage Rules**.

7. On the **Rules** task pane, click **New ➤ Formatting**.

8. On the **Rules** task pane under the **Formatting** section, select the **Hide this control** check box.

9. On the **Rules** task pane under the **Condition** section, click on the text **None**.

10. On the **Condition** dialog box, select **isSectionVisible** from the first drop-down list box, select **is equal to** from the second drop-down list box, select **Type text** from the third drop-down list box, type **0** in the text box, and then click **OK**. The following condition should now appear on the **Rules** task pane under the **Condition** section:

    ```
    isSectionVisible = "0"
    ```

    This condition allows the rule to run to hide the section if the value of the **isSectionVisible** field is equal to **0**.

11. Click **Data ➤ Submit Form ➤ Submit Options**.

12. On the **Submit Options** dialog box, select the **Allow users to submit the form** check box, select the **Perform custom action using Rules** radio button, click **Advanced**, select **Leave the form open** from the **After submit** drop-down list box, and click **OK**. With this you have configured the form to be submitted using rules and to have the form remain open once it has been submitted.

13. Click **Data ➤ Rules ➤ Form Submit**.

14. On the **Rules** task pane ensure that **Form Submit** is being shown below the title bar, and then click **New ➤ Action**.

15. On the **Rules** task pane under **Condition**, click the text **None – Rule runs when form is submitted**.

16. On the **Condition** dialog box, select **termsConditionsCheck** from the first drop-down list box, select **is equal to** from the second drop-down list box, select **TRUE** from the third drop-down list box, and click **OK**. The following condition should now appear on the **Rules** task pane under the **Condition** section:

    ```
    termsConditionsCheck = TRUE
    ```

This condition allows the **Form Submit** rule to run if the **termsConditionsCheck** check box has been selected.

17. On the **Rules** task pane under the **Run these actions** section, click **Add ➤ Switch views**.

18. On the **Rule Details** dialog box, select **Submit View** from the **View** drop-down list box, and click **OK**. The following action should now appear on the **Rules** task pane under the **Run these actions** section:

```
Switch to view: Submit View
```

Note: This recipe simulates submitting the form by switching to a different view for testing purposes. If you have a destination to submit to, you could configure a **Submit data** action (instead of a **Switch views** action) with a corresponding data connection that does a real submit.

19. On the **Rules** task pane, select the **Don't run remaining rules if the condition of this rule is met** check box, because after the form has been submitted, you do not want any more rules to run.

20. On the **Rules** task pane, click **New ➤ Action** to add a second action rule.

21. On the **Rules** task pane under **Condition**, add a condition just like you did in step 16 that says:

```
termsConditionsCheck = FALSE
```

This condition allows the rule that sets the value of the **isSectionVisible** field equal to **1** to run if the **termsConditionsCheck** check box has not been selected, which means that if a user tries to submit the form and the check box has not been selected, the section will be made visible.

22. On the **Rules** task pane under **Run these actions**, click **Add ➤ Set a field's value**.

23. On the **Rule Details** dialog box, click the button behind the **Field** text box.

24. On the **Select a Field or Group** dialog box, select **isSectionVisible**, and click **OK**.

25. On the **Rule Details** dialog box, type **1** in the **Value** text box, and click **OK**. The following action should now appear on the **Rules** task pane under the **Run these actions** section:

```
Set a field's value: isSectionVisible = "1"
```

26. Preview the form.

When the form opens, click the **Submit** button on the ribbon. The section should appear displaying the message that you must accept the terms and conditions. Select the check box and click the **Submit** button again. The **Submit View** should now be displayed to indicate that the form has been submitted.

Discussion

The recipe described above is a typical example of running a rule based on whether a certain condition has been met or not. In this case, if a user has not selected the check box, the form should not be submitted, but instead, a message should appear.

This recipe contains both **Action** and **Formatting** rules. Let us try to identify them by dissecting the requirement.

The form is submitted. This is an action, a **Submit data** action on a **Form Submit** rule to be more precise. Note: You used a **Switch views** action instead of a **Submit data** action in this recipe for testing purposes.

The submitting of the form depends on whether the check box is selected or not. This is a condition for submitting the form, so a condition that should go on the **Form Submit** rule. This results in a **Submit Form** rule with the condition

```
termsConditionsCheck = TRUE
```

and the action

```
Switch to view: Submit View
```

when submitting the form. And because you do not want any more rules to run if the condition for this rule is met, you need to disable all other rules that are run after this rule by checking the **Don't run remaining rules if the condition of this rule is met** check box.

A message should appear if the user tries to submit the form, but has not selected the check box. The appearing of a message on a section control can only be done through the use of a **Formatting** rule. And **Formatting** rules are set on targets instead of sources. You used a section control to show the message, so you have to add a formatting rule on the section control (the target).

The showing/hiding of the section depends on whether the check box is selected and should only be shown when the form is being submitted. This means that you have to create a hidden field (**isSectionVisible**) that is set to a value that indicates that the section should be shown. The value of the hidden field should be set by the **Submit Form** rule to the value (any value unequal to 0; you used a value of 1) that makes the section visible if the check box has not been selected. This is why you must set the condition

```
termsConditionCheck = FALSE
```

and the action

```
Set a field's value: isSectionVisible = "1"
```

on a second rule for submitting the form.

The entire submit form logic with conditions is visualized in the following flow chart.

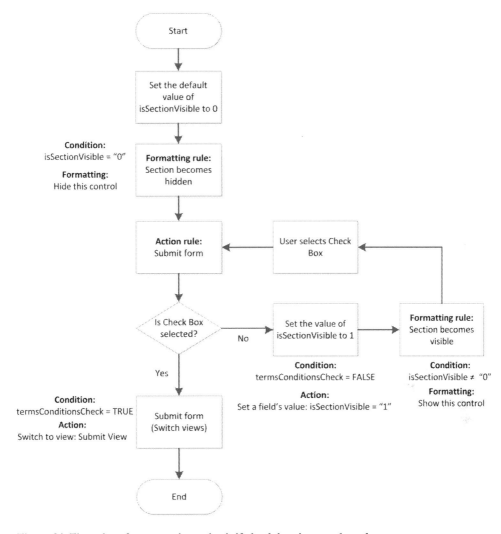

Figure 84. Flow chart for preventing submit if check box is not selected.

38. Submit InfoPath data to a single Microsoft Access database table

Problem

You want to use InfoPath to create, update, and delete records in an Access database table.

Solution

You can use the **Database** form template in InfoPath to design a form to collect data that is stored in an Access database.

Suppose you have an Access database named **RunningShoes.accdb**, which has a table named **Brand** and another table named **Model** in it.

Brand has two columns:

1. BrandID (autonumber; primary key)

2. BrandName (text).

Model has three columns:

1. ModelID (autonumber; primary key)

2. ModelName (text)

3. BrandID (number; foreign key related to BrandID column in Brand)

To submit data to the **Brand** Access database table:

1. In InfoPath, click **File ➤ New ➤ Database** to create a new **Database** form template. When you select **Database** and click **Design Form** in the **Backstage**, the **Data Connection Wizard** will open.

2. On the **Data Connection Wizard**, click **Select Database**, and browse to and select the **RunningShoes.accdb** Access database file. After you have selected the database, the **Select Table** dialog box will open.

3. On the **Select Table** dialog box, select **Brand**, and click **OK**.

4. On the **Data Connection Wizard**, click **Next**.

5. On the **Data Connection Wizard**, you can read that InfoPath created a submit connection for the form template, and gave it the name **Main connection submit**. Ensure that the **Enable submit for this connection** check box is selected, and click **Finish**.

6. InfoPath automatically adds a **New Record** and **Run Query** button to the form template. The **New Record** button is used to clear form fields in preparation to enter data for a new record, and the **Run Query** button is used to retrieve data

from the database. But before you can do all this, you must add a few fields to the template.

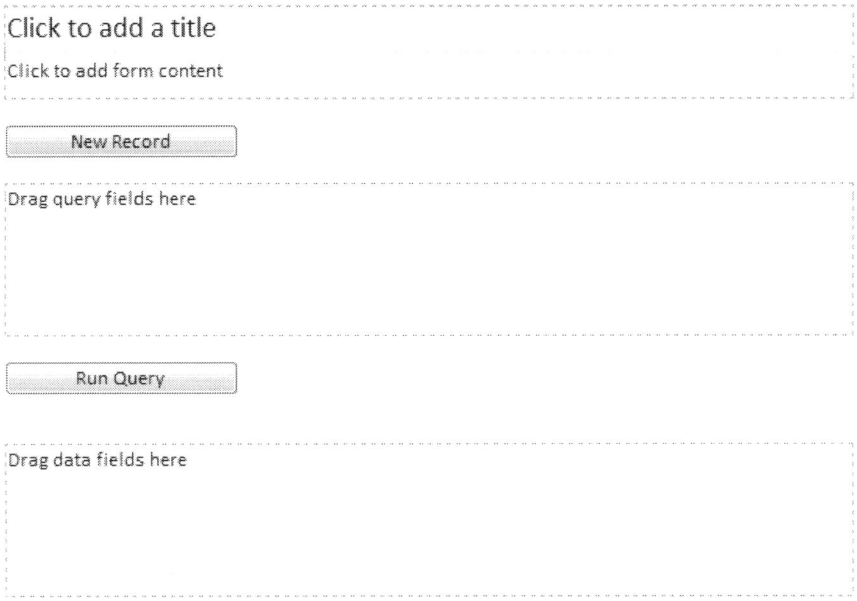

Click to add a title

Click to add form content

New Record

Drag query fields here

Run Query

Drag data fields here

Figure 85. InfoPath design canvas after binding the form template to a database table.

7.   On the **Fields** task pane, you will see two groups in the Main data source: **queryFields** and **dataFields**. The **queryFields** group contains fields you can use for querying data in the database table, and the **dataFields** group contains fields and groups that can be used to enter data in or display data from the database table.

On the **Fields** task pane, expand all of the groups, and examine the fields and groups under **queryFields** and **dataFields**.

Figure 86. Main data source of an InfoPath form bound to a database table.

8. On the **Fields** task pane under **dataFields**, click the **Brand** repeating group, drag it to the form template, drop it on the text that says "Drag data fields here", and select **Repeating Section** from the context menu that appears.

9. On the **Fields** task pane under **dataFields** under **Brand**, click **BrandName**, drag it to the form template, and drop it inside of the repeating section you added in the previous step.

10. Preview the form. When the form opens, click the **Run Query** button to view all of the data in the table. You may see the following message appear when you click the **Run Query** button.

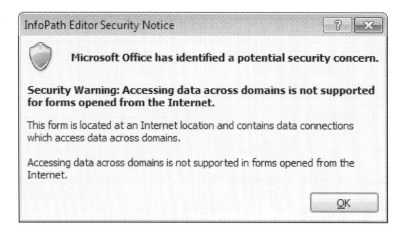

Figure 87. Security warning in InfoPath when trying to connect to a local Access database.

To bypass security warnings when previewing the form, give the form template **Full Trust** as follows:

   a. Click **File ➤ Form Options**.

   b. On the **Form Options** dialog box, select **Security and Trust** under **Category**, deselect the **Automatically determine security level (recommended)** check box, select **Full Trust**, select the **Sign this form template** check box, click **Create Certificate** to create a self-signed certificate, and click **OK**.

   c. Preview the form again.

11. To add a new record to the database table, click **New Record**, type in a brand name, and click **Submit**. After you click **Submit**, the form will close, because it is configured by default to close after submit, but you can configure it to remain open by going to **Data ➤ Submit Options ➤ Advanced** and selecting **Leave the form open** from the **After submit** drop-down list box.

12. Now that you have seen how to retrieve all records and add a new one, it is time to add a query filter, to retrieve one specific record. On the **Fields** task pane,

expand the **queryFields** group under **Brand**, drag **BrandName** to the form template, and drop it on the text that says "Drag query fields here".

13. Preview the form.

When the form opens, type a brand name into the text box under the **New Record** button and then click **Run Query**. If an exact match can be found in the database table for the brand name you typed in, then its details should appear in the text box below the **Run Query** button.

Discussion

As you saw in the recipe above, you can add a filter to query records from a database table. However, wildcard searches are not supported when you use the method described above. If you want to design a form template that can perform wildcard searches on a database table, you will have to write code to provide such functionality.

The error message "Accessing data across domains is not supported from forms opened from the Internet" is displayed because InfoPath identifies the form and data source as being located in two different domains. InfoPath checks cross-domain access if the security for the form is set to **Domain** or **Automatically determine security level (recommended)**, which it was set to before you set it to **Full Trust**. The solution is to put the InfoPath form template and Access database in the same domain.

InfoPath uses the security model of Internet Explorer to apply security to forms, so before you publish the InfoPath form template to the same domain as where the Access database is located, you must configure the Internet Security on your computer.

Suppose the Access database is located somewhere on the network. It makes sense then to publish the form template to a network location in the same domain as where the Access database is located.

The recognition of network (UNC) paths is not enabled by default in the Internet Options, so you must enable this as follows:

1. In InfoPath, click **File ➤ Options**.

2. On the **InfoPath Options** dialog box, click **More Options**.

3. On the **Options** dialog box on the **General** tab, click **Internet Options**. Note: You can also open the **Internet Properties** dialog box via Internet Explorer's **Tools** menu or by clicking the Windows 7 start button, typing in **change security settings** in the search box, and pressing **ENTER**.

4. On the **Internet Properties** dialog box, click the **Security** tab, select **Local Intranet**, and click **Sites**.

5. On the **Local intranet** dialog box, deselect the **Automatically detect intranet network** check box, select the **Include all network paths (UNCs)** check box, and click **Advanced**.

Figure 88. Local intranet dialog box including network paths as websites.

6. On the **Local intranet** dialog box, type in the UNC path to the network location, click **Add**, and then click **Close**.

7. On the **Local intranet** dialog box, click **OK**.

8. On the **Internet Properties** dialog box, click **OK**.

9. On the **Options** dialog box, click **OK**.

10. On the **InfoPath Options** dialog box, click **OK**.

11. Click **File ➤ Form Options**.

12. On the **Form Options** dialog box, select **Security and Trust ➤ Domain**, and click **OK**. This will set the form template's security level back to **Domain** trust instead of **Full Trust**.

Now you must publish the form template to the network location in the same domain as where the Access database is located, and then you should be able to open an InfoPath form without getting the cross-domain access error. Be careful with using mapped network drives for the network location, since not all users may be using the same drive letter mappings for a certain network location.

It is always best to use the full network path when publishing a form template instead of a mapped network drive to a network location, because in the latter case, InfoPath may still see the form template and data source as being located in different domains.

To see the location to where a form template has been published, look at the bottom left corner in **InfoPath Filler 2010**. That location should be the same location where the Access database is located.

Figure 89. Publish location for form template in InfoPath Filler 2010.

Tip:

Whenever you have included external data sources in an InfoPath form template and get data source access errors, check that the security level of the form template has been set to **Domain** (and not **Restricted**), and then analyze where you have published the form template and whether the external data sources that the form is trying to access are located in the same domain as the form template. If not, make sure that they are.

39. Submit to Access database tables with a one-to-many relationship

Problem

You want to use InfoPath to create, update, and delete records in two Access database tables that have a one-to-many relationship defined between them.

Solution

You can use the **Database** form template in InfoPath to design a form to collect data that is stored in two related Access database tables that have a one-to-many relationship between them.

Suppose you have an Access database named **RunningShoes.accdb**, which has a table named **Brand** and another table named **Model** in it.

Brand has two columns:

1. BrandID (autonumber; primary key)
2. BrandName (text).

Model has three columns:

1. ModelID (autonumber; primary key)
2. ModelName (text)
3. BrandID (number; foreign key related to BrandID column in Brand)

To submit data to the **Brand** and **Model** Access database tables:

1. In InfoPath, create a new **Database** form template. When you click **File ➤ Database ➤ Design Form**, the **Data Connection Wizard** will open.

2. On the **Data Connection Wizard**, click **Select Database**, and browse to and select the **RunningShoes.accdb** Access database file. After you have selected the database, the **Select Table** dialog box will open.

3. On the **Select Table** dialog box, select **Brand** (which covers the "one" side of the relationship between the tables), and click **OK**.

4. On the **Data Connection Wizard**, click **Add Table**.

5. On the **Add Table or Query** dialog box, select **Model** (which covers the "many" side of the relationship between the tables), and click **Next**.

6. On the **Edit Relationship** dialog box, click **Finish**.

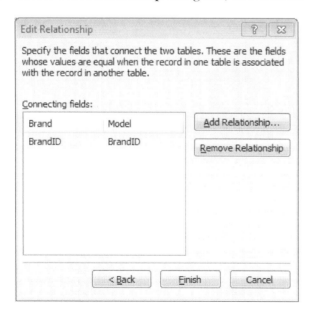

Figure 90. Edit Relationship dialog box in InfoPath 2010.

Note: If you gave the columns that bind the two tables together the same name, InfoPath will automatically find the correct fields to relate to each other. In this case, InfoPath found **BrandID** in **Brand** and related it to **BrandID** in **Model**. If InfoPath automatically created an incorrect relationship, because the fields do not have the same name, you must select the relationship in the **Connecting fields** list, and then click **Remove Relationship**. Once you have deleted the incorrect relationship, click **Add Relationship** and choose the correct field from each table to relate to each other.

7. On the **Data Connection Wizard**, click **Next**.

8. On the **Data Connection Wizard**, you can read that InfoPath created a submit connection for the form template, and gave it the name **Main connection submit**. Ensure that the **Enable submit for this connection** check box is selected, and click **Finish**.

9. InfoPath automatically adds a **New Record** and **Run Query** button to the form template. The **New Record** button can be used to clear form fields in preparation to enter data for a new record, and the **Run Query** button can be used to retrieve data from the database. But before you can do all this, you must add a few fields to the form template.

10. On the **Fields** task pane, you will see two groups in the Main data source: **queryFields** and **dataFields**. The **queryFields** group contains fields you can use for querying data in the database table, and the **dataFields** group contains fields and groups that can be used to enter data in or display data from the database table. On the **Fields** task pane, expand all of the groups, and examine the fields and groups under **queryFields** and **dataFields**.

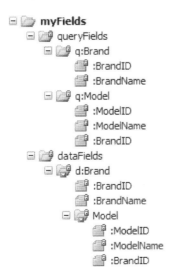

Figure 91. Main data source of an InfoPath form bound to two related database tables.

11. On the **Fields** task pane under **dataFields**, click the **Brand** repeating group, drag it to the form template, drop it on the text that says "Drag data fields here", and select **Repeating Section** from the context menu that appears.

12. On the **Fields** task pane under **dataFields** under **Brand**, click **BrandName**, drag it to the form template, and drop it inside of the repeating section you added in the previous step.

13. On the **Fields** task pane under **dataFields** under **Brand**, click **Model**, drag it to the form template, drop it below the **BrandName** text box, and select **Repeating Table** from the context menu that appears. Delete the **ModelID** and **BrandID** columns from the repeating table, because they are not required to be able to enter new records, since these fields have the **autonumber** data type in the database. To delete a column from a repeating table, right-click anywhere in the column you want to delete, and select **Delete ➤ Columns** from the context menu or click anywhere in the column you want to delete and then select **Layout ➤ Rows & Columns ➤ Delete ➤ Columns** under **Table Tools** on the ribbon.

14. Preview the form.

When the form opens, click the **Run Query** button to view all of the data in the table. If you get a security warning, follow the instructions in step 10 of *38 Submit InfoPath data to a single Microsoft Access database table*.

To add a new record to the database table, click **New Record**, type in a brand name, add a few model names to the repeating table, and then click **Submit**.

Discussion

Submitting to Access database tables that have a many-to-many relationship with each other is not supported in InfoPath. You will have to write custom code, if you want to submit data to tables that have a many-to-many relationship with each other.

And always remember to set primary keys on any tables you want to submit to from an InfoPath form, otherwise the submit action might fail.

Note that you must always have data that is new or that has changed on a form before submitting the form. If you click **Submit** without performing any changes to the data in the form, you will see an error message appear saying "The form cannot be submitted because of an error". And if you look at the details for the error message, it will say "InfoPath cannot submit the form. The form does not contain any new data to submit to the data source".

Read-only views and controls after submit

Often times you may want to make one or more controls or an entire view with controls read-only immediately after an InfoPath form has been submitted or after a form has been submitted and is subsequently reopened.

The following three recipes discuss how you can make a control or an entire view read-only after a submit action has taken place.

40. Switch to read-only view on submit

Problem

You added a read-only view to an InfoPath form template. Now you want to have the form switch to the read-only view when the form is submitted.

Solution

You can use rules to submit an InfoPath form and then switch to a read-only view after submit.

To switch to a read-only view on submit:

1. In InfoPath, create a new **Blank Form** template.

2. Add a read-only view to the form template (see *14 Add a read-only view*) and remove the ability for users to switch views through the menu (deselect the **Show on the View menu when filling out this form** check box on the **View Properties** dialog box). When you are done, switch back to the default view via the **View** drop-down list box on the **Page Design** tab.

3. Click **Data ➤ Submit Form ➤ Submit Options**.

4. On the **Submit Options** dialog box, select the **Allow users to submit this form** check box, select the **Perform custom action using Rules** radio button, click **Advanced**, select **Leave the form open** in the **After submit** drop-down list box, and click **OK**. This will cause the form to remain open once it has been submitted.

5. On the **Rules** task pane, click **New ➤ Action**.

6. On the **Rules** task pane, click **Add ➤ Submit data** to add an action to submit the form to a destination of your choice. This could be to a list of email recipients (see *35 Submit a form to a single destination using rules*) or to a SharePoint Form Library (see *36 Submit a form to multiple destinations using rules*) for example.

7. On the **Rules** task pane, click **Add** to add a second action to the rule, and then select **Switch views** from the drop-down menu.

8. On the **Rule Details** dialog box, select the read-only view from the **View** drop-down list box, and click **OK**.

9. Preview the form.

When the form opens, click the **Submit** button. The form should switch to and display the read-only view and remain open after it has been submitted.

Discussion

There are two things you must be aware of for this recipe:

1. Because you want to switch to and display a read-only view when the form is submitted, you need to keep the form open after submit.

2. Because you want to switch views when the form is submitted, you must use rules for submitting the form and add a **Switch views** action rule as the last rule to run during the form submit event.

41. Switch to read-only view when form opens after submit

Problem

You added a read-only view to an InfoPath form template. Now you want to have the form switch to the read-only view as soon as a user opens the form after it has been submitted.

Solution

Switching to a specific view when a form is opened on subsequent times after it has been submitted, is a conditional action, which means that you must first set a flag to track whether the form has been submitted and then when the form is opened, check the flag and if it has been set to a particular value that indicates that the form has been submitted, switch to the read-only view.

To switch to a read-only view when a form opens after it has been submitted:

1. In InfoPath, create a new **Blank Form** template.

2. Add a read-only view to the form template (see *14 Add a read-only view*) and remove the ability for users to switch views through the menu (deselect the **Show on the View menu when filling out this form** check box on the **View Properties** dialog box). When you are done, switch back to the default view via the **View** drop-down list box on the **Page Design** tab.

3. Add a hidden field named **isFormSubmitted** (see *10 Add a hidden field*).

4. Click **Data ➤ Submit Form ➤ Submit Options**.

5. On the **Submit Options** dialog box, select the **Allow users to submit this form** check box, select the **Perform custom action using Rules** radio button, and click **OK**.

6. On the **Rules** task pane, ensure that **Form Submit** is listed under the title bar, and then click **New ➤ Action**.

7. On the **Rules** task pane, click **Add ➤ Set a field's value**.

8. On the **Rule Details** dialog box, click the button behind the **Field** text box and select the **isFormSubmitted** field.

9. On the **Rule Details** dialog box, type **submitted** in the **Value** text box, and click **OK**. With this you are setting the value of the **isFormSubmitted** field to the text **submitted** once the form has been submitted.

10. On the **Rules** task pane, click **Add ➤ Submit data** to add an action to submit the form to a destination of your choice. This could be to a list of email recipients (select the **Attach the form template to ensure that users can open the form** check box on the e-mail **Data Connection Wizard**, and send the email to yourself for testing purposes) or to a SharePoint Form Library for example.

11. Click **Data ➤ Rules ➤ Form Load**.

12. On the **Rules** task pane, ensure that **Form Load** is listed under the title bar, and then click **New ➤ Action**.

13. On the **Rules** task pane, click **Add ➤ Switch views**.

14. On the **Rule Details** dialog box, select the read-only view from the **View** drop-down list box, and click **OK**.

15. On the **Rules** task pane under **Condition**, click the text **None – Rule runs when form is opened**.

16. On the **Condition** dialog box, select **isFormSubmitted** from the first drop-down list box, leave **is equal to** selected in the second drop-down list box, select **Type text** in the third drop-down list box, type **submitted** in the text box, and click **OK**. With this you have created a rule that will run when the form opens, check whether the **isFormSubmitted** field contains the text **submitted**, and if it does, switch to the read-only view.

17. Preview the form.

When the form opens, click **Submit** to submit it. When you reopen the form, it should display the read-only view.

42. Make a control read-only upon submit

Problem

You have a text box control on an InfoPath form which you want the user to be able to edit the first time the form is opened, but then after the form is submitted and subsequently reopened, you do not want the user to be able to edit the text in the text box anymore.

Solution

You can use conditional formatting and a hidden field to make a control read-only upon submit.

To make a text box control read-only upon submit:

1. In InfoPath, create a new **Blank Form** template.

2. Add a **Text Box** control to the form template.

3. On the **Fields** task pane under the **myFields** group, add a field with the name **isSubmitted** and data type **True/False (boolean)**.

4. Click the **Text Box** to select it.

5. Click **Home ➤ Rules ➤ Manage Rules**.

6. On the **Rules** task pane, click **New ➤ Formatting**.

7. On the **Rules** task pane, select the **Disable this control** check box.

8. On the **Rules** task pane, click the text **None** under **Condition**, and add a condition that says:

    ```
    isSubmitted = TRUE
    ```

    With this you have added a rule that will disable the text box whenever the value of the **isSubmitted** field is equal to **TRUE**.

9. Click **Data ➤ Submit Form ➤ Submit Options**.

10. On the **Submit Options** dialog box, select the **Allow users to submit this form** check box, select the **Perform custom action using Rules** radio button, and click **OK**.

11. On the **Rules** task pane, create a new **Action** rule that sets the value of **isSubmitted** to **true** (Note: You must type the text **true** in the **Value** text box on the **Rule Details** dialog box and not use the formula button behind the **Value** field).

12. On the **Rules** task pane, create a second **Action** rule to **Submit data** to the data connection of your choice, for example a submit data connection to a SharePoint

Library or be to a list of email recipients (select the **Attach the form template to ensure that users can open the form** check box on the e-mail **Data Connection Wizard**, and send the email to yourself for testing purposes).

13. Preview the form.

When the form opens, the text box should be editable. Once you submit the form and reopen it thereafter, the text box should be read-only.

Discussion

In the recipe above, you used a Boolean hidden field in the Main data source to keep track of whether the form had been submitted or not. The value of the hidden field is set through an action rule that runs just before the form is submitted. Because rules do not run after a form has been submitted, you must always set the value of fields before the submit action takes place.

Chapter 7: Input Controls

Input controls are controls that can store data in the Main data source of an InfoPath form. Input controls, a few of which include text boxes, date pickers, and drop-down list boxes, are the most frequently used type of controls in InfoPath.

Check Boxes and Option Buttons

Check boxes and option or radio buttons allow users to select one or more options that they are presented with on a form. So when do you use check boxes and when do you use option (radio) buttons?

Use check boxes when you want to present a user with multiple options, which are not mutually exclusive. For example, a set of options such as Word/Access/Excel/InfoPath asking users to select all of the Microsoft Office applications they are familiar with would be a good candidate for check boxes, because in this case a user can select none, one, or several options.

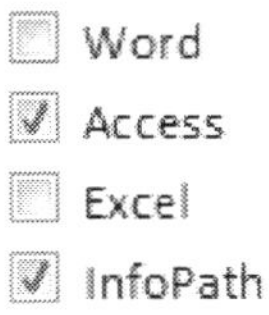

Figure 92. Check Box controls on an InfoPath form.

Use option buttons when you want to present a user with multiple options, which are mutually exclusive, meaning that the user is only allowed to select one option. For example, yes/no questions are good candidates for option buttons, and so is a set of options such as male/female/unspecified, because in such cases only one option should be selected by the user.

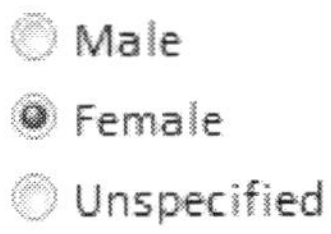

○ Male
◉ Female
○ Unspecified

Figure 93. Option Button control on an InfoPath form.

43.   Validate a check box

Problem

You have a check box control on an InfoPath form and want to determine whether the check box is selected or not.

Solution

You can use a **Validation** rule to determine whether a check box has been selected or not.

To validate a check box:

1.   In InfoPath, create a new **Blank Form** template.

2.   Add a **Check Box** control to the form template and name it **isSelected**.

3.   Add a **Text Box** control to the form template, and name it **checkBoxMustBeSelected**.

4.   Add a **Validation** rule to the check box control with a **Condition** that says:

   ```
   isSelected = FALSE
   and
   checkBoxMustBeSelected is not blank
   ```

   and a **ScreenTip** that says: **You must select the check box**. What this rule does is display the screen tip and a red dashed border around the check box if you type a piece of text in the text box without first selecting the check box.

5.   Preview the form.

When the form opens, type a piece of text into the text box without first selecting the check box. A red dashed border should appear around the check box and when you hover with the mouse over it, you should see the screen tip. Now select the check box and watch the red dashed border disappear.

Discussion

The key to understanding check box validation lies in paying close attention to what has been set as the **Value when cleared** and **Value when checked** properties on the check box.

The aforementioned two properties can be set to one of 5 values when the **Data type** for the check box is set to **True/False (boolean)**:

1.   (Blank)

2.   TRUE

3.   FALSE

4. 1

5. 0

When you first add a check box to a form template, the **Value when cleared** is set to **FALSE** by default, and the **Value when checked** is set to **TRUE** by default.

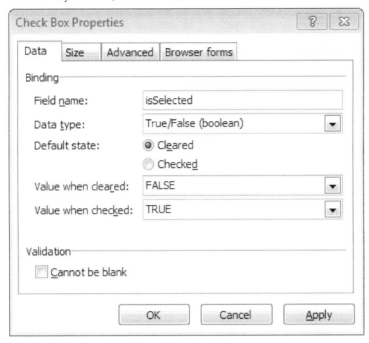

Figure 94. Checked and unchecked states of a check box set to TRUE and FALSE.

TRUE and **FALSE** is a good pair to use for the checked and unchecked states of a check box, but can easily result in validation errors on the check box itself if you do not know that you should set the value of the check box using the **true()** or **false()** function instead of just setting the value to the text **TRUE** or **FALSE** when using the **Set a field's value** action in a rule. However, setting the value to the text **true** or **false** would work.

When you use **1** and **0** as the pair of values for the checked and unchecked states of a check box, you can avoid the ambiguity of using **TRUE** and **FALSE** and are less likely to make the mistake of incorrectly setting the value of the check box or not knowing whether to use text, a number, or a function to set the value, because 1 is equal to "1" (text) in InfoPath.

As you may have noticed from the **Check Box Properties** dialog box, InfoPath does not restrict you to only use the **True/False (boolean)** data type for a check box control. For example, you could also select **Date (date)** as the data type for a check box and define two dates for the **Value when cleared** and **Value when checked**, so that if a user selects the check box, a certain date instead of TRUE or 1 is stored in the field bound to the check box. This also applies to option buttons (see *47 Select an option on one view and have a text box appear on another view*).

Note that the data validation on a check box must match the data type of the field bound to the check box. For example, if you use a date as the data type, you must perform a date validation instead of a validation on whether the field is equal to TRUE/FALSE or 1/0.

44. Toggle a check box on and off when a button is clicked

Problem

You have a check box on an InfoPath form and you want to be able to click a button and select the check box if it is deselected, or deselect the check box if it is selected.

Solution

You can use an **Action** rule on the button to change the value of the check box depending on the current value of the check box.

To toggle a check box on and off when a button is clicked:

1. In InfoPath, create a new **Blank Form** template.

2. Add a **Check Box** and a **Button** control to the form template. Name the check box control **isChecked**.

3. Add an **Action** rule to the button with a **Condition** that says:

    ```
    isChecked = FALSE
    ```

    and an action that says:

    ```
    Set a field's value: isChecked = "true"
    ```

    and select the **Don't run remaining rules if the condition of this rule is met** check box. The condition allows the rule to run if the **isChecked** check box has not been selected and then stops all remaining rules on the button from running. If the condition is met, the rule sets the **isChecked** check box to be selected.

4. Add a second **Action** rule to the button with a **Condition** that says:

    ```
    isChecked = TRUE
    ```

    and an action that says:

    ```
    Set a field's value: isChecked = "false"
    ```

and select the **Don't run remaining rules if the condition of this rule is met** check box. The condition allows the rule to run if the **isChecked** check box has been selected and then stops all remaining rules on the button from running. If the condition is met, the rule sets the **isChecked** check box to be deselected.

5. Preview the form.

When the form opens, click the button. The check box should be selected. When you click the button again, the check box should be deselected.

Discussion

In the recipe above, you made use of the **Don't run remaining rules if the condition of this rule is met** check box on a rule.

InfoPath generally runs action rules on a control one after the other from top to bottom. And because you added two rules to the button and these two rules could inadvertently affect each other (and cause unexpected behavior) because they are setting the value of the same control, i.e. the check box, you must select the option to stop running any other rules as soon as the condition for one of these two rules has been met.

45. Make a field required based on a check box selection

Problem

You have a date picker control on an InfoPath form and want to force the user to enter a date in this date picker if a check box has been selected.

Solution

You can use data validation with a condition to check whether the check box has been selected and if it has whether a date has been entered and display a message if it has not.

To make a field required based on a check box selection:

1. In InfoPath, create a **Blank Form** template.

2. Add a **Date Picker** and **Check Box** control to the form template. Name the date picker control **dueDate** and the check box control **isUrgent**.

3. Because you want to check whether a date has been entered if the check box has been selected, you must add a **Validation** rule on the date picker control. Add a **Validation** rule on the date picker with a **Condition** that says:

```
isUrgent = TRUE
and
dueDate is blank
```

and a **ScreenTip** that says: **Please enter a due date**. The condition allows the rule to run when the **isUrgent** check box has been selected and the **dueDate** date picker does not contain a date.

4. Preview the form.

When the form opens, the date picker control is not a required field, because there is no red asterisk being displayed in it. Once you select the check box, a red asterisk appears in the date picker and when you hover over the date picker, you will see the screen tip you specified earlier.

Discussion

In the recipe above, a field was made required based on a condition. If you have a field that must be required and does not depend on a condition being met for it to be required, it is best to select the **Cannot be blank** check box on the **Properties** dialog box of either the field or the control instead of adding a **Validation** rule on the field.

In summary:

- If you do not have any conditions that should be met for a field to be required, select the **Cannot be blank** property of the field.

- If you have a condition that should be met for a field to be required, use a **Validation** rule on the field.

46. Select a check box to move text from one field to another

Problem

You have two text boxes and one check box on an InfoPath form. When you select the check box, you want the text from the first text box to be moved to the second text box.

Solution

Moving is a combination of two actions: Copying and deleting. You can use an **Action** rule in InfoPath to first set the value of the second text box to be the same value as the first text box, and then set the value of the first text box to an empty string. This will simulate the copying and deleting that is required for moving text.

To move text from one field to another:

1. In InfoPath, create a new **Blank Form** template.

2. Add two **Text Box** controls and one **Check Box** control to the form template. Name the check box **moveText**, the first text box **textToMove**, and the second text box **copiedText**.

3. Add an **Action** rule on the check box that has the following condition:

```
moveText = TRUE
and
textToMove is not blank
```

and two actions:

```
Set a field's value: copiedText = textToMove
Set a field's value: textToMove = ""
```

4. Preview the form.

When the form opens, type a piece of text in the first text box, and then select the check box to move the text over to the second text box.

Note: You could have also used a button instead of a check box to perform this action.

47. Select an option on one view and have a text box appear on another view

Problem

You have a radio button group on the default view of an InfoPath form template. Each option from the radio button group has a corresponding text box on a second view of the form template. When you select one of the options on the first view, you want a corresponding text box to appear on the second view and you do not want the text boxes for the other non-selected options to appear on the second view.

Solution

You can use conditional formatting to show/hide controls in InfoPath independent of the view on which they are located.

To select options on one view and have corresponding text boxes appear on a second view:

1. In InfoPath, create a new **Blank Form** template.

2. Add an **Option Button** control with 3 option buttons to **View 1** of the form template. Name the option button control **color**. Note: While you will see three option buttons on the form, the Main data source of the form only contains one field for those three option buttons, so the value of only one option button – the selected option – will eventually be stored in the form.

3. Type the text **Red** behind the first option button, **Yellow** behind the second option, and **Blue** behind the third option button.

4. Select the first option button, open its **Properties** dialog box, change its **Value when selected** property on the **Data** tab of the **Option Button Properties** dialog box to the text **red**, and select the **This button is selected by default** check box.

5. Select the second option button, open its **Properties** dialog box, and change its **Value when selected** property on the **Data** tab of the **Option Button Properties** dialog box to the text **yellow**.

6. Select the third option button, open its **Properties** dialog box, and change its **Value when selected** property on the **Data** tab of the **Option Button Properties** dialog box to the text **blue**.

7. Add a second view named **View 2** to the form template (see *12 Add a second view to a form template*).

8. Add 3 **Text Box** controls to **View 2** of the form template. Name the text boxes **red**, **yellow**, and **blue**, respectively, and make the background color of each text box the same color as the name you gave the text box (Right-click the text box, and then select **Borders and Shading ➤ Shading ➤ Color**).

9. Click the **red** text box to select it, and then add a **Formatting** rule with a **Condition** that says:

   ```
   color ≠ "red"
   ```

   and a **Formatting** to **Hide this control**. You can compose the condition for this rule by selecting **is not equal to** from the second drop-down list box on the **Condition** dialog box and selecting **Type text** from the third drop-down list box, and then type the text **red** in the text box. This rule will hide the **red** text box on **View 2** if the **red color** option button on **View 1** is not selected.

10. Click the **yellow** text box to select it, and then add a **Formatting** rule with a **Condition** that says:

    ```
    color ≠ "yellow"
    ```

    and a **Formatting** to **Hide this control**. This rule will hide the **yellow** text box on **View 2** if the **yellow color** option button on **View 1** is not selected.

11. Click the **blue** text box to select it, and then add a **Formatting** rule with a **Condition** that says:

    ```
    color ≠ "blue"
    ```

and a **Formatting** to **Hide this control**. This rule will hide the **blue** text box on **View 2** if the **blue color** option button on **View 1** is not selected.

12. Switch back to **View 1** (select **Page Design ➤ Views ➤ View ➤ View 1**) and add a **Button** control with an **Action** rule to switch to **View 2**.

13. Preview the form.

When the form opens, select the yellow option button and then click the button to switch to the second view. The yellow text box should be visible and the other text boxes should be hidden.

Discussion

The recipe described above makes use of the principle that an InfoPath form has only one Main data source in which all of its data is stored, and that you can use views and controls to expose whatever data that is stored within the Main data source.

In this example, controls exposing different fields in the Main data source are located on two different views, but you are still able to add rules (business logic) to the controls and have them depend on each other even if they are located on different views.

Remember:

> Views and controls are visual elements that you can add and place wherever you want to on a form template. Business rules do not depend on the placing of controls themselves, but rather on the corresponding values of those controls stored in fields in the Main data source of the InfoPath form.

Drop-down List Boxes

Drop-down list boxes in InfoPath allow you to display items to a user in a list that takes up the space of only one row, but can temporarily be expanded to display a list of multiple items.

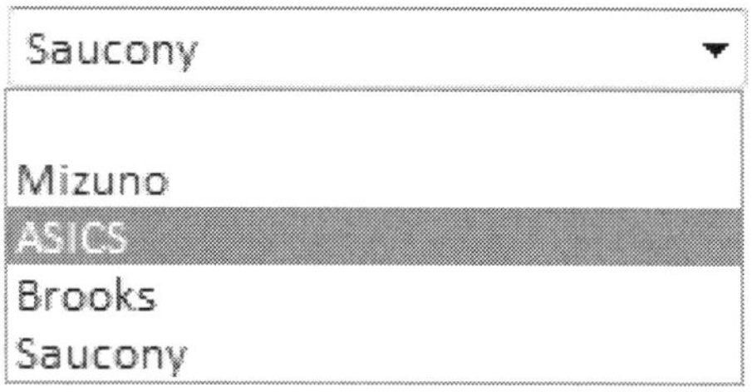

Figure 95. Drop-down list box in InfoPath 2010.

Drop-down list boxes are not difficult to work with once you understand how they function and understand the following two things:

1. You can fill a drop-down list box with items (also called "entries" in InfoPath). This can be one or multiple items, but is typically the latter. These items can be entered either manually, can come from a repeating group in the Main data source of the form, or can come from an external data source as demonstrated in *48 Populate a drop-down list box from an XML file*.

2. While a drop-down list box can display a list of multiple items, you can only select one item at a time from this list to be stored in the form. And it is the value of the selected item that is stored in the field that is bound to the drop-down list box.

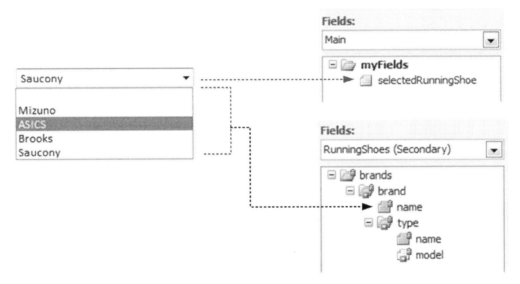

Figure 96. Relationship between a drop-down list box and the Main and a Secondary data source.

In the figure above, the drop-down list box is populated from a Secondary data source named **RunningShoes**, and Saucony is the currently selected item in the drop-down list box, so this value is stored in the **selectedRunningShoe** field in the Main data source of the InfoPath form.

Remember:

> The field that is bound to a drop-down list box can contain only one value, i.e. the value of the selected item in the drop-down list box. This "rule" also applies to combo boxes and list boxes, but not to multiple-selection list boxes.

48.   Populate a drop-down list box from an XML file

Problem

You have a drop-down list box on an InfoPath form and want to fill it with items that are contained in an XML file.

Solution

You can configure the items displayed in a drop-down list box to come from an external data source such as an XML file.

Suppose you have an XML file named **RunningShoes.xml** that has the following contents:

```
<?xml version="1.0" encoding="UTF-8"?>
<brands xmlns="uri:sym">
  <brand name="Mizuno">
    <type name="Control">
      <model>Wave Alchemy</model>
      <model>Wave Renegade</model>
    </type>
    <type name="Stability">
      <model>Wave Nirvana</model>
      <model>Wave Inspire</model>
      <model>Wave Nexus</model>
      <model>Wave Elixir</model>
    </type>
  </brand>
  <brand name="ASICS">
    <type name="Control">
      <model>GEL-Evolution</model>
      <model>GEL-Foundation</model>
    </type>
    <type name="Stability">
      <model>GEL-Kayano</model>
      <model>GEL-3020</model>
      <model>GEL-Turbulent</model>
      <model>GT-2150</model>
      <model>GEL-Phoenix 2</model>
      <model>GEL-1150</model>
    </type>
  </brand>
  <brand name="Brooks">
    <type name="Control">
      <model>Ariel</model>
      <model>Addiction</model>
    </type>
    <type name="Stability">
      <model>Trance</model>
      <model>Adrenaline</model>
    </type>
  </brand>
  <brand name="Saucony">
    <type name="Control">
      <model>ProGrid Stabil CS</model>
```

```
    </type>
    <type name="Stability">
      <model>ProGrid Omni</model>
      <model>ProGrid Hurricane</model>
      <model>Grid Tangent</model>
    </type>
  </brand>
</brands>
```

To populate a drop-down list box from an XML file:

1. In InfoPath, create a new **Blank Form** template.

2. Add a **Drop-Down List Box** control to the form template and name it **selectedRunningShoe**.

3. Right-click the **Drop-Down List Box** and select **Drop-Down List Box Properties** from the context menu.

4. On the **Drop-Down List Box Properties** dialog box on the **Data** tab under **List box choices**, select **Get choices from an external data source**, and then click **Add**. Note: If the form template already contains links to external data sources, they will appear in the **Data source** drop-down list box, and you would not have to add any new ones unless the one you want to connect to is not listed. But because you just created a new form template, your form template should not contain any Secondary data sources, so you have to add one here.

5. On the **Data Connection Wizard**, leave **Receive data** selected and click **Next**.

6. On the **Data Connection Wizard**, select **XML document**, and click **Next**.

7. On the **Data Connection Wizard**, click **Browse**, browse to and select the **RunningShoes.xml** file, and click **Next**.

8. On the **Data Connection Wizard**, click **Next**.

9. On the **Data Connection Wizard**, name the data connection **RunningShoes**, leave the **Automatically retrieve data when form is opened** check box selected, and click **Finish**.

10. On the **Drop-Down List Box Properties** dialog box on the **Data** tab under **List box choices**, click the button behind the **Entries** text box.

11. On the **Select a Field or Group** dialog box, select a repeating group such as for example **brand**, and click **OK**. Selecting **brand** in this case will allow you to show brands in the drop-down list box.

12. On the **Drop-Down List Box Properties** dialog box, the **Value** and **Display name** text boxes should automatically be populated with the **@name** attribute, which is what you want to use in this case, because you are going to display the names of running shoe brands in the drop-down list box. If you want to configure the value and display name yourself or if they were not automatically

populated with the correct field, you can click the buttons behind the corresponding text boxes, and select a field of your choice.

13. On the **Drop-Down List Box Properties** dialog box, click **OK**.

14. Preview the form.

When the form opens the drop-down list box should contain the list of running shoe brands.

Discussion

Populating a drop-down list box with data from an external data source can be done in one of two ways:

1. You can pre-add a data connection to the form template (see e.g. *32 Get data from an XML file*), and then use this data source to configure the choices for the drop-down list box.

2. You can add a new data connection when you are configuring the choices for the drop-down list box.

The recipe above uses the second method.

The field from the external data source you select for the **Display name** of a drop-down list box contains the values that users will be able to see in the drop-down list box. The field from the external data source you select for the **Value** of a drop-down list box remains invisible to users, but is the field that contains the value that will eventually be used as the value for the selected item in the drop-down list box.

On the **Drop-Down List Box Properties** dialog box, you may have noticed a check box with the label **Show only entries with unique display names** at the bottom of the **Data** tab.

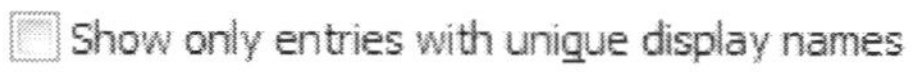

☐ Show only entries with unique display names

Figure 97. Show only entries with unique display names check box.

Select this option if the external data source contains duplicate values for the field you are using as the **Display name**.

Important:

> Always use a field from the external data source that contains unique values for the **Value** of a drop-down list box. If you use a data source that contains duplicate values in a field and use this field to provide the value for the drop-down list box, you may experience unexpected behavior for the drop-down list box.

49. Filter a drop-down list based on the first character

Problem

You have a drop-down list box and text box on an InfoPath form and you want to type a character into the text box (for example, A, B, or C) and then have only those items that start with the character you specified appear as an item in the drop-down list box.

Solution

You can apply a filter to the repeating group that you use to populate the drop-down list box when configuring the drop-down to get choices from either the form or an external data source.

To filter a drop-down list box on the first character of items in the drop-down list box:

1. In InfoPath, create a new **Blank Form** template.

2. Add a **Text Box** and **Drop-Down List Box** control to the form template. Name the text box **filterOnFirstLetter** and the drop-down list box **runningShoes**.

3. Add a receive data connection (see *32 Get data from an XML file*) to the same XML file you used in *48 Populate a drop-down list box from an XML file*, and name the data connection **RunningShoes**.

4. Right-click the drop-down list box and select **Drop-Down List Box Properties** from the context menu that appears.

5. On the **Drop-Down List Box Properties** dialog box on the **Data** tab under the **List box choices** section, select **Get choices from an external data source**, select **RunningShoes** from the **Data source** drop-down list box, and click the button behind the **Entries** text box.

6. On the **Select a Field or Group** dialog box, select **brand**, and then click **Filter Data**.

7. On the **Filter Data** dialog box, click **Add**.

8. On the **Specify Filter Conditions** dialog box, select **name** from the first drop-down list box, select **begins with** from the second drop-down list box, and select **Use a formula** from the third drop-down list box.

9. On the **Insert Formula** dialog box, click **Insert Field or Group**.

10. On the **Select a Field or Group** dialog box, select **Main** from the **Fields** drop-down list box, select **filterOnFirstLetter**, and then click **OK**.

11. On the **Insert Formula** dialog box, click **OK**.

12. On the **Specify Filter Conditions** dialog box, click **OK**.

13. On the **Filter Data** dialog box, the filter should now say:

```
name begins with filterOnFirstLetter
```

which means that you have created a filter on the **brand** nodes in the XML file to only show those brands of which the name starts with the character specified in the **filterOnFirstLetter** field which is located in the Main data source of the form. Click **OK**.

14. On the **Select a Field or Group** dialog box, click **OK**.

15. On the **Drop-Down List Box Properties** dialog box, ensure that **@name** has been selected for the **Value** and **Display name** fields, and then click **OK**.

16. Preview the form.

When the form opens, type the first letter of any of the items in the drop-down list box into the text box. The items in the drop-down list box should be filtered to contain the matching items.

Discussion

In the recipe above, you used the **Filter Data** option on the **Select a Field or Group** dialog box to filter the entries within a Secondary data source based on the value of a field in the Main data source of the InfoPath form. You can use this option whenever you want to select specific items within a Secondary data source through filtering.

To complete this recipe, you should restrict users to only be able to enter one character into the text box by setting a maximum length on the text box through a validation rule (see *30 Set a maximum length on a text box*).

If filtering on the first letter of items is too restrictive, you could also use **contains** in the filter condition instead of **begins with**. The filter would then look for an occurrence of the text that you typed into the text box in any item of the drop-down list box.

50. Automatically select the first item in a drop down list box

Problem

You have a drop-down list box on an InfoPath form and want to have it automatically display the first item as selected.

Solution

You can set the **Default Value** of the field bound to the drop-down list box to be equal to the value of the first item in the list of items in the drop-down list box.

To select the first item in a drop-down list box:

1. In InfoPath, create a new **Blank Form** template.

2. Add a **Drop-Down List Box** control to the form template.

3. Fill the drop-down list box with items from an external data source, with items from a repeating group in the form, or with items that have been entered manually (static entries). Here you will use the XML file from *48 Populate a drop-down list box from an XML file* to fill the drop-down list box with items from an external data source.

4. Click the drop-down list box to select it, and then click **Properties** ➤ **Properties** ➤ **Default Value**.

5. On the **Field or Group Properties** dialog box on the **Data** tab under **Default Value**, do the following:

   a. If the drop-down list box contains static entries, that is, you entered the items manually when configuring the choices for the drop-down list box, type the value of the first item in the **Value** text box under **Default Value**.

   b. If the drop-down list box contains dynamic entries, that is, you configured the items in the drop-down list box to come from either a repeating group in the form or from an external data source, click the function button behind the **Value** text box under **Default Value**. You will use the external data source from *48 Populate a drop-down list box from an XML file* here to construct the default value:

      i. On the **Insert Formula** dialog box, click **Insert Field or Group**.

      ii. On the **Select a Field or Group** dialog box, select **RunningShoes (Secondary)** from the **Fields** drop-down list box, expand the **brand** node, select **name**, and click **OK**.

iii. On the **Insert Formula** dialog box, select the **Edit XPath (advanced)** check box, and modify the formula from:

```
xdXDocument:GetDOM("RunningShoes")/ns1:brands/ns1:brand/@
name
```

to

```
xdXDocument:GetDOM("RunningShoes")/ns1:brands/ns1:brand[1
]/@name
```

What this does is select the name of the first **brand** node by using an index filter (**[1]**) on **brand**. Remember that **@name** was configured to be the **Value** for the drop-down list box, so you must set the default value to the first **@name** attribute in the list of brand names in the drop-down list box.

iv. On the **Insert Formula** dialog box, click **OK**. The formula for the default value on the **Field or Group Properties** dialog box should now say:

```
brand[1]/@name
```

v. On the **Field or Group Properties** dialog box, click **OK**.

6. Preview the form.

When the form opens, the first item should appear as the selected item in the drop-down list box.

Discussion

You can use either rules or default values for setting the value of a field.

Use default values if you want a field to start up with a particular (default) value that does not depend on any conditions.

Use rules when the setting of the value of a field is triggered by clicking or changing data on another field and/or if the setting of the value of the field depends on a condition. Because you cannot add conditions to default values, you must use rules to be able to set conditions that need to be met before setting the value of a field.

Filters in XPath expressions are specified between square brackets ([ ]). In the recipe above, you used **[1]** as a filter on the **brand** repeating group to find the first item in the Secondary data source. Always remember that in XPath, counting always starts at 1, and not at 0.

51.   Clear the selected value in a drop-down list

Problem

You have a drop-down list box on an InfoPath form and have selected an item in it. Now you want to click a button and clear the selected item in the drop-down list box.

Solution

You can use a rule to set the value of the field that is bound to the drop-down list box to an empty string. This will clear the drop-down list box selection.

To clear the selected value in a drop-down list box:

1.   In InfoPath, create a new **Blank Form** template.

2.   Add a **Drop-Down List Box** and a **Button** control to the form template.

3.   Configure the drop-down list box to be filled with items from an external data source, with items from a repeating group in the form, or with items that have been entered manually (static entries).

4.   Add an **Action** rule to the button that says:

    ```
    Set a field's value: field1 = ""
    ```

    where **field1** represents the field that is bound to the drop-down list box.

5.   Preview the form.

When the form opens, select any item from the drop-down list box and then click the button. The drop-down list box should be reset to display an empty item or its non-selected state.

52.   Count the number of items in a drop down list box

Problem

You have filled a drop-down list box on an InfoPath form with data from an external data source and want to know how many items are in the drop-down list box.

Solution

When you fill a drop-down list box with items from a data source, you typically bind the drop-down list box to a repeating group either in the Main or in a Secondary data source. So to find out how many items are in a drop-down list box, you must use the **count** function on the repeating group used to fill the drop-down list box.

To count the number of items in a drop-down list box:

1. In InfoPath, create a new **Blank Form** template.

2. Add a **Drop-Down List Box** control to the form template and populate it with items from an external data source (see *48 Populate a drop-down list box from an XML file*).

3. Add a **Text Box** control to the form template. You will use this text box to display the amount of items in the drop-down list box.

4. Right-click the text box and select **Text Box Properties** from the context menu that appears.

5. On the **Text Box Properties** dialog box, click the button behind the **Value** text box under **Default Value**.

6. On the **Insert Formula** dialog box, type **count(**, and then click **Insert Field or Group**.

7. On the **Select a Field or Group** dialog box, select the Secondary data source from the **Fields** drop-down list box (if you followed the steps in see *48 Populate a drop-down list box from an XML file*, this would be **RunningShoes (Secondary)**), click the repeating group (**brand** in this case), and click **OK**.

8. On the **Insert Formula** dialog box, type **)** to close the **count** function. The formula should now resemble the following:

    ```
    count(brand)
    ```

    or

    ```
    count(xdXDocument:GetDOM("RunningShoes")/ns1:brands/ns1:brand)
    ```

    if you select the **Edit XPath (advanced)** check box. Click **Verify Formula** to check that the formula does not contain any errors, and then click **OK**.

9. On the **Text Box Properties** dialog box, click **OK**.

10. Preview the form.

When the form opens, the text box should display the number of items in the drop-down list box.

Discussion

The **count** function in InfoPath takes a field or group as its argument and counts the number of instances of that field or group.

In the recipe above, **brand** is the repeating group that is used to populate the drop-down list box, and represents items in the Secondary data source. If you want to count the number of items in the Secondary data source, you must count the number of instances of the **brand** group in the Secondary data source, which the recipe does by using the formula:

```
count (brand)
```

You can use the technique described in the recipe above if you populate a drop-down list box with items from a repeating group in the Main data source of the form or in a Secondary data source. The latter was used in the recipe above.

You cannot use this technique if you have manually populated a drop-down list box with items. When you manually add items to a drop-down list box, these items become part of the view and not part of the data source of a form, and therefore you cannot access static items in a drop-down list box using rules in InfoPath.

Important:

> You can only use rules in InfoPath on fields that are located in either the Main or Secondary data sources of a form; not on views. Views are static elements of a form template. Their appearance is stored and defined in a **view.xsl** file that is part of the form template. The **view.xsl** file is constructed at design time and is not accessible via rules in InfoPath at runtime.

You can verify that items that have been entered manually to populate a drop-down list box are indeed part of the view by exporting the source files (via **File ➤ Publish ➤ Export Source Files**), opening the **view.xsl** file in Notepad, and searching for the items from the drop-down list box.

53.   Check if an item exists in a drop-down list box

Problem

You have a drop-down list box that is populated from an external data source. You want to know whether a particular item exists in the drop-down list box.

Solution

To check whether an item exists in a drop-down list box:

1.   In InfoPath, create a new **Blank Form** template.

2.   Add a **Drop-Down List Box**, a **Text Box**, and a **Section** control to the form template. Name the drop-down list box **selectedItem** and the text box **itemToLookup**.

3.   Type the text "Item exists" on the section control. The section control will be used to display the message as to whether the piece of text typed into the text box exists in the drop-down list box.

4. Configure the drop-down list box to be filled with items as demonstrated in *48 Populate a drop-down list box from an XML file*. Select **@name** under **brand** for both the **Value** and **Display name** of the drop-down list box.

5. Click the section control to select it, and then click **Home ➤ Rules ➤ Manage Rules**.

6. On the **Rules** task pane, ensure **group1** (the group representing the section control) is displayed below the title bar of the **Rules** task pane as the group you are adding the rule to, and then click **New ➤ Formatting**.

7. On the **Rules** task pane, select the **Hide this control** check box. This will hide the section control if the item does not exist in the drop-down list box, so does not exist in the Secondary data source that the drop-down list box is populated from.

8. To determine whether an item exists you can count the number of items in the drop-down list box that have a value that is equal to the value typed into the **itemToLookup** text box. If the count is zero, no item exists that has the value of the text string you typed in, so the section must be hidden. You can now use this information to construct a condition for the rule. On the **Rules** task pane under **Condition**, click on the text **None**.

9. On the **Condition** dialog box, select **Use a formula** from the third drop-down list box. You are going to misuse the **Insert Formula** dialog box to construct a formula to count the items that have a value equal to the value of **itemToLookup**.

10. On the **Insert Formula** dialog box, type

    ```
    count(
    ```

    and then click **Insert Field or Group**.

11. On the **Select a Field or Group** dialog box, select **RunningShoes (Secondary)** from the **Fields** drop-down list box, select **brand**, and then click **Filter Data**.

12. On the **Filter Data** dialog box, click **Add**.

13. On the **Specify Filter Conditions** dialog box, leave **name** selected in the first drop-down list box, leave **is equal to** selected in the second drop-down list box, and then select **Select a field or group** from the third drop-down list box.

14. On the **Select a Field or Group** dialog box, select **Main** from the **Fields** drop-down list box, select **itemToLookup**, and click **OK**. This filter condition compares the brand **name** from the Secondary data source to the value of the **itemToLookup** field, which is bound to the text box and which is located in the Main data source of the form.

15. On the **Specify Filter Conditions** dialog box, click **OK**.

16. On the **Filter Data** dialog box, click **OK**.

17. On the **Select a Field or Group** dialog box, click **OK**.

18. On the **Insert Formula** dialog box, type

    ```
    ) = 0
    ```

    to close the formula. The formula should now resemble the following:

    ```
    count(brand[@name = itemToLookup]) = 0
    ```

    This formula counts the **brand** nodes in the Secondary data source that are used to populate the drop-down list box where the **name** attribute is equal to the **itemToLookup** field in the Main data source of the InfoPath form and checks whether the result is 0, so whether there are no brand nodes that have a name that is the same as the text typed into the **itemToLookup** text box. Note that the constructed XPath expression is using square brackets ([ ]) as an indication that the **brand** nodes are being filtered on their **name** attribute being equal to **itemToLookup**.

19. On the **Insert Formula** dialog box, click **OK**.

20. On the **Condition** dialog box, select **The expression** from the first drop-down list box, and then delete the last round bracket and everything before **count** in the expression. You are then left with the following expression:

    ```
    count(xdXDocument:GetDOM("RunningShoes")/ns1:brands/ns1:brand[@name =
    xdXDocument:get-DOM()/my:myFields/my:itemToLookup]) = 0
    ```

21. On the **Condition** dialog box, click **OK**.

22. Preview the form.

When the form opens, type the name of an item that exists in the drop-down list box in the text box and tab or click away from the text box. The section with the text "Item exists" should appear. Now type a text string that does not exist in the drop-down list box. The section should disappear.

Discussion

To check whether an item exist in a drop-down list box, you must populate the drop-down list box with items from either an external (Secondary) data source or from a repeating group in the Main data source of the form, because you cannot use rules to look up items in a drop-down list box that has been populated manually with items, since such items become part of the view and not part of the data source of a form (see the discussion section of *52 Count the number of items in a drop down list box*).

54.   Populate a text box based on a drop-down list box

Problem

You have a drop-down list box that is filled with items from an XML file. Not all of the data from the XML file can be displayed through the drop-down list box, so you want to be able to select an item from the drop-down list box, and then have a text box be filled with additional information from the XML file that corresponds to the item you selected.

Solution

You can use a filter condition to perform a lookup in the Secondary data source that is used to populate the drop-down list box, to find additional information that pertains to the selected item in the drop-down list box, and then populate the text box with this information.

In this recipe you will use an XML file named **MonthNames.xml** that has the following contents:

```xml
<?xml version="1.0" encoding="UTF-8" ?>
<months>
   <month>
      <number>01</number>
      <name>January</name>
   </month>
   <month>
      <number>02</number>
      <name>February</name>
   </month>
   <month>
      <number>03</number>
      <name>March</name>
   </month>
   <month>
      <number>04</number>
      <name>April</name>
   </month>
   <month>
      <number>05</number>
      <name>May</name>
   </month>
   <month>
      <number>06</number>
      <name>June</name>
   </month>
   <month>
      <number>07</number>
      <name>July</name>
   </month>
   <month>
      <number>08</number>
      <name>August</name>
   </month>
   <month>
```

```
    <number>09</number>
    <name>September</name>
  </month>
  <month>
    <number>10</number>
    <name>October</name>
  </month>
  <month>
    <number>11</number>
    <name>November</name>
  </month>
  <month>
    <number>12</number>
    <name>December</name>
  </month>
</months>
```

To populate a text box based on the item selected in a drop-down list box:

1. In InfoPath, create a new **Blank Form** template.

2. Add a **Drop-Down List Box** control to the form template and populate it with data from an XML file (see *48 Populate a drop-down list box from an XML file*). Use the **MonthNames.xml** to populate the drop-down list box and select **number** as the **Value** and **name** as the **Display name** for the drop-down list box. Name the drop-down list box **selectedMonthNumber**.

3. Add a **Text Box** control to the form template and name the text box **monthName**.

4. Add an **Action** rule to the drop-down list box that sets the value of the text box to the value of the drop-down list box. The action for the rule should say:

   ```
   Set a field's value: monthName = .
   ```

   where **monthName** is the field bound to the text box and . represents the field bound to the control the rule is running on, which in this case is the drop-down list box.

5. When you preview the form, and select a month from the drop-down list box, you will see that the number appears in the text box instead of the month name. This is because while you see a month name (**Display name**) in the drop-down, in reality, the **Value** (the month number) of the drop-down list box is stored in the field (**selectedMonthNumber**) bound to the drop-down list box when you select an item. So you must perform an extra lookup in the data source of the drop-down list box to find the month name based on the month number that was selected and stored in the field bound to the drop-down list box. And doing a lookup basically means filtering the Secondary data source that is used to fill the drop-down list box on the selected month number. You will do that next.

6. Click on the action you added in step 4.

7. On the **Rule Details** dialog box, click the formula button behind the **Value** text box.

8. On the **Insert Formula** dialog box, clear the **Formula** text box by deleting the formula you constructed previously, and then click **Insert Field or Group**.

9. On the **Select a Field or Group** dialog box, select **MonthNames (secondary)** from the **Fields** drop-down list box, expand all of the nodes, click **name**, and then click **Filter Data**.

10. On the **Filter Data** dialog box, click **Add**. You want to add a filter where the number in the XML file is the same as the selected month number in the drop-down list box. The first number should come from the Secondary data source containing month names, and the second number should come from the **selectedMonthNumber** field in the Main data source that is bound to the drop-down list box.

11. On the **Specify Filter Conditions** dialog box, select **Select a field or group** from the first drop-down list box.

12. On the **Select a Field or Group** dialog box, ensure **MonthNames (Secondary)** has been selected in the **Data source** drop-down list box, select **number**, and then click **OK**.

13. On the **Specify Filter Conditions** dialog box, leave **is equal to** selected in the second drop-down list box, and then select **Select a field or group** from the third drop-down list box.

14. On the **Select a Field or Group** dialog box, select **Main** from the **Fields** drop-down list box, select **selectedMonthNumber** (which is bound to the drop-down list box), and then click **OK**.

15. On the **Specify Filter Conditions** dialog box, click **OK**.

16. On the **Filter Data** dialog box, click **OK**.

17. On the **Select a Field or Group** dialog box, click **OK**.

18. On the **Insert Formula** dialog box, select the **Edit XPath (advanced)** check box. The formula should now look as follows:

```
xdXDocument:GetDOM("MonthNames")/months/month/name[../number =
xdXDocument:get-DOM()/my:myFields/my:selectedMonthNumber]
```

What the expression above does is look at all of the **name** nodes in the **MonthNames** Secondary data source and then filter out only those names where the value of the **number** node in the Secondary data source is equal to the value of the **selectedMonthNumber** field in the Main data source, which contains selected month number from the drop-down list box.

19. Click **OK** when closing all open dialog boxes.

20. Preview the form.

When the form opens, select a month from the drop-down list box. The same month name as shown in the drop-down list box should appear in the text box.

Discussion

In the formula in step 18 in the recipe above, you can see that **xdXDocument:get-DOM()** gives you a reference to the Main data source when you are writing XPath expressions, while **xdXDocument:GetDOM("MonthNames")** gives you a reference to a Secondary data source called **MonthNames**.

You need not be concerned with these references when you are constructing XPath expressions through the dialog boxes in InfoPath, but just be aware of them in case you want to manually start writing and/or modifying XPath expressions later down the track.

55. Cascading drop-down list boxes using an XML file

Problem

You have an XML file containing the names, types, and models of running shoes. You want to add three drop-down list boxes to an InfoPath form and have the first one be populated with all of the running shoe brand names, the second one with only the running shoe types belonging to the selected brand in the first drop-down list box, and the third one with only the running shoe models belonging to the selected brand in the first drop-down list box and the selected type in the second drop-down list box.

Solution

Creating cascading or dependent drop-down list boxes entails filtering the data sources used to populate the drop-down list boxes on values that are selected elsewhere and which are often times located in the Main data source of an InfoPath form.

To create cascading drop-down list boxes using data contained in one XML file:

1. In InfoPath, create a new **Blank Form** template.

2. Add a **Drop-Down List Box** control to the form template, populate it with data from an XML file (see *48 Populate a drop-down list box from an XML file*), and name it **shoeBrand**. A user can select a running shoe brand from this drop-down list box.

3. Add a second **Drop-Down List Box** control to the form template and name it **shoeType**. This drop-down list box should be populated with the types of running shoes that are available for a chosen running shoe brand.

4. Open the **Drop-Down List Box** properties dialog box for the **shoeType** drop-down list box.

5. On the **Drop-Down List Box** properties dialog box on the **Data** tab, select **Get choices from an external data source**, select **RunningShoes** from the **Data source** drop-down list box, and click the button behind the **Entries** text box.

6. On the **Select a Field or Group** dialog box, expand the **brand** repeating group, select the **type** repeating group, and click **Filter Data**.

7. On the **Filter Data** dialog box, click **Add**.

8. You want to add a filter that will return only those **type** repeating groups that fall under the selected **brand** from the first drop-down list box. For this you must add a filter that compares the brand **name** from the XML file to the **shoeBrand** value selected in the first drop-down list box on the form. On the **Specify Filter Conditions** dialog box, select **Select a field or group** from the first drop-down list box.

9. On the **Select a Field or Group** dialog box, ensure that **RunningShoes (Secondary)** is selected in the **Data source** drop-down list box, select the **name** field that is located under the **brand** repeating group, and click **OK**.

10. On the **Specify Filter Conditions** dialog box, leave **is equal to** selected in the second drop-down list box, and then select **Select a field or group** from the third drop-down list box.

11. On the **Select a Field or Group** dialog box, select **Main** from the **Fields** drop-down list box, select **shoeBrand**, and click **OK**.

12. On the **Specify Filter Conditions** dialog box, click **OK**.

13. On the **Filter Data** dialog box, click **OK**.

14. On the **Select a Field or Group** dialog box, click **OK**.

15. On the **Drop-Down List Box** properties dialog box, the **@name** for the type has been automatically selected for the **Value** and **Display** name fields. Leave this as is, and click **OK**.

16. Before you continue, preview the form to see whether the types for each brand are automatically populated in the **shoeType** drop-down list box when you select a **shoeBrand**.

17. Add a third **Drop-Down List Box** control to the form template and name it **shoeModel**.

18. Do the same thing as you did for the **shoeType** drop-down list box, but then instead of the **type** repeating group, select the **model** repeating field, and add a filter that compares the type's name in the XML file (**name** field under the **type** repeating group in the **RunningShoes** Secondary data source) to the type's name selected in the **shoeType** drop-down list box in the **Main** data source, and a

second filter that compares the brand's name from the XML file (**name** field under the **brand** repeating group in the **RunningShoes** Secondary data source) to the brand's name selected in the **shoeBrand** drop-down list box in the **Main** data source. The resulting filter should resemble the following:

```
name = shoeType
and
name = shoeBrand
```

where the first **name** is the **name** under the **type** repeating group, and the second **name** is the **name** under the **brand** repeating group in the **RunningShoes** Secondary data source. Note: To join the two filter conditions together you must click the **And** button behind the first filter condition when you are on the **Specify Filter Conditions** dialog box (see the discussion section of *31 Show/hide sections based on a drop-down list box*).

19. Add an **Action** rule to the **shoeBrand** drop-down list box with two actions that say:

```
Set a field's value: shoeType = ""
Set a field's value: shoeModel = ""
```

These two actions ensure that any previously selected values from the **shoeType** and **shoeModel** drop-down list boxes are cleared. This is necessary to prevent items that do not exist in the list of filtered items from appearing in the drop-down list boxes.

20. Add an **Action** rule to the **shoeType** drop-down list box with an action that says:

```
Set a field's value: shoeModel = ""
```

This action ensures that any previously selected value from the **shoeModel** drop-down list box is cleared. This is necessary to prevent items that do not exist in the list of filtered items from appearing in the **shoeModel** drop-down list box.

21. Preview the form.

When the form opens, the second and third drop-down list boxes should be empty. Select a brand from the first drop-down list box. The second drop-down list box should now contain running shoe types. Select a type from the second drop-down list box. The third drop-down list box should now contain running shoe models for the selected shoe brand and shoe type you selected in the first and second drop-down list boxes.

Discussion

The figure below is a visual representation of how cascading drop-down list boxes are set up in InfoPath.

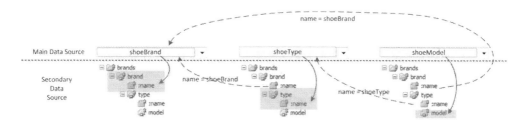

Figure 98. Relationship between Main and Secondary data sources with filters for cascading lists.

In this figure, **shoeBrand**, **shoeType**, and **shoeModel** are all fields in the Main data source and are bound to drop-down list box controls. These fields store the selected value for each drop-down list box.

The **shoeBrand** drop-down list box is populated with the **name** field under the **brand** repeating group in the Secondary data source, the **shoeType** drop-down list box is populated with the **name** field under the **type** repeating group in the Secondary data source, and the **shoeModel** drop-down list box is populated with the **model** repeating field in the Secondary data source.

The **shoeType** drop-down list box has a filter set on it to only show those type names where the brand **name** in the Secondary data source is equal to the **shoeBrand** in the Main data source.

The **shoeModel** drop-down list box has a filter set on it to only show those models where the brand **name** in the Secondary data source is equal to the **shoeBrand** in the Main data source and the type **name** in the Secondary data source is equal to the **shoeType** in the Main data source.

Date Pickers and Date and Time Pickers

InfoPath 2010 comes with two date controls: **Date Picker** and **Date and Time Picker**.

Date Picker controls in InfoPath allow you to select or enter dates, while **Date and Time Picker** controls allow you to select or enter dates in addition to entering times. A **Date and Time Picker** control is a control that is a combination of a **Date Picker** control for entering a date and a **Text Box** control for entering a time.

When selecting a date from a date picker or a date and time picker control, you can make use of a calendar to select a date.

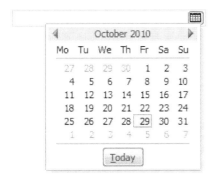

Figure 99. Date Picker calendar in InfoPath 2010.

A drawback of the date picker controls in InfoPath is that you cannot select a specific year from the calendar. For example, if you currently have the calendar open on the year 2010 and you want to select a date in 2012 or 1997, you would have to click on the forward or backward arrows on the calendar to navigate through each month and arrive at the desired year. A workaround is to use a drop-down list box to select the starting year for the date picker (see *62 Select a date picker's year via a drop-down selection*).

56.   Change a text box control into a date picker control

Problem

You have a text box control on an InfoPath form and you want to change it into a date picker control.

Solution

You can change the data type of the field bound to the text box control into a date so that you can change the text box control into a date picker control.

To change a text box control into a date picker control:

1.   In InfoPath, create a new **Blank Form** template.

2.   Add a **Text Box** control to the form template.

3.   Click **Properties ➤ Properties ➤ Field Properties**.

4.   On the **Field or Group Properties** dialog box on the **Data** tab, change the **Data type** from **Text (string)** to **Date (date)**, and click **OK**.

5.   Right-click the **Text Box** control, select **Change Control ➤ Date Picker** from the context menu that appears.

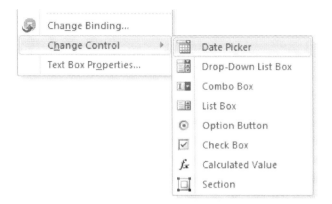

Figure 100. Change Control menu item on the context menu of a text box control.

6.   Preview the form.

The text box should now have been converted into a date picker and you should be able to select and enter a date into the date picker control.

Discussion

You can change any control from one type to another by first changing the data type of the field that is bound to the control and then changing the control to the desired control.

Exercise

Try changing the **Date Picker** control into a **Rich Text Box** control. Hint: The data type of a **Rich Text Box** control is **Rich Text (XHTML)**.

Tip:

To learn what kind a data type you must assign to a field to be able to bind it to the type of control you want to bind it to, first place the type of control you want to use by dragging it from the **Controls** section on the **Home** tab, dropping it on the form template, and then examining the data type of the field bound to that control. Do this for each type of control that is available in InfoPath and soon you will know which data type is required for each type of control.

57.   Add a date picker to a repeating table

Problem

You have added a repeating table control to an InfoPath form and you want to add a date picker control to the repeating table.

Solution

You can add a date picker control to a repeating table by changing an existing control that is in a column of the repeating table into a date picker control as demonstrated in *56 Change a text box control into a date picker*.

You can also add a field of type **Date (date)** under the repeating group bound to the repeating table, and then drag-and-drop this field into a column of the repeating table as you will do next.

To add a date picker control to a repeating table control:

1.   In InfoPath, create a new **Blank Form** template.

2.   Add a **Repeating Table** control to the form template.

3.   On the **Fields** task pane, click the down arrow behind **group2** (the repeating group bound to the repeating table), and select **Add** from the drop-down menu.

Figure 101. Add menu item on drop-down menu of repeating group in InfoPath.

4. On the **Add Field or Group** dialog box, type a **Name** for the field (for example **dueDate**), select **Date (date)** from the **Data type** drop-down list box, and click **OK**.

5. Right-click any column in the repeating table, and select **Insert ➤ Columns to the Right** from the context menu that appears.

6. InfoPath automatically adds a text box in the newly added column (if you have the **Automatically create data source** check box selected on the **Controls** task pane). Because you want to place your own control in the column, you must delete the text box that InfoPath added. So select the text box control and press **Delete** on your keyboard. And because the field that the text box was bound to still exists in the Main data source, you must click on the drop-down arrow on the right-hand side of that field on the **Fields** task pane, and select **Delete** from the drop-down menu that appears to delete the field from the Main data source.

7. On the **Fields** task pane, drag the **dueDate** field to the form template and drop it into a cell in the column you just added.

Discussion

InfoPath automatically adds a text box control to a repeating table when you add a new column to the repeating table and have the **Automatically create data source** check box selected on the **Controls** task pane. You can either delete this field from the **Fields** task pane if you do not need or want it, or you can use the technique described in *56 Change a text box control into a date picker* to change the text box control into the type of control you want.

The technique described in the recipe described above can be used to add any type of control to a repeating table.

Exercise

Try adding a **Rich Text Box** control to a column of the repeating table. Hint: The data type for a **Rich Text Box** control is **Rich Text (XHTML)**.

58. Display the current date in a date picker

Problem

You have a date picker on an InfoPath form and you want this date picker to display the current date when the form is opened.

Solution

You can set the **Default Value** of the date picker to a formula that uses the **today** function.

To set a date picker to display the current date:

1. In InfoPath, create a new **Blank Form** template.

2. Add a **Date Picker** control to the form template.

3. Right-click the date picker control and select **Date Picker Properties** from the context menu that appears.

4. On the **Date Picker Properties** dialog box on the **Data** tab, use the formula button to set the **Default Value** to the following formula:

   ```
   today()
   ```

5. Preview the form.

When the form opens, the current date should appear in the date picker control.

Discussion

You can also apply the technique described in the recipe above if you are using a **Date and Time Picker** instead of a **Date Picker**.

The **now** function returns the current system date and time, while the **today** function only returns the current system date.

Because a **Date and Time Picker** control consists of two controls (a date and a time) you must use the **now** function instead of the **today** function if you want to set its **Default Value**.

Exercise

Add a **Date and Time Picker** control to the form template and set its value to the current date and time using the **now** function in a formula. As a test, also try setting the default value using the **today** function and see what happens.

59. Display the current time on a form when it opens

Problem

You want to display the current time (without the date) whenever you open an InfoPath form.

Solution

You can use the **now** and **substring** functions to extract the current time and then use a text box with the **Time** data type to display the time.

To display the current time when an InfoPath form opens:

1. In InfoPath, create a new **Blank Form** template.

2. Add a **Text Box** control to the form template, name it **currentTime**, change its data type to **Time (time)**, and make it **Read-only**.

3. Set the following formula as the **Default Value** for the text box:

```
substring(now(), 12)
```

   This formula extracts all of the characters from the date and time string starting from the character at position 12 until the end of the string.

4. On the **Text Box Properties** dialog box on the **Data** tab, click the **Format** button behind the **Data type** field.

5. On the **Time Format** dialog box, select **Display the time like this**, select the time format you want to use to display the time as, and then click **OK**.

Figure 102. Time Format dialog box in InfoPath 2010.

6. On the **Text Box Properties** dialog box, click **OK**.

7. Preview the form.

When the form opens, the current time should be displayed in the text box.

Discussion

The **now** function returns the current date and time with the following format: **yyyy-MM-ddThh:mm:ss**. The part of this string that comes after the **T**, represents the time. So **yyyy** represents the year, **MM** represents the month, **dd** represents the day, **hh** represents the hours, **mm** represents the minutes, and **ss** represents the seconds.

So to get the current time, you must use the **substring** function to extract the time by returning the part of the date and time string that starts at position 12 (so after the **T**) and runs until the end of the string. By not specifying the third argument in the **substring** function, you are telling InfoPath that the function should run till the end of the string.

You could have also specified the amount of characters to extract from the date and time string by using the following formula:

```
substring(now(), 12, 8)
```

A second way to display the current time on an InfoPath form is by using a **Calculated Value** control instead of a **Text Box** control.

A **Calculated Value** control is read-only by default, which is what you are after when you are displaying the current time.

You have two options when using a **Calculated Value** control. You can:

1. Add a field to the Main data source and then bind it to a **Calculated Value** control.

2. Use a formula to display the result of a calculation in a **Calculated Value** control.

The first option works similar to using a text box control. This option would allow you to store the current time in the form when the form is saved or submitted.

With the second option, the time would not be stored in the InfoPath form once the form is saved or submitted, because there is no field in the Main data source to store it in (it is not bound to any field). You can use the second option if you want to show the current time at startup, but not save it in the form itself.

After you have added a **Calculated Value** control to the form template, you would have to do the following to be able to display the current time:

1. Open the **Calculated Value Properties** dialog box.

2. On the **Calculated Value Properties** dialog box on the **General** tab, click the formula button behind the **XPath** field.

3. On the **Insert Formula** dialog box, enter the following formula

```
substring(now(), 12, 8)
```

and click **OK**.

4. On the **Calculated Value Properties** dialog box on the **General** tab under **Result**, select **Time** from the **Format as** drop-down list box, and click **Format**.

5. On the **Time Format** dialog box, select the time format you want to use to display the time as, and then click **OK**.

6. On the **Calculated Value Properties** dialog box, click **OK**.

Note: When you click on a **Calculated Value** control to add it to a form template, the **Insert Calculated Value** dialog box is opened. You can add the formula via this dialog box, but will still have to open the **Calculated Value Properties** dialog box after the control has been added to the form template to be able to format the time.

Alternatively, you can just click **OK** on the **Insert Calculated Value** dialog box immediately after you clicked on the **Calculated Value** control to add it to the form template without entering a formula, and then open the **Calculated Value Properties** dialog box to configure the properties on the control.

Tip:

If you want to see the format of the date and time that InfoPath uses or exactly what the **now** function returns, you can add a text box control to a form template and then set the **Default Value** on the control to a formula with the **now** function. You can use this technique to test any function in InfoPath.

60. Add 7 days to a date in a date picker

Problem

You have two date picker controls on an InfoPath form. You want the user to be able to select a date in one date picker and have the other date picker automatically populate itself with a date that lies 7 days in the future.

Solution

You can use the **addDays** function to add an amount of days to a date.

To add 7 days to the date displayed in a date picker:

1. In InfoPath, create a new **Blank Form** template.

2. Add two **Date Picker** controls to the form template. Name the first date picker **selectedDate**, and the second date picker **calculatedDate**.

3. On the **Date Picker Properties** dialog box of the **calculatedDate** date picker, set the **Default Value** to the following formula:

```
addDays(selectedDate, 7)
```

This formula adds 7 days to **selectedDate** and returns the result as a date.

4. Preview the form.

When the form opens, select a date for the first date picker. The date in the second date picker should be automatically calculated and set to 7 days in the future.

Discussion

The **addDays** function adds days to a date or date and time value. The **addDays** function accepts two arguments: The first argument is the date you want to add a number of days to, and the second argument is the amount of days you want to add to the date.

Exercise

The same way you can add days to a date, you can subtract days from a date by adding a minus sign before the amount of days, so for example `addDays(selectedDate, -7)`. Try it out!

If you want to add an amount of days to the date of a **Date and Time Picker** control instead of a **Date Picker** control, you can use the **addSeconds** function instead of the **addDays** function.

The **addSeconds** function adds seconds to a time or date and time, and takes two arguments: A time and the amount of seconds to add.

There are 60 seconds in a minute, 60 minutes in an hour, and 24 hours in a day. Suppose you want to add 3 days and 5 hours to the date and time specified in a **Date and Time Picker** control, you would have to specify a total amount of 277200 (3 days x 24 hours x 60 minutes x 60 seconds + 5 hours x 60 minutes x 60 seconds) seconds as the second argument of the **addSeconds** function.

Exercise

Add a **Date and Time Picker** control to the form template and set its **Default Value** to 9 days and 3 hours in the future starting from today. Hint: You must use the **now** function as the first argument of the **addSeconds** function.

61.   Extract the year from a date picker

Problem

You have a date picker control on an InfoPath form and you want to extract the year number from the date that has been selected in the date picker and put this year number in a text box.

Solution

You can use the **substring** function to extract the year number from a date.

To extract the year from a date picker:

1. In InfoPath, create a new **Blank Form** template.

2. Add a **Date Picker** and **Text Box** control to the form template. Name the date picker **selectedDate** and the text box **selectedYear**.

3. Click the **Date Picker** control to select it, and then select **Home ➤ Rules ➤ Add Rule ➤ This Field Changes ➤ Set a Field's Value**.

4. On the **Rule Details** dialog box, click the button behind the **Field** text box.

5. On the **Select a Field or Group** dialog box, select **selectedYear** (which is bound to the text box control), and click **OK**.

6. On the **Rule Details** dialog box, click the button behind the **Value** text box.

7. On the **Insert Formula** dialog box, type a formula that says:

    ```
    substring(., 1, 4)
    ```

    This formula extracts the first 4 characters from the string representation of the date. InfoPath date fields have the format **yyyy-MM-dd** and InfoPath date/time fields have the format **yyyy-MM-ddThh:mm:ss**, where **yyyy** represents the year, **MM** represents the month, **dd** represents the day, **hh** represents the hours, **mm** represents the minutes, and **ss** represents the seconds. For example September 15, 2010 at 3 p.m. would be represented by **2010-09-15** as the value of a date picker and by **2010-09-15T15:00:00** as the value of a date and time picker in InfoPath. So to extract the year, you must retrieve the part of the date string that starts at position 1 and is 4 characters long.

8. On the **Insert Function** dialog box, click **Verify Formula** to check for any errors. Click **OK** on the message box that says "The formula does not contain any errors." If your formula contains errors, try to fix them.

9. On the **Insert Formula** dialog box, click **OK**.

10. On the **Rule Details** dialog box, click **OK**. The **Rules** task pane automatically opens where you can see the rule InfoPath has added for you with the following

action:

```
Set a field's value: selectedYear = substring(., 1, 4)
```

11. Preview the form.

When the form opens, select a date from the date picker. The year number for the selected date should appear in the text box.

Discussion

The **substring** function can be used to retrieve part of or an entire text string. The **substring** function takes 2 or 3 arguments:

1. The text string to retrieve part of or the whole string.

2. The position in the text string where the substring should start. The position number always starts at 1 (and not 0) for the first character. If the piece of string you are looking for starts at position 3, enter a 3.

3. Optionally, the amount of characters contained in the piece of text string you want to retrieve. If you do not specify an amount, all of the characters starting from the starting position you defined up to the end of the string will be returned.

Here are a few examples of how the **substring** function works:

- substring("InfoPath is fun", 1, 8) returns "InfoPath"

- substring("InfoPath is fun", 12) returns "fun"

Having extracted the year from a date string, you now also know how to extract the day number, month number, hours, minutes, and seconds. The month starts at position 6 in the date string and has a length of 2 characters. The day starts at position 9 and has a length of 2 characters, etc.

Exercise

With what you have learned about the **substring** function, try to extract the month number and day number from the date picker, and then try to extract the hour from a date and time picker control.

62. Select a date picker's year via a drop-down selection

Problem

You have a date picker control on an InfoPath form and want to be able to select a year from a drop-down list box and have the date picker automatically display the 1st of January of that year.

Solution

You can use the **concat** function to construct a date string based on the selected year value in the drop-down list box and then use a rule to set the value of the date picker to the constructed date string.

To select the year for a date picker control using a drop-down list box:

1. In InfoPath, create a new **Blank Form** template.

2. Add a **Drop-Down List Box** and **Date Picker** control to the form template. Name the drop-down list box **selectedYear** and the date picker **selectedDate**.

3. Right-click the drop-down list box and select **Drop-Down List Box Properties** from the context menu that appears.

4. On the **Drop-Down List Box Properties** dialog box on the **Data** tab under **List box choices**, leave **Enter choices manually**, and then click **Add**.

5. On the **Add Choice** dialog box, type a year, for example 2011, in the **Value** and **Display name** text boxes, and click **OK**.

6. Repeat steps 4 and 5 to add more years, for example, 2012, 2013, etc. On the **Drop-Down List Box Properties** dialog box, click **OK** when you are done adding the years.

7. Click the drop-down list box to select it, and then select **Home ➤ Add Rule ➤ This Field Changes ➤ Set a Field's Value**.

8. On the **Rule Details** dialog box, click the button behind the **Field** text box, select the **selectedDate** field, and click **OK**.

9. On the **Rule Details** dialog box, click the button behind the **Value** text box, and via the **Insert Formula** dialog box, enter the following formula:

```
concat(., "-01-01")
```

   What this formula does is take the year value from the selected item in the drop-down list box and append "-01-01" to it. A sample result would be 2011-01-01, which has the correct format for a date that can be displayed in a date picker control in InfoPath.

10. Click **OK** to close all open dialog boxes.

11. Preview the form.

When the form opens, select a year from the drop-down list box. The date should be populated in the date picker control. And when you click on the calendar icon on the right-hand side of the date picker control, the calendar should open and display the 1st of January of whichever year you selected from the drop-down list box.

Discussion

InfoPath date fields have the format **yyyy-MM-dd** and InfoPath date/time fields have the format **yyyy-MM-ddThh:mm:ss**, where **yyyy** represents the year, **MM** represents the month, **dd** represents the day, **hh** represents the hours, **mm** represents the minutes, and **ss** represents the seconds.

For example, September 15, 2010 at 3 p.m. would be represented by **2010-09-15** as the value of a date picker and by **2010-09-15T15:00:00** as the value of a date and time picker in InfoPath.

So had you used a date and time picker control instead of a date picker control in the recipe above, you would have had to change the formula to be the following:

```
concat(., "-01-01T00:00:00")
```

or set the time part of the date and time picker to be whatever you wanted it to be, but in any case to a valid time. Otherwise InfoPath would reject the constructed date and time value as a valid value for a date and time picker control.

63. Extract the month name from a date picker

Problem

You have a date picker control on an InfoPath form and want to extract the month number from the date and display the month name elsewhere on the form.

Solution

Because InfoPath does not offer a function to retrieve the month name from a date, you must use a workaround that uses the **substring** function to extract the month number from a date, and then look up the month name in either an external data source (e.g. an XML file) or a repeating field in the form. In this recipe you will use the **MonthNames.xml** file that was used in *54 Populate a text box based on a drop-down list box*.

To extract the month name from a date picker:

1. In InfoPath, create a new **Blank Form** template.

2. Add a **Date Picker** control to the form template and name it **completionDate**.

3. On the **Fields** task pane, right-click **completionDate**, and then drag-and-drop it onto the form template. When you drop it, select **Calculated Value** from the context menu that appears.

4. Add a **Receive data** connection to the **MonthNames.xml** file (see *32 Get data from an XML file*).

5. Double-click the **Calculated Value** control, which will bring forward the **Properties** tab on the ribbon, and then click **Properties ➤ Control Properties**.

6. On the **Calculated Value Properties** dialog box on the **General** tab, click the formula button behind the **XPath** text box.

7. On the **Insert Formula** dialog box, delete `completionDate`, and click **Insert Field or Group**.

8. On the **Select a Field or Group** dialog box, select **MonthNames (Secondary)** from the **Fields** drop-down list box, expand the **month** repeating group, select the **name** field, and click **Filter Data**.

9. On the **Filter Data** dialog box, click **Add**.

10. You are going to construct a formula that retrieves all of the names of the months, but with a filter that will look for the month name that has the same number as the month number of the date that is selected in the date picker. On the **Specify Filter Conditions** dialog box, select **number** from the first drop-down list box, leave **is equal to** selected in the second drop-down list box, and select **Use a formula** from the third drop-down list box.

11. On the **Insert Formula** dialog box, type **substring(**, and click **Insert Field or Group**.

12. On the **Select a Field or Group** dialog box, select **Main** from the **Fields** drop-down list box, select **completionDate**, and click **OK**.

13. On the **Insert Formula** dialog box, type **, 6, 2)** to complete the formula. The final formula should resemble the following:

    ```
    substring(completionDate, 6, 2)
    ```

    or the following if you have the **Edit XPath (advanced)** check box selected:

    ```
    substring(xdXDocument:get-DOM()/my:myFields/my:completionDate, 6, 2)
    ```

    What this formula does is extract the month number from the **completionDate** date picker. Remember that dates in InfoPath have the format **yyyy-MM-dd**, so the **substring** function extracts 2 characters starting from position 6 in the date string. This results in **MM** being returned, so the number for the month.

14. Click **OK** to close the **Insert Formula** dialog box.

15. On the **Specify Filter Conditions** dialog box, click **OK**.

16. On the **Filter Data** dialog box, the filter should say:

```
number = substring(completionDate, 6, 2)
```

This filter says that the month number in the XML file (Secondary data source) should be the same as the month number extracted from the **completionDate** field. Click **OK**.

17. On the **Select a Field or Group** dialog box, click **OK**. The final formula should now say:

```
name[number = substring(completionDate, 6, 2)]
```

or the following if you have the **Edit XPath (advanced)** check box selected:

```
xdXDocument:GetDOM("MonthNames")/months/month/name[../number =
substring(xdXDocument:get-DOM()/my:myFields/my:completionDate, 6, 2)]
```

With this you have added a filter on the month names to perform a lookup in the Secondary data source to find only that month name for which its corresponding month number in the XML file (Secondary data source) is the same as the month number extracted from the date that is selected in the **completionDate** date picker, which is located in the Main data source of the form.

18. On the **Insert Formula** dialog box, click **OK**.

19. On the **Calculated Value Properties** dialog box on the **General** tab, select **Text** from the **Format as** drop-down list box, and click **OK**.

20. Preview the form.

When the form opens, select a date from the date picker. The month name should be retrieved from the XML file and displayed in the calculated value control.

64. Set a date picker to display the previous month in its calendar

Problem

You have a date picker on an InfoPath form and want it to display the 1st of the previous month instead of the current month.

Solution

You can use rules, functions, and formulas to set the date of the date picker to the first of the previous month.

To set a date picker to display the previous month in its calendar:

1. In InfoPath, create a new **Blank Form** template.

2. Add a **Date Picker** control to the form template and name it **datePreviousMonth**.

3. The logic to calculate the date for the previous month is as follows:

   a. If it is currently January, you want the date in the date picker to be the 1st of December of the previous year.

   b. If it is currently not January, you want the date in the date picker to be the 1st of the previous month in the same year.

   What this logic means is that you must set conditions on rules, and the conditions must determine whether it is currently January or not. And because you have to set conditions on rules, you cannot use a **Default Value** on the date picker, but must rather use an **Action** rule on another control or on the form itself to trigger setting the date of the date picker. Here you will set the date when the form opens.

4. Click **Data ➤ Rules ➤ Form Load**. This will open the **Rules** task pane.

5. On the **Rules** task pane, add an **Action** rule with an action that says:

   ```
   Set a field's value: datePreviousMonth = today()
   ```

   This rule initializes the date picker to contain the current date. This rule does not have conditions and should always be the first rule in the list of rules.

6. On the **Rules** task pane, add a second **Action** rule with the **Condition**:

   ```
   number(substring(my:datePreviousMonth, 6, 2)) > 1
   and
   number(substring(my:datePreviousMonth, 6, 2)) < 11
   ```

   and an action that says:

   ```
   Set a field's value: datePreviousMonth =
   concat(substring(datePreviousMonth, 1, 4), "-0",
   string(number(substring(datePreviousMonth, 6, 2)) - 1), "-01")
   ```

   and select the **Don't run remaining rules if the condition of this rule is met** check box.

   This rule sets the **datePreviousMonth** field when the current month falls between February and October (inclusive). This rule is added to make the concatenation easier as a zero should be added before any month number less than 10. Remember that dates in InfoPath have the format **yyyy-MM-dd**, so any month number is expected to consist of 2 characters, and not 1. Note: You must use the **The expression** option to define the expressions for the condition on the rule.

7. On the **Rules** task pane, add a third **Action** rule with the **Condition**:

```
number(substring(my:datePreviousMonth, 6, 2)) >= 11
```

and an action that says:

```
Set a field's value: datePreviousMonth =
concat(substring(datePreviousMonth, 1, 4), "-",
string(number(substring(datePreviousMonth, 6, 2)) - 1), "-01")
```

and select the **Don't run remaining rules if the condition of this rule is met** check box.

This rule sets the **datePreviousMonth** field when the current month falls in or after November. This rule is added to make the concatenation easier as a zero should not be added before any month number greater than 9. Note: You must use the **The expression** option to define the expressions for the condition on the rule.

8. On the **Rules** task pane, add a fourth **Action** rule with the **Condition**:

```
number(substring(my:datePreviousMonth, 6, 2)) = 1
```

and an action that says:

```
Set a field's value: datePreviousMonth =
concat(string(number(substring(datePreviousMonth, 1, 4)) - 1), "-12-01")
```

and select the **Don't run remaining rules if the condition of this rule is met** check box.

This rule sets the **datePreviousMonth** field to December of the previous year when the current month is January. Note: You must use the **The expression** option to define the expressions for the condition on the rule.

9. Preview the form.

When you open the form, the first of the previous month should be displayed in the date picker, depending on the date that is currently set on your system. To test other months, you could change your system date and then reopen the form to see whether it displays the correct previous month.

Discussion

In the recipe above, you used the following InfoPath functions to construct the date for the previous month:

- **number**, which converts a string to a number so that you can perform math calculations.

- **string**, which converts a number to a text string, so that you can use the result in the **concat** function.

- **concat**, which combines two or more fields or text strings into one text string.

- **substring**, which returns a specific part of a text string.

Tip:

When you use the **The expression** option on the **Condition** dialog box, there is no facility to construct an expression. It is best to select the **Use a formula** option in the third drop-down list box as soon as you open the **Condition** dialog box.

This will open the **Insert Formula** dialog box where you can select fields and insert functions. Once you are happy with your constructed formula, you can click **OK**, and then on the **Condition** dialog box, select **The expression** from the first drop-down list box.

InfoPath will add a field (whichever field was selected in the first drop-down list box before you selected **The expression** from the first drop-down list box) and an equal sign in front of your constructed formula, so you must correct the expression in the text box by removing these additions. See for example *30 Set a maximum length on a text box*.

---

65. Extract the name of the day for a selected date

Problem

You have a date picker control on an InfoPath form and want to select a date from the date picker and have the name of the day corresponding to the date be displayed on the form.

Solution

You can use the **substring** function and a formula that is based on using the year, month, and day to calculate a day number where Sunday is 0 and Saturday is 6.

To display the name of the day for a selected date:

1. In InfoPath, create a new **Blank Form** template.

2. Add a **Date Picker** control to the form template, name the date picker control **myDate**, and set its **Default Value** to

```
today()
```

3. On the **Fields** task pane, add a text field named **dayName** under the **myFields** group, right-click it, drag it to the form template, and when you drop it select **Calculated Value** from the context menu that appears.

4. On the **Fields** task pane under the **dayName** field, add a field of type **Field (attribute)** with the name **day** and data type **Whole Number (integer)**.

5. Once added, double-click the **day** field, and then on the **Field or Group Properties** dialog box, set its default value to

```
number(substring(myDate, 9, 2))
```

and ensure that the **Refresh value when formula is recalculated** check box is selected for the default value. This formula extracts the day number from the **myDate** date picker.

6. On the **Fields** task pane under the **dayName** field, add a field of type **Field (attribute)** with the name **month** and data type **Whole Number (integer)**.

7. Once added, double-click the **month** field, and then on the **Field or Group Properties** dialog box, set its default value to

```
number(substring(myDate, 6, 2))
```

and ensure that the **Refresh value when formula is recalculated** check box is selected for the default value. This formula extracts the month number from the **myDate** date picker.

8. On the **Fields** task pane under the **dayName** field, add a field of type **Field (attribute)** with the name **year** and data type **Whole Number (integer)**.

9. Once added, double-click the **year** field, and then on the **Field or Group Properties** dialog box, set its default value to

```
number(substring(myDate, 1, 4))
```

and ensure that the **Refresh value when formula is recalculated** check box is selected for the default value. This formula extracts the year number from the **myDate** date picker.

10. Set the **Default Value** of the **dayName** field to the following formula:

```
(@my:day + number(@my:year - (floor((14 - @my:month) div 12))) +
floor(number(@my:year - (floor((14 - @my:month) div 12))) div 4) -
floor(number(@my:year - (floor((14 - @my:month) div 12))) div 100) +
floor(number(@my:year - (floor((14 - @my:month) div 12))) div 400) +
floor((31 * number(@my:month + 12 * (floor((14 - @my:month) div 12)) -
2)) div 12)) mod 7
```

and ensure that the **Refresh value when formula is recalculated** check box is selected. This is a formula used to calculate a number for a day of the week. It uses the value of the **myDate** date picker to calculate a number between 0 and 6, with 0 representing Sunday and 6 representing Saturday.

11. Add 7 **Action** rules to the **dayName** calculated value control with the following conditions and actions:

    a. Condition: dayName = "0"
        Action: Set a field's value: . = "Sunday"

    b. Condition: dayName = "1"
        Action: Set a field's value: . = "Monday"

    c. Condition: dayName = "2"
        Action: Set a field's value: . = "Tuesday"

    d. Condition: dayName = "3"
        Action: Set a field's value: . = "Wednesday"

    e. Condition: dayName = "4"
        Action: Set a field's value: . = "Thursday"

    f. Condition: dayName = "5"
        Action: Set a field's value: . = "Friday"

    g. Condition: dayName = "6"
        Action: Set a field's value: . = "Saturday"

Ensure that the **Don't run remaining rules if the condition of this rule is met** check box is selected for each one of the rules above.

12. Preview the form.

When the form opens, the date of today should be displayed in the date picker and the name of the week day should be displayed in the calculated value control. Select a different date from the date picker and see how the week day name changes.

Discussion

In the recipe above, you used attributes on a field to help make a formula shorter and more legible. However, you could have also just referenced the **myDate** field in each **substring** function and arrive at the following formula as the **Default Value** for the **myDate** field.

```
(number(substring(../my:myDate, 9, 2)) + number(number(substring(../my:myDate,
1, 4)) - (floor((14 - number(substring(../my:myDate, 6, 2))) div 12))) +
floor(number(number(substring(../my:myDate, 1, 4)) - (floor((14 -
number(substring(../my:myDate, 6, 2))) div 12))) div 4) -
floor(number(number(substring(../my:myDate, 1, 4)) - (floor((14 -
number(substring(../my:myDate, 6, 2))) div 12))) div 100) +
floor(number(number(substring(../my:myDate, 1, 4)) - (floor((14 -
```

```
number(substring(../my:myDate, 6, 2))) div 12))) div 400) + floor((31 *
number(number(substring(../my:myDate, 6, 2)) + 12 * (floor((14 -
number(substring(../my:myDate, 6, 2))) div 12)) - 2)) div 12)) mod 7
```

There are two types of fields you can create in InfoPath:

1. Elements

2. Attributes

An attribute can be seen as a property of an element, and can be used to provide additional information for an element.

You can add an attribute to either a **group** or an element **field** in InfoPath.

Figure 103. Day, month, and year attributes under the dayName element.

While creating fields as elements instead of attributes will suit most of your needs, there might be instances where you want to describe properties of an element. In such cases, you can add fields as attributes on an element as shown in the recipe above.

66. Force Sundays to be selected from a date picker

Problem

You have a date picker control on an InfoPath form and want to force users to always select a date that falls on a Sunday.

Solution

You can use a **Validation** rule to check whether the date that is selected in a date picker falls on a Sunday.

To force a Sunday to be selected from a date picker control:

1. In InfoPath, create a new **Blank Form** template.

2. Add a **Date Picker** control to the form template, name the date picker control **myDate**, and set its **Default Value** to

    ```
    today()
    ```

3. On the **Fields** task pane, add a hidden text field named **dateParts** (see *10 Add a hidden field*) under the **myFields** group.

4. On the **Fields** task pane under the **dateParts** field, add a field of type **Field (attribute)** with the name **day** and data type **Whole Number (integer)**.

5. Once added, double-click the **day** field, and then on the **Field or Group Properties** dialog box, set its default value to

```
number(substring(myDate, 9, 2))
```

   and ensure that the **Refresh value when formula is recalculated** check box is selected for the default value. This formula extracts the day number from the **myDate** date picker.

6. On the **Fields** task pane under the **dateParts** field, add a field of type **Field (attribute)** with the name **month** and data type **Whole Number (integer)**.

7. Once added, double-click the **month** field, and then on the **Field or Group Properties** dialog box, set its default value to

```
number(substring(myDate, 6, 2))
```

   and ensure that the **Refresh value when formula is recalculated** check box is selected for the default value. This formula extracts the month number from the **myDate** date picker.

8. On the **Fields** task pane under the **dateParts** field, add a field of type **Field (attribute)** with the name **year** and data type **Whole Number (integer)**.

9. Once added, double-click the **year** field, and then on the **Field or Group Properties** dialog box, set its default value to

```
number(substring(myDate, 1, 4))
```

   and ensure that the **Refresh value when formula is recalculated** check box is selected for the default value. This formula extracts the year number from the **myDate** date picker.

10. Set the **Default Value** of the **dateParts** field to the following formula:

```
(@my:day + number(@my:year - (floor((14 - @my:month) div 12))) +
floor(number(@my:year - (floor((14 - @my:month) div 12))) div 4) -
floor(number(@my:year - (floor((14 - @my:month) div 12))) div 100) +
floor(number(@my:year - (floor((14 - @my:month) div 12))) div 400) +
floor((31 * number(@my:month + 12 * (floor((14 - @my:month) div 12)) -
2)) div 12)) mod 7
```

   and ensure that the **Refresh value when formula is recalculated** check box is selected. This is a formula used to calculate a number for a day of the week. It uses the value of the **myDate** date picker to calculate a number between 0 and 6, with 0 representing Sunday and 6 representing Saturday.

11. Add a **Validation** rule to the **myDate** date picker with a **Condition** that says:

   ```
   dateParts ≠ "0"
   ```

   (**dateParts** is not equal to 0) and a **ScreenTip** that says: "You must select a Sunday". This rule checks whether the selected date is not a Sunday and then displays a message.

12. Preview the form.

When the form opens, select a date that does not fall on a Sunday. A red dashed border should appear around the date picker and when you hover over the date picker you should see the screen tip message appear. Then select a date that falls on a Sunday. The red dashed border should disappear.

Discussion

See *65 Extract the name of the day for a selected date* for the discussion of the difference between elements and attributes in InfoPath.

67. Change the time text box of a date and time picker into a drop-down list box

Problem

You have a date and time picker control on an InfoPath form and want to change the text box of the time part of the date and time picker control into a drop-down list box control for easy selection of a certain time within a day.

Solution

You can use a Secondary data source that contains times and bind this to a drop-down list box control to provide the hours for a date and time picker control.

To change the time text box of a date and time picker control into a drop-down list box:

1. In InfoPath, create a new **Blank Form** template.

2. Add a **Date and Time Picker** control to the form template and name it **theDateAndTime**.

3. Select the text box control (time part) of the date and time picker control and press **Delete** on your keyboard to delete it.

4. Add a data connection to an XML file (see *32 Get data from an XML file*) that has the following contents:

   ```
   <?xml version="1.0" encoding="UTF-8"?>
   ```

```
<datetimetimes xmlns="urn:sym">
  <selectedTime/>
  <times><date/><time>01:00</time><datetime/></times>
  <times><date/><time>02:00</time><datetime/></times>
  <times><date/><time>03:00</time><datetime/></times>
  <times><date/><time>04:00</time><datetime/></times>
  <times><date/><time>05:00</time><datetime/></times>
  <times><date/><time>06:00</time><datetime/></times>
  <times><date/><time>07:00</time><datetime/></times>
  <times><date/><time>08:00</time><datetime/></times>
  <times><date/><time>09:00</time><datetime/></times>
  <times><date/><time>10:00</time><datetime/></times>
  <times><date/><time>11:00</time><datetime/></times>
  <times><date/><time>12:00</time><datetime/></times>
  <times><date/><time>13:00</time><datetime/></times>
  <times><date/><time>14:00</time><datetime/></times>
  <times><date/><time>15:00</time><datetime/></times>
  <times><date/><time>16:00</time><datetime/></times>
  <times><date/><time>17:00</time><datetime/></times>
  <times><date/><time>18:00</time><datetime/></times>
  <times><date/><time>19:00</time><datetime/></times>
  <times><date/><time>20:00</time><datetime/></times>
  <times><date/><time>21:00</time><datetime/></times>
  <times><date/><time>22:00</time><datetime/></times>
  <times><date/><time>23:00</time><datetime/></times>
  <times><date/><time>00:00</time><datetime/></times>
</datetimetimes>
```

and name the data connection **DateTimeTimes**.

5. Click the date picker to select it, and then click **Home ➤ Rules ➤ Manage Rules**.

6. On the **Rules** task pane, click **New ➤ Action**, add a **Condition** that says:

```
theDateAndTime is not blank
```

and then click **Add ➤ Set a field's value**.

7. On the **Rule Details** dialog box, click the button behind the **Field** text box.

8. On the **Select a Field or Group** dialog box, select **DateTimeTimes (Secondary)** from the **Fields** drop-down list box, expand all nodes, select the **date** node under the **times** repeating group, and click **OK**. With this you are setting all of the **date** fields in the Secondary data source.

9. On the **Rule Details** dialog box, click the button behind the **Value** field, and construct a formula that says:

```
substring(., 1, 10)
```

This formula extracts the first 10 characters from the date and time string, which is the same as extracting only the date part from the date and time string.

10. On the **Rule Details** dialog box, click **OK**. The action on the **Rules** task pane should now say:

```
Set a field's value: date = substring(., 1, 10)
```

where **date** is the **date** field under the **times** repeating group in the **DateTimeTimes** Secondary data source. This rule sets all of the **date** fields in the Secondary data source to the date part of the date and time picker control. The date part has the format of **yyyy-MM-dd**. If you look at the XML file, you will see that all of the **date** nodes start out as empty fields.

11. On the **Fields** task pane, select **DateTimeTimes (Secondary)** from the **Fields** drop-down list box, right-click the **selectedTime** field, and then drag-and-drop it to the form template. When you drop it, select **Drop-Down List Box** from the context menu.

12. Open the **Drop-Down Properties** dialog box, and then set the list box choices to come from the **DateTimeTimes** Secondary data source and to have the **times** repeating group as the **Entries**, the **datetime** field as the **Value** and the **time** field as the **Display name** for the drop-down list box (also see *48 Populate a drop-down list box from an XML file*). Click **OK** when you are done.

Figure 104. Drop-down list box bound to Secondary data source containing times.

13. Add a **Formatting** rule to the **selectedTime** drop-down list box with a **Condition** that says:

```
theDateAndTime is blank
```

and a **Formatting** to **Disable this control**. This rule is to disable the drop-down list box if no date has been selected or entered in the date part of the date and time picker control. Note: Remember that **theDateAndTime** field is located in the Main data source of the form, so you must select **Main** from the **Data source** drop-down list box on the **Select a Field or Group** dialog box when constructing the condition for the rule.

14. On the **Fields** task pane, select **DateTimeTimes (Secondary)** from the **Fields** drop-down list box, and then click **date** under the **times** repeating group to select it. Then on the **Rules** task pane, add an **Action** rule that says:

```
Set a field's value: datetime = concat(.,"T", time, ":00")
```

This rule sets the values of all of the **datetime** fields in the Secondary data source by concatenating the **date** and **time** values from the Secondary data source with a resulting format of **yyyy-MM-ddThh:mm:ss**, which is suitable to be used as the format for the value of a date and time picker control.

15. Add a second **Action** rule to the **date** node under the **times** repeating group in the Secondary data source with a **Condition** that says:

```
selectedTime is not blank
and
theDateAndTime is not blank
```

and an action that says:

```
Set a field's value: selectedTime =
concat(substring(theDateAndTime,1,10), substring(selectedTime,11))
```

This rule ensures that if a time has previously been selected, and you select a different date, the selected time in the drop-down list box is refreshed to reflect the new date and the previously selected time, because the formula concatenates the date part from the date picker and the time part from the drop-down list box. While you may only see a date in the date picker and a time in the drop-down list box, both controls store a date and time as their value. So **substring(theDateAndTime, 1, 10)** results in the date part of the date picker being extracted, and **substring(selectedTime, 11)** results in the time part of the value of the selected item in the drop-down list box being extracted.

16. Add a third **Action** rule to the **date** node under the **times** repeating group in the Secondary data source with a **Condition** that says:

```
selectedTime is blank
and
theDateAndTime is not blank
```

and an action that says:

```
Set a field's value: selectedTime = theDateAndTime
```

This rule ensures that the first time a date is selected from the date picker, the time in the drop-down list box is automatically set to 12 a.m. if no time has been selected.

17. Click the drop-down list box to select it, and then add an **Action** rule to it with an action that says:

```
Set a field's value: theDateAndTime = .
```

This rule sets the value of the field bound to the date and time picker control to the date and time value of the item selected in the drop-down list box. This is necessary, because the date and time picker control will have a time of 00:00 when you select a date from the date picker, because its time part will not have been set yet. Its time part should be set when you select a time from the drop-down list box.

18. Click **Data ➤ Rules ➤ Form Load**.

19. On the **Rules** task pane, ensure that **Form Load** is listed under the title bar, and then click **New ➤ Action**, and add two actions that say:

```
Set a field's value: date = substring(theDateAndTime, 1, 10)
Set a field's value: selectedTime = theDateAndTime
```

This rule ensures that when a previously saved form is opened with a previously selected date and time, the correct time is displayed in the drop-down list box.

20. Preview the form.

When the form opens, the drop-down should be disabled and you should see 00:00 in it as the time. When you select a date from the date picker control, the drop-down list box should be enabled. Select a time from the drop-down list box, and then save the form somewhere locally on disk. Open the form (XML) you just saved in Notepad. You should see the date and time picker field with a value that contains your selected date from the date picker and your selected time from the drop-down list box. Double-click the form you saved to open it again in InfoPath Filler 2010. The date and time should be correctly displayed both in the date picker and in the drop-down list box.

Discussion

The trick to understanding the recipe described above is to realize that while you are seeing a date in the date picker and a time in the drop-down list box control, the fields that these controls are bound to store a date and time as their value. So any rule you add to set the value of these controls should have a date and time format (yyyy-MM-ddThh:mm:ss).

Data from Secondary data sources is never persisted (stored) in the InfoPath form (XML) itself. In the recipe above, you used a Secondary data source to be able to display a drop-down list box with times and then select a time from this drop-down list box without having all of the date and time values stored in the form once the form was saved. This is a best practice that will keep your forms uncluttered, light, and containing only relevant data.

Tip:

> If you need to use a field purely as a way to perform a calculation or any other processing, and do not need to store the final value of this field in the Main data source of the form, you can use a Secondary data source that contains "helper fields" such as this field. This will keep data in your forms uncluttered and relevant.

In the recipe above, there are several rules being applied on fields. Whenever you have so many rules that can affect each other, you need to be careful and aware of which field change triggers which rule. You can click **Data** ➤ **Rules** ➤ **Rule Inspector** to open the **Rule Inspector** to view these rules. And if you click on any of the fields (for example **date**) on the left-hand side of the **Rule Inspector**, the right-hand side will show all of the rules that depend on the field you selected, rules that are triggered by a change in the field, and rules that may change the field. You can always use this information to try to troubleshoot a form that has many rules and is showing unexpected behavior.

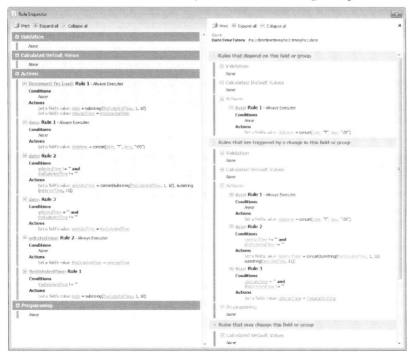

Figure 105. Rule Inspector showing dependencies on the right-hand side.

The date picker has one rule that can be triggered:

1. If **theDateAndTime** is not blank (so a date has been entered into the date picker), an action will set the **date** field in the Secondary data source to be equal to the date part of the date picker.

The **date** field in the Secondary data source has 3 rules that can be triggered:

1. If a change takes place on the **date** field, the **datetime** fields in the Secondary data source are set. This rule always runs.

2. If **selectedTime** in the Secondary data source is not blank (so a time has been selected once before from the drop-down list box) and **theDateAndTime** is not blank (so a date has been entered into the date picker), then the **selectedTime** field will be set to a concatenation of the date part of the date picker and the time part of itself.

3. If **selectedTime** is blank (so a time has yet to be selected from the drop-down list box for the first time) and **theDateAndTime** is not blank (a date has been entered into the date picker), then the **selectedTime** field will be set to the value of the date picker.

The **selectedTime** field in the Secondary data source has one rule that can be triggered:

1. If a change takes place on the **selectedTime** field, the date picker (**theDateAndTime** field) is set to the same value as the value of the **selectedTime** field. This rule always runs.

Now let us take a look at a few scenarios to see how these rules are triggered and work.

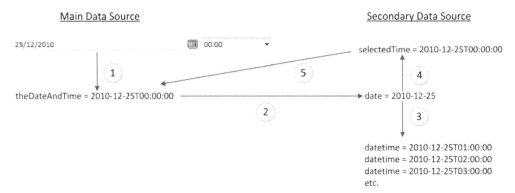

In the figure above, a user enters a date of December 25, 2010 in the date picker. This action causes the following chain of events:

1. The value of the **theDateAndTime** field is set to 2010-12-25T00:00:00. The time is set to 00:00:00, because no time has been selected.

2. Because the value of the **theDateAndTime** field changed from blank to 2010-12-25T00:00:00, it triggers the rule that sets the value of the **date** field in the Secondary data source.

3. Because the value of the **date** field in the Secondary data source changed from an empty string to 2010-12-25, it triggers the rule that sets the **datetime** fields in the Secondary data source.

4. Because the value of the **date** field in the Secondary data source changed from an empty string to 2010-12-25 and **selectedTime** is blank and **theDateAndTime** is not blank, it triggers rule number 3 on the **date** field that sets the value of the **selectedTime** field.

5. Because the value of the **selectedTime** field changed from blank to 2010-12-25T00:00:00, it triggers the rule on the **selectedTime** field that sets the value of the **theDateAndTime** field. And because the **theDateAndTime** field was already set to 2010-12-25T00:00:00, no change takes place, so the rule on the **theDateAndTime** field does not run again, and all actions stop.

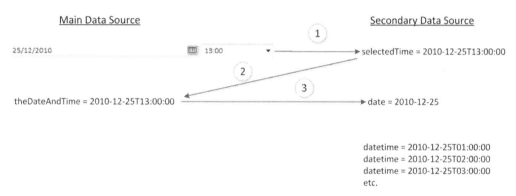

In the figure above, a user selects a time of 13:00 from the drop-down list box. This action causes the following chain of events:

1. The value of the **selectedTime** field is set to 2010-12-25T13:00:00.

2. Because the value of the **selectedTime** field changed from 2010-12-25T00:00:00 to 2010-12-25T13:00:00, it triggers the rule on the **selectedTime** field that sets the value of the **theDateAndTime** field to 2010-12-25T13:00:00.

3. Because the value of the **theDateAndTime** field changed from 2010-12-25T00:00:00 to 2010-12-25T13:00:00, it triggers the rule that sets the value of the **date** field in the Secondary data source. But because the date part of the **theDateAndTime** field is equal to 2010-12-25 and the **date** field in the Secondary data source was already set to this value, no change takes place, so none of the rules on the **date** field are triggered, and all actions stop.

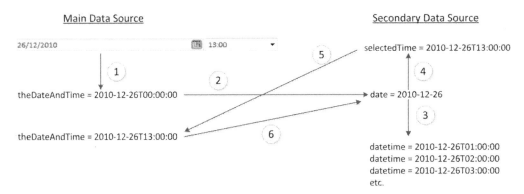

In the figure above, a user changes the date to December 26, 2010 in the date picker. This action causes the following chain of events:

1. The value of the **theDateAndTime** field is set to 2010-12-26T00:00:00. The time is set to 00:00:00, because no time has been selected (no time can be selected from the date picker alone). Remember that we deleted the text box to enter a time for the date and time picker control, so technically speaking, we cannot enter times for the **theDateAndTime** field, so the time is always 00:00:00 when a new date is selected.

2. Because the value of the **theDateAndTime** field changed from 2010-12-25T13:00:00 to 2010-12-26T00:00:00, it triggers the rule that sets the value of the **date** field in the Secondary data source.

3. Because the value of the **date** field in the Secondary data source changed from 2010-12-25 to 2010-12-26, it triggers the rule that sets the **datetime** fields in the Secondary data source.

4. Because the value of the **date** field in the Secondary data source changed from 2010-12-25 to 2010-12-26 and **selectedTime** is not blank and **theDateAndTime** is not blank, it triggers rule number 2 on the **date** field that sets the value of the **selectedTime** field.

5. Because the value of the **selectedTime** field changed from 2010-12-25T13:00:00 to 2010-12-26T13:00:00, it triggers the rule on the **selectedTime** field that sets the value of **theDateAndTime** field.

6. Because the value of the **theDateAndTime** field changed from 2010-12-26T00:00:00 to 2010-12-26T13:00:00, it triggers the rule that sets the value of the **date** field in the Secondary data source. But because the date part of the **theDateAndTime** field is equal to 2010-12-26 and the **date** field in the Secondary data source was already set to this value, no change takes place, so none of the rules on the **date** field are triggered again, and all actions stop.

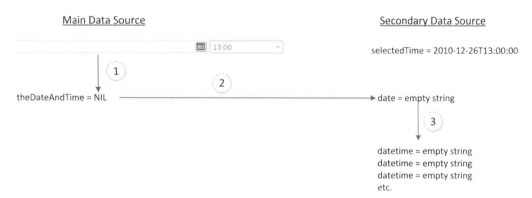

In the figure above, a user clears the date picker. This action causes the following chain of events:

1. The value of the **theDateAndTime** field is set to NIL (blank).

2. Because the value of the **theDateAndTime** field changed from 2010-12-26T13:00:00 to blank, this triggers the rule that sets the value of the **date** field in the Secondary data source.

3. Because the value of the **date** field in the Secondary data source changed from 2010-12-26 to an empty string, this triggers the rule that sets the **datetime** fields in the Secondary data source. And because the conditions for the other 2 rules on the **date** field are not met, those rules are not triggered, and all actions stop.

Hopefully the scenarios explained above have increased your understanding of how rules are triggered and how changes on one field can have a cascading effect on the values of other fields.

68. Check whether start date falls before end date

Problem

You have start and end date picker controls on an InfoPath form and want to ensure that the start date always falls before the end date.

Solution

You can use data validation and the fact that dates in InfoPath are represented by strings that can be easily compared with each other to check whether the start date falls before the end date.

To check whether a start date falls before an end date:

1. In InfoPath, create a new **Blank Form** template.

2. Add two **Date Picker** controls to the form template. Name the first date picker **startDate** and the second date picker **endDate**.

3. Click the **startDate** date picker to select it, and then select **Home ➤ Rules ➤ Add Rule ➤ Is After ➤ Show Validation Error**.

4. On the **Rule Details** dialog box, click the formula button behind the text box.

5. On the **Insert Formula** dialog box, click **Insert Field or Group**.

6. On the **Select a Field or Group** dialog box, select **endDate**, and click **OK**.

7. On the **Insert Formula** dialog box, click **OK**.

8. On the **Rule Details** dialog box, click **OK**. The **Rules** task pane should automatically open if it was not already being displayed.

9. On the **Rules** task pane, InfoPath should have created a **Validation** rule for you that has the **Condition**:

```
startDate > endDate
and
startDate is not blank
```

and the **ScreenTip** "Enter a date on or before endDate". You can change the screen tip if you wish.

10. Preview the form.

When the form opens, select an end date and then enter a start date that falls after the end date. A red dashed border should appear around the start date and when you hover with the cursor over it, you should see the screen tip appear.

Discussion

In a similar way as described in the recipe above, you can also add a **Validation** rule to the end date to check that the start date falls before the end date. The only difference is that you must use the **Is Before** option instead of the **Is After** option when adding the rule on the **endDate** date picker.

Remember, the **Add Rule** option on the **Home** tab under the **Rules** group provides shortcuts to adding rules in InfoPath. You can also use the **Manage Rules** option to construct and add similar rules yourself.

69. Keeping two date pickers within a 7-day date range of each other

Problem

You have two date pickers on an InfoPath form and want to check whether the dates are within 7 days of each other.

Solution

You can use data validation to prevent two dates from being more than 7 days apart from each other.

To maintain a 7-day interval between two date pickers:

1. In InfoPath, create a new **Blank Form** template.

2. Add two **Date Picker** controls to the form template and name them **startDate** and **endDate**, respectively.

3. Add a **Validation** rule to **endDate** that has the following **Condition**:

   ```
   startDate is not blank
   and
   endDate is not blank
   and
   endDate > addDays(startDate, 7)
   ```

   and the **ScreenTip** "Enter a date that falls within 7 days from the start date".

   Note: To construct the third condition, on the **Condition** dialog box, you must select **endDate** from the first drop-down list box, select **is greater than** from the second drop-down list box, select **Use a formula** from the third drop-down list box, and then construct the formula using the **addDays** function.

4. Preview the form.

When the form opens, select a start date, and then select an end date that lies more than 7 days in the future. A red dashed border should appear around the end date, and when you hover over the end date, the screen tip message you specified earlier should appear. Now select an end date that is within 7 days from the start date. The red dashed border should disappear.

Discussion

The condition on the **Validation** rule in this recipe prevents the rule from running if either the start date or end date has not been entered through the use of the following expressions:

```
startDate is not blank
and
endDate is not blank
```

You can use the technique described in the recipe above to also check dates in the past by subtracting days using the **addDays** function. For example, if you want to check whether the start date falls in the past but stays within 7 days of the end date, then you can use the following formula

```
addDays(endDate, -7)
```

when constructing the condition for a **Validation** rule on **startDate**.

70.   Calculate a person's age from a date of birth in a date picker control

Problem

You have a date picker on an InfoPath form that is used to enter a date of birth. You want to be able to calculate a person's age from the selected date of birth.

Solution

You can use **Action** rules with conditions to calculate an age based on a date of birth selected in a date picker control.

To calculate a person's age from a date of birth in a date picker control:

1.   In InfoPath, create a new **Blank Form** template.

2.   Add a **Date Picker** control to the form template and name it **dob**.

3.   Add a **Text Box** control to the form template and name it **age**. Change the data type of **age** to **Whole Number (integer)** and set the text box to be **Read-only**.

4.   Add an **Action** rule to the date picker control with no conditions and the following action:

     ```
     Set a field's value: age = number(substring(today(), 1, 4)) -
     number(substring(., 1, 4))
     ```

     This rule calculates the amount of years between the current year and the birth year.

5.   Add a second **Action** rule to the date picker control that has the following **Condition**:

     ```
     number(substring(xdDate:Today(), 9, 2)) < number(substring(../my:dob, 9,
     2))
     ```

```
and
number(substring(xdDate:Today(), 6, 2)) = number(substring(../my:dob, 6,
2))
or
number(substring(xdDate:Today(), 6, 2)) < number(substring(../my:dob, 6,
2))
```

and the following action:

```
Set a field's value: age = number(substring(today(), 1, 4)) -
number(substring(., 1, 4)) - 1
```

This rule subtracts 1 year from the age if the current date falls within the same month but before the day of birth or if the current month falls before the month of the date of birth. Note: To construct each expression for the condition listed above, select **The expression** from the first dropdown list box on the **Condition** dialog box and then enter the condition.

6. Add a third **Action** rule to the date picker control that has the following **Condition**:

```
age < 0
```

and the following action:

```
Set a field's value: age = 0
```

This rule sets the age to 0 if the calculated age is less than 0.

7. Preview the form.

When the form opens, enter any date of birth and see whether the age is calculated correctly.

Discussion

The recipe described above makes use of the fact that **Action** rules run in order from top to bottom (see the section on *Action rules*). This means that when the first rule has run, the age is set to a certain amount of years. This value is overwritten by rule 2 (the one that subtracts 1 year from the age) if the person's day of birth has yet to take place in the current year. And finally, rule 3 overwrites the age with a zero, if the calculated age from any of the two previous rules resulted in a number less than zero.

If the expressions for the conditions in the recipe above look like magic to you, review the tip given in *64 Set a date picker to display the previous month in its calendar* that explains making use of a trick when constructing formulas to be used as expressions in conditions for rules.

71. Calculate the difference in days between a date picker and today

Problem

You have a date picker control on an InfoPath form and want to know how many days there are between the current date (today) and the selected date in the date picker.

Solution

You can use the Julian Day formula as described on Wikipedia (see http://en.wikipedia.org/wiki/Julian_day) to calculate the difference between today and a date picker using **Action** rules.

To calculate the difference between the selected date in a date picker and today:

1. In InfoPath, create a new **Blank Form** template.

2. Add a **Date Picker** control to the form template and name it **selectedDate**.

3. On the **Fields** task pane under the **selectedDate** field, add a **Field (attribute)** named **jdn_selectedDate** of data type **Text (string)**.

4. On the **Fields** task pane under the **myFields** group, add a **Field (element)** with the name **currentDate**, the data type **Date (date)**, and the **Default Value** equal to **today()**.

5. On the **Fields** task pane under the **currentDate** field, add a **Field (attribute)** named **jdn_currentDate** of data type **Text (string)**.

6. Add a **Text Box** control named **difference** to the form template. Make the text box **Read-only**.

7. On the **Fields** task pane under the **myFields** group, add a group named **JulianDayCalculator**.

8. On the **Fields** task pane under the **JulianDayCalculator** group, add 7 fields of type **Field (element)** with the data type **Whole Number (integer)** and the following names: **day, month, year, a, y, m, JDN**.

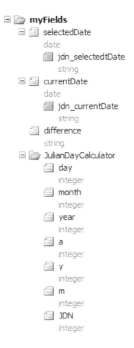

Figure 106. Main data source of the InfoPath form.

9. Set the **Default Value** of field **a** to the following formula:

```
(14 - ../my:month) div 12
```

10. Set the **Default Value** of field **y** to the following formula:

```
../my:year + 4800 - ../my:a
```

11. Set the **Default Value** of field **m** to the following formula:

```
../my:month + 12 * ../my:a - 3
```

12. Set the **Default Value** of field **JDN** to the following formula:

```
../my:day + ((153 * ../my:m + 2) div 5) + 365 * ../my:y + (../my:y div
4) - (../my:y div 100) + (../my:y div 400) - 32045
```

13. Add an **Action** rule to the **selectedDate** field with the following actions:

```
Set a field's value: day = number(substring(., 9, 2))
Set a field's value: month = number(substring(., 6, 2))
Set a field's value: year = number(substring(., 1, 4))
Set a field's value: @jdn_selectedDate = JDN
```

This rule sets the day, month, and year for the Julian Day calculator based on the values from the selected date and then calculates the Julian Day Number (JDN) for the selected date.

14. Add a second **Action** rule to the **selectedDate** field with the following actions:

```
Set a field's value: day = number(substring(currentDate, 9, 2))
Set a field's value: month = number(substring(currentDate, 6, 2))
Set a field's value: year = number(substring(currentDate, 1, 4))
Set a field's value: @jdn_currentDate = JDN
Set a field's value: difference = floor(number(@jdn_selectedDate) -
number(@jdn_currentDate))
```

This rule sets the day, month, and year for the Julian Day calculator based on the values from the current date, calculates the Julian Day Number (JDN) for the current date, and then calculates the difference between the selected date and the current date.

15. Preview the form.

When the form opens, select a date that lies in the future. A positive amount of days should appear in the **difference** text box. And then select a date that lies in the past. A negative amount of days should appear in the **difference** text box.

Discussion

The Julian Day formula calculates a number for a certain date in time. The recipe described above calculates the Julian Day Number for the selected date and the Julian Day Number for the current date and then subtracts them from each other to find the difference.

The first **Action** rule calculates the Julian Day Number for the selected date. By setting the values of the **day**, **month**, and **year** fields under the **JulianDayCalculator** group, the values of the **a**, **y**, **m**, and **JDN** fields are recalculated. And then the last action in this rule is to temporarily store the result of the calculation in the **@jdn_selectedDate** attribute under the **selectedDate** field.

The second **Action** rule calculates the Julian Day Number for the current date. By setting the values of the **day**, **month**, and **year** fields under the **JulianDayCalculator** group, the values of the **a**, **y**, **m**, and **JDN** fields are recalculated. The result of the calculation is then temporarily stored in the **@jdn_currentDate** attribute under the **currentDate** field.

And finally, the difference between **@jdn_selectedDate** and **@jdn_currentDate** is calculated to give you the date difference. The **floor** function is used in the final date difference calculation to round the difference down to the nearest integer and prevent decimals from appearing in the result.

Note: Because actions in a rule are also executed from top to bottom just like rules are executed from top to bottom, you could have combined the two **Action** rules into one big **Action** rule containing 9 actions. The recipe above split them up into two **Action** rules for clarity reasons.

72. Calculate the difference in days between two date pickers

Problem

You have two date picker controls on an InfoPath form and want to know how many days there are between the two dates.

Solution

You can use the Julian Day formula as described on Wikipedia (see http://en.wikipedia.org/wiki/Julian_day) to calculate the difference between two date picker controls using **Action** rules.

To calculate the difference between two date picker controls:

1. In InfoPath, create a new **Blank Form** template.

2. Add a **Date Picker** control to the form template and name it **startDate**.

3. On the **Fields** task pane under the **startDate** field, add a **Field (attribute)** named **jdn_startDate** of data type **Text (string)**.

4. Add a **Date Picker** control to the form template and name it **endDate**.

5. On the **Fields** task pane under the **endDate** field, add a **Field (attribute)** named **jdn_endDate** of data type **Text (string)**.

6. Add a **Text Box** control named **difference** to the form template. Make the text box **Read-only**.

7. On the **Fields** task pane under the **myFields** group, add a group named **JulianDayCalculator**.

8. On the **Fields** task pane under the **JulianDayCalculator** group, add 7 **Field (element)** fields with the data type **Whole Number (integer)** and the following names: **day, month, year, a, y, m, JDN**.

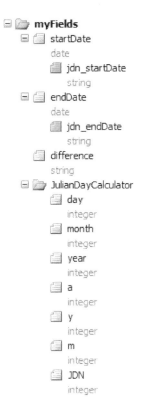

Figure 107. Main data source of the InfoPath form.

9. Set the **Default Value** of field **a** to the following formula:

```
(14 - ../my:month) div 12
```

10. Set the **Default Value** of field **y** to the following formula:

```
../my:year + 4800 - ../my:a
```

11. Set the **Default Value** of field **m** to the following formula:

```
../my:month + 12 * ../my:a - 3
```

12. Set the **Default Value** of field **JDN** to the following formula:

```
../my:day + ((153 * ../my:m + 2) div 5) + 365 * ../my:y + (../my:y div
4) - (../my:y div 100) + (../my:y div 400) - 32045
```

13. Add an **Action** rule to the **startDate** field with the following actions:

```
Set a field's value: day = number(substring(., 9, 2))
Set a field's value: month = number(substring(., 6, 2))
Set a field's value: year = number(substring(., 1, 4))
Set a field's value: @jdn_startDate = JDN
Set a field's value: day = number(substring(endDate, 9, 2))
Set a field's value: month = number(substring(endDate, 6, 2))
Set a field's value: year = number(substring(endDate, 1, 4))
Set a field's value: @jdn_endDate = JDN
```

This rule calculates the Julian Day Number (JDN) first for the start date and then for the end date when a start date is entered.

14. Add a second **Action** rule to the **startDate** field with the **Condition**:

```
startDate is not blank
and
endDate is not blank
```

and the following action:

```
Set a field's value: difference = floor(number(@jdn_endDate) -
number(@jdn_startDate))
```

This rule calculates the date difference if both the start date and end date have been entered.

15. Add an **Action** rule to the **endDate** field with the following actions:

```
Set a field's value: day = number(substring(., 9, 2))
Set a field's value: month = number(substring(., 6, 2))
Set a field's value: year = number(substring(., 1, 4))
Set a field's value: @jdn_endDate = JDN
Set a field's value: day = number(substring(startDate, 9, 2))
Set a field's value: month = number(substring(startDate, 6, 2))
Set a field's value: year = number(substring(startDate, 1, 4))
Set a field's value: @jdn_startDate = JDN
```

This rule calculates the Julian Day Number (JDN) first for the end date and then for the start date when the end date is entered.

16. Add a second **Action** rule to the **endDate** field with the **Condition**:

```
startDate is not blank
and
endDate is not blank
```

and the following action:

```
Set a field's value: difference = floor(number(@jdn_endDate) -
number(@jdn_startDate))
```

This rule calculates the date difference if both the start date and end date have been entered.

17. Preview the form.

When the form opens, select a date for the start date and then a date that lies in the future for the end date. The date difference should be a positive amount of days. Select an end date that lies in the past. The date difference should be a negative amount of days.

Discussion

The Julian Day formula calculates a number for a certain date in time. The recipe described above follows the same logic as that described in the discussion of *71 Calculate the difference in days between a date picker and today* where the selected date can be seen as the end date and current date can be seen as the start date.

Multiple-Section List Boxes

A **Multiple-Selection List Box** is a close cousin of the **Drop-Down List Box** and the normal **List Box** with the difference that you have the ability to select and store multiple items in it instead of just one.

Figure 108. Multiple-Selection List Box in InfoPath 2010.

And because a multiple-selection list box is a close cousin of the other types of list boxes in InfoPath, you can populate it by using the same technique you used to populate a drop-down list box (see *48 Populate a drop-down list box from an XML file*).

The big difference between a multiple-selection list box and the other types of list boxes in InfoPath is the data source structure. A multiple-selection list box must be bound to a repeating field instead of a non-repeating field as is the case with other types of list boxes.

When you look at the data source structure for a field bound to a multiple-selection list box, you will see a similar structure on the **Fields** task pane as shown in the following figure.

Figure 109. Data source structure for a field bound to a Multiple-Selection List Box in InfoPath 2010.

In the figure shown above, **field1** is the field that is bound to a multiple-selection list box. As you can see from the small blue icon with an arrow on the field, the field is a repeating field, which means that **group1**, which serves as the container for **field1**, will contain multiple **field1** nodes in it once you select multiple items from the multiple-selection list box. To fully understand how this works, add a multiple-selection list box to a form template, populate it with a few items, preview the form, save the form locally on disk, and then open the form (XML file) in Notepad.

73.   Filter data from an external data source using multiple selections

Problem

You have data in an XML file and you want to use a multiple-selection list box to show data from that XML file based on the items that are selected in the multiple-selection list box.

Solution

You can use a conditional formatting on a repeating section to filter and display data based on selections from a multiple-selection list box.

In this recipe, you will use the **RunningShoes** XML file that you used in *48 Populate a drop-down list box from an XML file*.

To filter data from an external data source using multiple selections:

1.   In InfoPath, create a new **Blank Form** template.

2.   Add a **Multiple-Selection List Box** to the form template. Name the multiple-selection list box **shoeBrand**.

3.   Add a data connection to the XML file used in *48 Populate a drop-down list box from an XML file* and follow the same steps to populate the multiple-selection list box with items from the Secondary data source. Select **brand** for the **Entries**, and **name** (under **brand**) for both the **Value** and the **Display name** of the multiple-selection list box.

4.   On the **Fields** task pane, select **RunningShoes (Secondary)** from the **Fields** drop-down list box, right-click the **brand** repeating group, and then drag-and-

drop it on the form template. Select **Repeating Section with Controls** from the context menu when you drop it.

5. Click the repeating section to select it, and then click **Home ➤ Rules ➤ Manage Rules**.

6. On the **Rules** task pane, ensure **brand** is displayed under the title bar, and then click **New ➤ Formatting** to add a **Formatting** rule to the **brand** repeating group.

7. On the **Rules** task pane, select the **Hide this control** check box. This will hide any repeating sections for which the condition on the rule has been met.

8. Because you want to hide all repeating sections for which the brand name has not been selected in the multiple-selection list box, you must add a condition that counts the amount of repeating sections (items in the Secondary data source) for which the brand name has been selected in the multiple-selection list box (**shoeBrand** repeating fields in the Main data source), and if the count is zero hide the repeating section. On the **Rules** task pane under **Condition**, click the text **None**.

9. On the **Condition** dialog box, select **Use a formula** from the third drop-down list box. You are going to misuse the **Insert Formula** dialog box to construct a formula that you can use as an expression on the **Condition** dialog box.

10. On the **Insert Formula** dialog box, type

    ```
    count(
    ```

    and then click **Insert Field or Group**.

11. On the **Select a Field or Group** dialog box, ensure **RunningShoes (Secondary)** is selected in the **Fields** drop-down list box, expand all of the nodes, select **name** under the **brand** repeating group, and then click **Filter Data**.

12. On the **Filter Data** dialog box, click **Add**.

13. On the **Specify Filter Conditions** dialog box, leave **name** selected in the first drop-down list box, leave **is equal to** selected in the second drop-down list box, and select **Select a field or group** from the third drop-down list box.

14. On the **Select a Field or Group** dialog box, select **Main** from the **Fields** drop-down list box, expand all of the nodes, select **shoeBrand**, and then click **OK**.

15. On the **Specify Filter Conditions** dialog box, click **OK**.

16. On the **Filter Data** dialog box, click **OK**.

17. On the **Select a Field or Group** dialog box, click **OK**.

18. The resulting formula on the **Insert Formula** dialog box now looks like the following:

```
count(@name[. = shoeBrand]
```

Type **)** to close the **count** function. The final formula now looks like the following:

```
count(@name[. = shoeBrand])
```

19. On the **Insert Formula** dialog box, select **Edit XPath (advanced)**, and then select the entire formula and copy it by pressing **Ctrl+C**.

20. On the **Insert Formula** dialog box, click **Cancel**.

21. On the **Condition** dialog box, select **The expression** from the first drop-down list box, delete the entire expression in the text box, and then press **Ctrl+V** to paste the formula you copied into the text box. Modify the expression to check whether the result of the **count** function is equal to 0. The resulting expression should look like the following:

```
count(@name[. = xdXDocument:get-
DOM()/my:myFields/my:group1/my:shoeBrand]) = 0
```

What this expression does is lookup or filter shoe brands in the Secondary data source where the name of the shoe brand in the Secondary data source is the same as the name of the shoe brand that has been selected in the multiple-selection list box, which is located in the Main data source. If a shoe brand is found in the Secondary data source for a selected shoe brand in the multiple-selection list box, the count will be unequal to 0, so the repeating section for that shoe brand should be displayed. If a shoe brand has not been selected in the multiple-selection list box, the count will be 0, so the repeating section for that shoe brand should be hidden.

22. On the **Condition** dialog box, click **OK**.

23. Preview the form.

When the form opens, no repeating sections should be visible. As you select shoe brands from the multiple-selection list box, their corresponding sections should appear.

Discussion

A good way to understand how multiple-selection list boxes work is to add one to an InfoPath form template with a couple of static items, preview the form, select a couple of items, save the form locally on disk, and then open the XML file for the form in Notepad.

If you do this, you will notice that the value stored in the field through the control is not one single value as is the case with drop-down list boxes, combo-boxes, and list boxes, but that it consists of several values including one that is empty.

If you look at the **Fields** task pane after you have added a multiple-selection list box to an InfoPath form template, you will also see that it is constructed using a repeating field under a group node.

Figure 110. Group and repeating field representing a multiple-selection list box in InfoPath.

Armed with the knowledge that a multiple-selection list box consists of repeating fields, you now also know that you can come up with creative solutions that make use of functions that take a repeating group or field as their arguments, such as the **count**, **sum**, **avg**, and **eval** functions do.

74. Display items from a multiple-selection list box as multi-line text

Problem

You have a multiple-selection list box on an InfoPath form and want to be able to select a few items from it, click on a button, and have the selected items be transferred to a multi-line text box and displayed as text with one item on each line.

Solution

You can use the **eval** function to evaluate a list of items in either a repeating field or repeating group and concatenate all of the items in one string. And to add line-breaks between the items, you can use the XML character for a line-break in a secondary data source and add it to the items when concatenating them through the **eval** function.

To display items from a multiple-selection list box as multi-line text:

1. In InfoPath, create a new **Blank Form** template.

2. Add a **Multiple-Selection List Box**, **Text Box**, and **Button** control to the form template. Name the multiple-selection list box **allItems** and name the text box **selectedItems**.

3. Populate the multiple-selection list box with either static or dynamic items. Keep it simple and just add 3 static items: Item 1, Item 2, and Item 3. Note: You can populate a multiple-selection list box the same way you populate a drop-down list box (see *48 Populate a drop-down list box from an XML file*).

4. Open the **Properties** dialog box for the text box, and then on the **Display** tab, select **Multi-line** to make the text box accept and display multiple lines of text.

5. Add a **Receive data** connection to an XML file (see *32 Get data from an XML file*) that has the following contents:

    ```
    <?xml version="1.0" encoding="UTF-8" ?>
    <break>&#xD;</break>
    ```

    The **break** node in this XML file, which will become a Secondary data source in InfoPath, will be used to add line-breaks to text added to the multi-line text box.

6. Add a hidden text field named **break** (see *10 Add a hidden field*) under the **myFields** group, and set its **Default Value** to be equal to the value of the **break** group in the Secondary data source to the XML file.

7. Add an **Action** rule to the button that sets the value of the text box to the following formula:

    ```
    eval(eval(allItems[text() != ""], "concat(., ../../my:break)"), "..")
    ```

    Where **allItems** is the field bound to the multiple-selection list box.

8. Preview the form.

When the form opens, select a few items in the multiple-selection list box and then click the button. The items you selected should be copied over to the text box and each item should be displayed on a separate line.

Discussion

The **eval** function returns the values of a field or group, and takes two arguments. The first argument defines the field or group the **eval** function should operate on, and the second argument defines the expression to calculate for the field or group. Usually, the **eval** function is nested within a function that operates on a field or group, such as **sum** or **avg**.

In the recipe above, you used the **eval** function twice. The first **eval** function (the inner one) was used as follows:

```
eval(allItems[text() != ""], "concat(., ../../my:break)")
```

The preceding formula takes a selected item in the multiple-selection list box that is not an empty string, and returns the concatenation of that item with a line-break.

The **allItems** in the formula represents the repeating field the **eval** function should work on, and the second argument represents the expression the **eval** function should perform on that repeating field, so the result of the evaluation.

Let us first dissect the expression for the first argument in the **eval** function above.

```
allItems[text() != ""]
```

The filter expression **[text() != ""]** prevents the **eval** function from evaluating any **allItems** repeating field that has an empty string as its value. Remember that all lists in InfoPath have at least one empty item, so that that item can be selected if a user wants to clear the value for the list. So to prevent empty items from appearing in the final multi-line text, you need to filter them out as the expression above does.

Let us now dissect the expression for the second argument in the **eval** function.

```
concat(., ../../my:break)
```

. represents the current item (**allItems** field) the **eval** function is working on, while **../../my:break** represents the field for the line-break. The field for the line-break is located under the **myFields** group in the Main data source, and if you have an **allItems** field as the context (starting) node, you must first navigate upwards to the **group1** parent node of the **allItems** node, and then upwards again to the **myFields** group node (which in turn is the parent node of the **group1** node), before you can navigate back down to the **break** node, which then results in the **../../my:break** XPath expression used in the **concat** function.

So finally, the **eval** function is used on a non-empty **allItems** node in the multiple-selection list box to return the value of the concatenation of that **allItems** node with a line-break (**break** node).

```
eval(allItems[text() != ""], "concat(., ../../my:break)")
```

The second **eval** function (the outer one) is used to retrieve the contents of all of the **allItems** nodes in the multiple-selection list box as a string. The most basic formula to do this is the following:

```
eval(allItems, "..")
```

The preceding formula returns the value of the anonymous parent (".."), which is a concatenated string of the contents of all of the parent's children (**allItems** nodes). The latter is a W3C standard.

In the final formula, you want to get the contents of all of the **allItems** nodes, but you also want to apply the concatenation you constructed earlier for each **allItems** node, so that the line-break is included between the concatenated **allItems** nodes.

So you must replace **<u>allItems</u>** in the previous formula by the **eval** formula you constructed earlier, because you want the **eval** function to work on the formula you constructed earlier, and the result of the evaluation to be the contents of the anonymous parent (**..**).

The final formula would then be the following when you combine the two **eval** functions:

```
eval(eval(allItems[text() != ""], "concat(., ../../my:break)"), ".."))
```

Chapter 8: Objects

Objects are controls in InfoPath that do not store any data in the Main data source of an InfoPath form, that store a special type of data, or that store data that can be converted into binary data such as images and files.

Buttons

Button controls in InfoPath do not store any data and are not linked to any fields in the Main data source of a form. The only purpose of buttons is to perform actions when the user clicks on them.

There are two types of button controls in InfoPath 2010:

1. A normal **Button** control that has a textual caption.

2. A **Picture Button** control that allows you to use images for a button.

Figure 111. Normal Button control in InfoPath 2010.

Figure 112. Picture Button control in InfoPath 2010.

These two types of button controls do not differ in functionality; only in the way they look, because one uses images and the other uses text.

A Picture Button must be configured to use images that define the way the button looks. Therefore, it has two properties you can set to point to images:

1. Picture
2. Hover Picture

The **Picture** property can be set to point to an image that defines the normal state of the button and the **Hover Picture** property can be set to point to an image that defines the way the button looks when the user hovers with a mouse pointer over the button. Note that setting the **Hover Picture** property on a picture button is optional.

Figure 113. A Picture Button control with its Picture property set to an image.

To set the image for a **Picture Button** control, you can either click **Properties ➤ Picture Button ➤ Picture** or on the **Picture Button Properties** dialog box, click **Browse** under the **Picture** section on the **General** tab.

If you want to use one and the same image for several picture buttons, it is best to first add that image as a resource file to the form template.

A resource file is a file that is used to display additional information in a form template. When you save or publish a form template, any resource files are included in the form template (the .XSN file).

Tip:

A best practice is to use resource files whenever you have external files your InfoPath forms need to access. By adding such files as InfoPath resource files, you remove the dependency of requiring access to external locations, which may become unavailable from time to time.

To add an image as a resource file to the form template:

1. Click **Data ➤ Form Data ➤ Resource Files**.

2. On the **Resource Files** dialog box, click **Add**.

3. Browse to and select the image file you want to add.

4. Repeat steps 2 and 3 to add as many images as you like, and then on the **Resource Files** dialog box, click **OK**.

All of the images you add as resources files to the form template should then appear in the **Picture** and **Hover picture** drop-down list boxes on the **General** tab of the **Picture Button Properties** dialog box of the **Picture Button** control. You can then select an image from either drop-down list box to be used as a picture or a hover picture for the **Picture Button** control.

75. Change button caption when button is clicked

Problem

You have a button on an InfoPath form and you want the caption of this button to display a certain piece of text when the button is clicked.

Solution

You can use a rule on the button to change the value of a field that is used as the source for the button caption (label).

To change a button caption (label) when the button is clicked:

1. In InfoPath, create a new **Blank Form** template.

2. Add a **Button** control to the form template.

3. Add a hidden field of data type **Text (string)**, with the name **buttonLabel**, and that has a **Default Value** equal to the text **Not Clicked** to the Main data source (also see *10 Add a hidden field*).

4. Right-click the button and select **Button Properties** from the context menu that appears.

5. On the **Button Properties** dialog box on the **General** tab, click the formula button behind the **Label** text box.

6. On the **Insert Formula** dialog box, click **Insert Field or Group**.

7. On the **Select a Field or Group** dialog box, select **buttonLabel**, and click **OK**.

8. Click **OK** when closing all open dialog boxes.

9. Add an **Action** rule to the button with an action that says:

   ```
   Set a field's value: buttonLabel = "Clicked"
   ```

   This rule sets the value of **buttonLabel** to the text **Clicked**.

10. Preview the form.

When the form opens for the first time, the button caption should display the text **Not Clicked**. When you click the button, the button caption should change to the text **Clicked**.

Discussion

The **Label** property of a button can be set either to a static piece of text or to the result of a calculation or to the value of a field as the recipe above demonstrates. So to create a dynamic button label, you must use the formula button behind the **Label** property on the **Button Properties** dialog box to construct a formula that returns a piece of text.

76.   Add line breaks to a button caption

Problem

You have a button on an InfoPath form with a very long label, for example "First Line Second Line Third Line". You want to break the button label into 3 lines of text with "First Line", "Second Line", and "Third Line" each on a separate line of text.

Solution

You can use a formula on the button label to break a button label into multiple lines of text.

To add line-breaks to a button caption:

1. In InfoPath, create a new **Blank Form** template.

2. Add a **Button** control to the form template.

3. Add a **Receive data** connection that gets data from an XML file (see *32 Get data from an XML file*) that has the following contents:

    ```
    <?xml version="1.0" encoding="UTF-8" ?>
    <break>&#xD;</break>
    ```

    Name the data connection **break**.

4. Right-click the button and select **Button Properties** from the context menu that appears.

5. On the **Button Properties** dialog box, click the formula button behind the **Label** text box.

6. On the **Insert Formula** dialog box, construct a formula that uses the **concat** function and says:

    ```
    concat("First Line", break, "Second Line", break, "Third Line")
    ```

    where the **break** group is from the Secondary data source to the XML file.

7. Click **OK** when closing all dialog boxes.

8. Preview the form.

When the form opens, the text of the button label should appear on 3 separate lines.

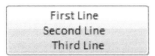

Figure 114. Button with label spread out on 3 separate lines.

Discussion

**** represents a carriage-return in XML. In the recipe above, you assigned this value to a group in an XML file (Secondary data source) and then used it in a formula to add line-breaks to text. Likewise, you could also use **	** in an XML file to add tab-stops to a piece of text.

File Attachments

File Attachment controls in InfoPath allow you to attach files to InfoPath forms.

Figure 115. File Attachment control in InfoPath 2010.

To add a file to a file attachment control, you must first open the InfoPath form and then do one of two things to attach a file to the control:

1. Click on the text that says "Click here to attach a file".

2. Hover with the cursor over the control until a paperclip icon appears in the upper left-hand corner, click on the icon to open the context menu, and then select **Attach** from the context menu.

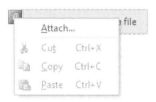

Figure 116. Attach menu item on the context menu of a File Attachment control.

Once you attach a file to a file attachment control, the context menu will be expanded to contain more menu items of which you can use the **Cut** or **Remove** menu items to delete the file contained within the attachment control.

Figure 117. Remove menu item to delete the file contained within the File Attachment control.

Any file you attach to an InfoPath form is stored within the InfoPath form itself as what is called a Base64 encoded string. To see what the contents of a file attachment control looks like: Save the InfoPath form locally on disk and then open it in Notepad. The contents of the file attachment control should look something like the following:

```
xO1GQRQAAAABAAAAAAAAABEAAAARAAAASQBuAGYAbwBQAGEAdABoADIAMAAxADAALgB0AHgAdAAAAElu
Zm9QYXRoOIGlzIGNvb2wh
```

Such a piece of text string, while illegible to you, can be converted back to a binary file by InfoPath or through the use of code.

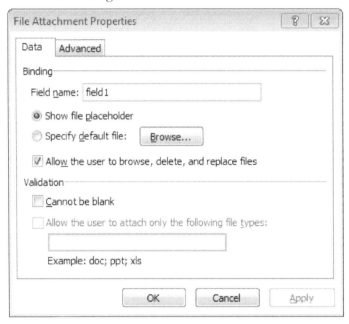

Figure 118. File Attachment control Properties dialog box in InfoPath 2010.

A file attachment control has several properties you can configure. If you look at the **Data** tab on the **File Attachment Properties** dialog box, you will find the following properties you can configure:

1. **Show file placeholder**
   This option allows the file attachment control to be empty at startup and displays the text "Click here to attach a file" in it.

2. **Specify default file**
   This option allows you to select a file to be included in the file attachment control by default. You are still able to replace the file when filling out the form.

3. **Allow the user to browse, delete, and replace files**
   When deselected, this option disables the **Attach**, **Remove**, **Cut**, and **Paste**

menu items on the context menu of the file attachment control. When selected, all menu items are enabled.

4. **Cannot be blank**
When selected, this option will make the file attachment control a mandatory field.

5. **Allow the user to attach only the following file types**
This option is enabled for InfoPath Filler Forms and is disabled for InfoPath Browser forms. When enabled, it allows you to specify the file extensions of files that are allowed to be placed in the file attachment control.

You may have noticed that the **Paste** menu item on the context menu of the file attachment control is not always enabled. This menu item only becomes enabled when you have previously used the **Copy** menu item on the same or another file attachment control on the form, and want to paste the file you copied to the same or another file attachment control on the form. The **Copy** and **Paste** menu items effectively allow you to copy and paste files between file attachment controls on an InfoPath form.

77. Check if a file has been attached

Problem

You have an attachment control on an InfoPath form and want to check whether the user has attached a file to the form.

Solution

To check whether a file is present within an attachment control, you must check whether the field bound to the file attachment control is not empty.

To check if a file has been attached to a file attachment control:

1. In InfoPath, create a new **Blank Form** template.

2. Add a **File Attachment**, a **Button**, and a **Text Box** control to the form template. Name the file attachment control **myAttachment** and the text box **message**.

3. Add an **Action** rule to the button with a **Condition** that says:

    ```
    myAttachment is blank
    ```

    and an action that says:

    ```
    Set a field's value: message = "Attachment is not present"
    ```

    This rule displays the message "Attachment is not present" in the text box when you click the button and no file has been attached to the file attachment control.

4. Add a second **Action** rule to the button with a **Condition** that says:

   ```
   myAttachment is not blank
   ```

   and an action that says:

   ```
   Set a field's value: message = "Attachment is present"
   ```

   This rule displays the message "Attachment is present" in the text box when you click the button and a file has been attached to the file attachment control.

5. Preview the form

When the form opens, click the button before attaching a file to the form. The message "Attachment is not present" should appear in the text box. Attach a file to the form and then click the button again. The message "Attachment is present" should appear in the text box.

Discussion

Checking whether an attachment is present is simply a matter of checking whether the field that is bound to the file attachment control is not blank.

78. Clear a file attachment field

Problem

You have an attachment control on an InfoPath form and want to be able to delete any file that has been added to this control as an attachment.

Solution

You can use an **Action** rule to clear a file attachment field.

To clear a file attachment field using rules:

1. In InfoPath, create a new **Blank Form** template.

2. Add a **File Attachment** and **Button** control to the form template. Name the file attachment control **myAttachment**.

3. Click the button to select it, and then select **Home ➤ Rules ➤ Add Rule ➤ When This Button Is Clicked ➤ Set a Field's Value**.

4. On the **Rule Details** dialog box, click the button behind the **Field** text box, select **myAttachment**, and click **OK**.

5. On the **Rule Details** dialog box, leave the **Value** text box empty, and click **OK**.

6. Preview the form.

When the form opens, click the file attachment control to attach a file. Once you have added an attachment, click the button to clear the file attachment field.

Discussion

You can clear a file attachment field by setting its value to an empty string as you have done in the recipe above.

79.   Make an attachment read-only – method 1

Problem

You have a file attachment control and a check box control on an InfoPath form. You want users to be able to add a file to the file attachment control, but when the check box is selected, you want to allow users to only view the attachment, but not change or delete the file that is stored within the file attachment control.

Solution

You can use conditional formatting on section controls containing file attachment controls to hide a modifiable file attachment control and show a read-only file attachment control containing the same file.

To make a file attachment control read-only based on a condition:

1. In InfoPath, create a new **Blank Form** template.

2. Add two **Section** controls, one **File Attachment** control, and one **Check Box** control to the form template. Name the file attachment control **myAttachment** and the check box control **isAttachmentReadOnly**.

3. Move the **File Attachment** control that is located on the form template from its current location outside of both **Section** controls to a location inside of the first **Section** control. Note: To move a control, click it, hold the left mouse button down, and then drag it to a new location on the form template.

4. On the **Fields** task pane, drag the **myAttachment** field and drop it into the second section control. Select **File Attachment** from the context menu when you drop the field on the form template. Now you have two **File Attachment** controls on the form template pointing to the same file attachment field in the Main data source of the form.

5. Delete all empty lines within and between the **Section** controls, so that when one section control is hidden the other will move up or down to seamlessly take its place.

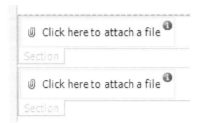

Figure 119. Two section controls without blank lines in or between them.

6. Right-click the second **File Attachment** control and select **File Attachment Properties** from the drop-down menu that appears.

7. On the **File Attachment Properties** dialog box on the **Data** tab, deselect the **Allow the user to browse, delete, and replace files**, and click **OK**. The attachment control in the second section is the read-only attachment control, so users should not be able to alter its contents.

8. Click the first **Section** control to select it, and then add a **Formatting** rule to it with a **Condition** that says:

    ```
    isAttachmentReadOnly = TRUE
    ```

    and a **Formatting** of **Hide this control**. This rule will hide the first **Section** control with the modifiable file attachment if the value of the **isAttachmentReadOnly** field is equal to **true**, and show the **Section** control if the value of the **isAttachmentReadOnly** field is equal to **false**. Note: Make sure you click on the text on the control that says "Section" and then on the **Rules** task pane double-check that **group1** is displayed below the title bar of the **Rules** task pane before you add the formatting rule.

9. Click the second **Section** control to select it, and then add a **Formatting** rule to it with a **Condition** that says:

    ```
    isAttachmentReadOnly = FALSE
    ```

    and a **Formatting** of **Hide this control**. This rule will hide the second **Section** control with the read-only attachment if the value of the **isAttachmentReadOnly** field is equal to **false**, and show the **Section** control if the value of the **isAttachmentReadOnly** field is equal to **true**. Note: Make sure you click on the text on the control that says "Section" and then on the **Rules** task pane double-check that **group2** is displayed below the title bar of the **Rules** task pane before you add the formatting rule.

10. Preview the form.

When the form opens, the modifiable file attachment control appears. Add a file to it. Then select the **isAttachmentReadOnly** check box. This action should hide the modifiable file attachment and show the read-only file attachment control. You should not see anything move on the form, because the second section control should seamlessly take the place of the first section control. When you hover above the file attachment control and then click on the attachment icon in its upper left-hand corner, you should only see options to **Open**, **Save As**, or **Copy** the file stored in the file attachment control, but not **Attach**, **Remove**, or **Cut** the file.

Figure 120. Menu of file attachment control containing a file that cannot be deleted or modified.

Discussion

A file attachment control does not have a read-only property you can set to make it read-only, neither does it support conditional formatting when it is placed on a Browser Form, but you can still make a file attachment control read-only based on a condition in one of two ways:

1. Use conditional formatting on a section control containing the file attachment control.

2. Place the file attachment control on a read-only view (see *14 Add a read-only view*).

The first method was used in the recipe above. The second method is explained in *80 Make an attachment read-only – method 2*.

Note that a file attachment control has a property called **Allow the user to browse, delete, and replace files** that you can turn on or off at design time to make the file stored in a file attachment control readable but not modifiable. You can use this property to make a file attachment control read-only if the state of the control does not depend on any conditions.

In the recipe above, the first file attachment control is used as a modifiable file attachment control so should be hidden if the check box, which indicates that the attachment is read-only, is selected.

The second file attachment control is used as a read-only file attachment control so should be hidden if the check box, which indicates that the attachment is read-only, is not selected.

You could delete the check box from the form template to make the field it is bound to a hidden field (see *10 Add a hidden field*). You could then set the value of this hidden field to TRUE, for example as soon as the form has been submitted (see *42 Make a control read-only upon submit*), so that the next time when the form opens, the attachment will be read-only. This is how you would go about making a file attachment control read-only when a form is submitted.

When section controls are hidden, they give up the space they normally take up on a form when they are visible. To make two section controls look like one and the same (without visual displacements when one is shown and the other hidden, or vice versa), you must ensure that there are no lines or spaces between the two section controls and that they have the same size. This trick was used in the recipe above to make two file attachment controls look like one and the same.

80.   Make an attachment read-only – method 2

Problem

You have a file attachment control on an InfoPath form and want users to be able to add a file to it, but once the form has been submitted, you want to allow users to only view the attachment, but not change or delete the file that is stored within the file attachment control.

Solution

You can use a read-only view with a modifiable file attachment control and a non-read-only view with a read-only file attachment control to make an attachment read-only.

To make a file attachment control read-only based on a condition:

1.   In InfoPath, create a new **Blank Form** template.

2.   Add a **File Attachment** control to the default view of the form template and name it **myAttachment**

3.   Add a view named **Read-Only View** to the form template and make it read-only (see *14 Add a read-only view*).

4.   Drag the **myAttachment** field from the **Fields** task pane, drop it onto the **Read-Only View**, and select **File Attachment** from the context menu when you

drop it. Note: Placing the file attachment control on the read-only view will make the file attachment control inaccessible and users will only be able to see that it contains a file, but not open or view the file it contains.

5. Add a **Button** control to the **Read-Only View**, and give it the **Label** "View Attachment". The read-only view will not affect the functioning of the button control, because buttons are not made read-only when placed on read-only views.

6. Add a third view named **Attachment View**. This view will be used as a view to limit access to the attachment control and allow users to view any file the attachment control contains, but not modify the file stored within the file attachment control.

7. Drag the **myAttachment** field from the **Fields** task pane, drop it onto the **Attachment View**, and select **File Attachment** from the context menu when you drop it.

8. Because the **Attachment View** is not read-only, you must disable the option for users to change the file in the attachment control. So right-click the file attachment control, select **File Attachment Properties** from the context menu, and then on the **File Attachment Properties** dialog box on the **Data** tab, deselect the **Allow the user to browse, delete, and replace files** check box.

9. Add a **Button** control to the **Attachment View**, and give it the **Label** "Back".

10. Add an **Action** rule to the button on the **Attachment View** that says:

```
Switch to view: Read-Only View
```

11. Add an **Action** rule to the button on the **Read-Only View** that says:

```
Switch to view: Attachment View
```

12. Configure the form to be submitted and then to switch to the **Read-Only View** on submit (see *40 Switch to read-only view on submit* and *41 Switch to read-only view when form opens after submit*).

13. Remove the **View menu** option on each one of the three views by deselecting the **Show on the View menu when filling out this form** check box on the **General** tab on the **View Properties** dialog box.

14. Ensure you have made **View 1 (default)** the startup view in the **View** drop-down list box on the **Page Design** tab.

15. Preview the form.

When the form opens, the default view should appear. Attach a file to the form by using the file attachment control and then click **Submit**. The form should then display the read-only view.

If you click the paperclip icon on the file attachment control, you will see that all of the menu items are disabled. And if you double-click the file in the file attachment control, the file should not open, so the user cannot read it.

Click the "View Attachment" button. The form should switch to the attachment view. If you now click the paperclip icon on the file attachment control, you should see the **Open**, **Save As**, and **Copy** menu items enabled, and when you double-click the file in the file attachment control, you should be able to open and view the file.

Discussion

A file attachment control does not have a read-only property you can set to make it read-only, neither does it support conditional formatting when it is placed on a Browser Form, but you can still make a file attachment control read-only based on a condition in one of two ways:

1. Use conditional formatting on a section control containing the file attachment control.

2. Place the file attachment control on a read-only view (see *14 Add a read-only view*).

The first method was explained in *79 Make an attachment read-only – method 1*. The second method is explained in the recipe above.

The drawback of placing a file attachment control on a read-only view is that you are then unable to open or view any file stored within the file attachment control.

To overcome this drawback, you can add a second (non-read-only) view to your form template, place a file attachment control on it, and bind the same attachment field that is bound to the file attachment control on the read-only view to it. This will allow you to open the file stored within the file attachment control.

And then to prevent users from modifying the contents of the file attachment control, you can disallow browsing, deleting, and replacing of files through the properties of the file attachment control.

The last step would be to add buttons on the views to allow the user to switch from the read-only view to the non-read-only view and vice versa.

81. Add multiple files to a file attachment control

Problem

You have a file attachment control on an InfoPath form and want to attach more than one file to the form by using this file attachment control.

Solution

A file attachment control can only contain one file at a time. To be able to store multiple files under the same field name in InfoPath, you must add a file attachment field to a repeating group, which you can then bind to either a **Repeating Table** or a **Repeating Section** control.

To add multiple files to a file attachment control:

1. In InfoPath, create a new **Blank Form** template.

2. Add a **Repeating Table** control with one column to the form template.

3. Delete the text box control that InfoPath automatically adds to the repeating table when you create it. Remember to also delete the field that the text box is bound to through the **Fields** task pane.

4. Place the cursor in the empty repeating table cell, then click **Home ➤ Controls ➤ File Attachment** to add a file attachment control to the repeating table. Name the file attachment control **myAttachment**.

5. Preview the form.

When the form opens, attach a file using the file attachment control in the repeating table. If you want to attach more files to the form, you can click **Insert item** on the repeating table to add a new row to the repeating table, and then attach a second file, etc.

Chapter 9: Container Controls

Container controls include sections, repeating tables, repeating sections, and regions. Container controls as the name suggests are controls that can serve as a container for other controls.

Repeating tables and repeating sections are among the most often used container controls in InfoPath, so in this chapter you will learn how to use these controls.

Sections

Section controls are controls that can contain other controls or on which you can write text. Section controls are often used to group related controls and can be bound to group nodes in a data source (Main or Secondary).

Section controls are ideal candidates to use for displaying error messages, because they give up their visible space when they are hidden. In addition, because the use of pop up error message boxes is discouraged when using InfoPath browser forms, you can instead use section controls to provide error display functionality in the browser when creating InfoPath Web Browser Forms.

And as you have already seen in *79 Make an attachment read-only – method 1*, section controls can also be used to perform swapping tricks in InfoPath, again because of the space that they give up when they are hidden.

82. Use sections to display error messages

Problem

You have an InfoPath form on which you want to use section controls to display error messages or other types of message to the user, but you do not want these messages to be stored in the InfoPath form itself.

Solution

To avoid storing error messages in the Main data source of an InfoPath form, you can use an XML file as a Secondary data source that can temporarily hold error messages to be displayed on an InfoPath form.

You must construct the XML file that will be used to display error messages in such a way that you can add section controls to the form template when you drag groups from the Secondary data source.

The following XML file will allow you to add section controls to a form template when you drag-and-drop one of its groups on the form template:

```
<?xml version="1.0" encoding="UTF-8"?>
<messages xmlns="uri:sym">
    <message1><placeholder/></message1>
    <message2><placeholder/></message2>
    <message3><placeholder/></message3>
    <message4><placeholder/></message4>
</messages>
```

To use section controls to display error messages:

1. In InfoPath, create a new **Blank Form** template.

2. Add a data connection to the **messages** XML file above (see *32 Get data from an XML file*) and name the data connection **Messages**.

3. Add a **Text Box** control to the form template and name it **myTextBox**.

4. On the **Fields** task pane, select **Messages (Secondary)** from the **Fields** drop-down list box.

5. Drag-and-drop the **message1** group from the **Fields** task pane to the form template and place it below the text box. Delete any empty lines within the section control. Also delete the **placeholder** text box control that is within the section control and replace it with the message you want to display, for example "You must enter a text string".

6. Add a second **Text Box** control to the form template and place it below the section control.

7. Click the section control to select it, and then add a **Formatting** rule to the section control with a **Condition** that says:

   ```
   myTextBox is not blank
   ```

   and a **Formatting** of **Hide this control**. This rule ensures that when the first text box is empty, the section will become visible, and soon after you type something into the first text box and move off it by clicking or tabbing away from the text box, the section will become hidden.

8. Preview the form.

When the form opens, the section with the message should be visible. Type something in the first text box and move to the second text box. The section should be hidden from view. Empty the first text box. The section should become visible again. Save the form to disk, open it in Notepad, and then verify that the message has not been stored in the InfoPath form (XML file).

Discussion

If you need to use fields or groups in InfoPath as a way to help you do something else or as in the recipe above to display error messages, it is best to use a Secondary data source (for example an XML) file instead of creating a field or group in the Main data source of the form.

If you use a Secondary data source, the data will not be stored in the form itself, so will also not unnecessarily make forms large, bulky, and/or contain data that is unrelated or irrelevant to other data contained in the form itself.

Important:

> All data that is part of the Main data source of a form will be permanently stored in the form itself (XML file). Any data that is stored in Secondary data sources you have added to a form template will not be stored in the form, so will be lost when you close the form. Only the XML schema definitions (XSD) of Secondary data sources are present within a form template (XSN). The data of Secondary data sources is never persisted in an InfoPath form (XML).

In the example above, the **placeholder** field within each **message** group was replaced by a static message saying "You must enter a text string". If you want to make error messages dynamic (so set them at runtime using rules), you can use the **placeholder** field within each **message** group, and change the **placeholder** text box to be a calculated value control so that it displays as a label without any borders around it and becomes read-only within the section control. And then you can use an **Action** rule to dynamically set the value of the **placeholder** field to the message you want to display.

Repeating Tables and Repeating Sections

A repeating control in InfoPath is a control to which you can add rows or sections, or from which you can remove rows or sections. A section is a control that can contain other controls and is often used to group related controls.

There are 4 types of repeating controls in InfoPath:

1. Repeating Table
2. Repeating Section
3. Horizontal Repeating Table (only available in InfoPath Filler Forms)
4. Repeating Recursive Section (only available in InfoPath Filler Forms)

Structurally, there is no difference between a **Repeating Table** and a **Repeating Section** control. While they may look different on an InfoPath form, their data source structure is similar. You can verify this by adding a **Repeating Table** control on an InfoPath form template and then looking at how the Main data source changed on the **Fields** task pane. Then add a **Repeating Section** control on the form template, add 3 **Text Box** controls in the repeating section, and then look at the Main data source on the **Fields** task pane again. You should see a similar structure for both the repeating table and the repeating section.

Figure 121. Data source of a repeating table or repeating section on the Fields task pane in InfoPath.

As you can see from the figure shown above, the data structure of a repeating table or a repeating section consists of:

1. A non-repeating group node (**group1**)
2. A repeating group node (**group2**)
3. One or more fields (**field1**, **field2**, **field3**)

If we now take a repeating table as shown in the figure below, **group1** would represent the table itself (so the container for all of the rows and columns), **group2** would represent a row in the table, and **field1**, **field2**, and **field3**, would represent the columns.

A table can have one or more rows, so one or more **group2** nodes, which is why **group2** is called a repeating node. **Field1**, **field2**, and **field3** are repeated along with the **group2** nodes to form table cells that contain data.

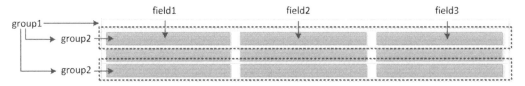

Figure 122. Relationship between a repeating table and nodes in the data source.

The name **Repeating Table** is a little bit misleading, because the table itself is not repeated, but its rows are.

Repeating tables and repeating sections are the most commonly used repeating controls in InfoPath.

83.   4 Ways to add a rich text box to a repeating table

Problem

You have a repeating table on an InfoPath form template or a repeating group in the Main data source of the form and want to add a rich text box control to one of its columns.

Solution

There are four ways you can add a rich text box control (or any other type of control) to a repeating table:

1. Add a **Repeating Table** control to the form template, delete one of the text box controls that is automatically added to a column of the repeating table, click in the empty column to place the cursor inside of the repeating table, and then click **Home ➤ Controls ➤ Rich Text Box** or if you have the **Controls** task pane open, click **Rich Text Box** to add a rich text box control to the column of the repeating table.

2. Add a **Repeating Table** control to the InfoPath form template, change the data type of the field that is bound to one of the text box controls in the repeating table to **Rich Text (XHTML)**, and then change the text box control into a **Rich Text Box** control. These are the steps you would have to follow:

    a. In InfoPath, create a new **Blank Form** template.

    b. Add a **Repeating Table** control to the form template.

    c. Click on the text box in the first column of the repeating table to select it, and then click **Properties ➤ Properties ➤ Field Properties**.

    d. On the **Field or Group Properties** dialog box on the **Data** tab, select **Rich Text (XHTML)** from the **Data type** drop-down list box, and click **OK**.

    e. The text box control in the repeating table now displays the message "Control cannot store this data type" when you hover over it. Right-click the text box and select **Change Control ➤ Rich Text Box** from the context menu that appears.

3. Construct the Main data source of the InfoPath form to contain a repeating group with a field of type **Rich Text (XHTML)** under it, and then drag-and-drop the repeating group onto the form template. These are the steps you would have to follow:

    a. In InfoPath, create a new **Blank Form** template.

b. On the **Fields** task pane, select the **myFields** group, click on the down arrow on the right-hand side of the group, and select **Add** from the drop-down menu.

c. On the **Add Field or Group** dialog box, type **group1** in the **Name** text box, select **Group** from the **Type** drop-down list box, and click **OK**.

d. On the **Fields** task pane, select the **group1** group, click on the down arrow on the right-hand side of the group, and select **Add** from the drop-down menu. **group1** will serve as the container for **group2** repeating groups. You can also see **group1** as the table and **group2** as a row in the table.

e. On the **Add Field or Group** dialog box, type **group2** in the **Name** text box, select **Group** from the **Type** drop-down list box, select the **Repeating** check box, and click **OK**.

f. On the **Fields** task pane, select the **group2** group, click on the down arrow on the right-hand side of the group, and select **Add** from the drop-down menu.

g. On the **Add Field or Group** dialog box, type **richtextbox** in the **Name** text box, leave **Field (element)** selected in the **Type** drop-down list box, select **Rich Text (XHTML)** from the **Data type** drop-down list box, and click **OK**.

h. On the **Fields** task pane, drag-and-drop **group2** onto the form template, and select **Repeating Table** from the context menu when you drop it. The repeating table should automatically contain a rich text box.

4. Add a **Repeating Table** control to the form template, add a **Rich Text Box** control to the form template, and then move the field that is bound to the rich text box to a location under the repeating group for the repeating table in the Main data source of the form. These are the steps you would have to follow:

a. In InfoPath, create a **Blank Form** template.

b. Add a **Repeating Table** control to the form template.

c. Add a **Rich Text Box** control to the form template. At this stage, the rich text box is located outside of the repeating table.

d. On the **Fields** task pane, select the field that is bound to the rich text box (this field is named **field4** if you started with a new form template and accepted the default of 3 columns in the repeating table), click on the down arrow on the right-hand side of the field, and select **Move** from the drop-down menu.

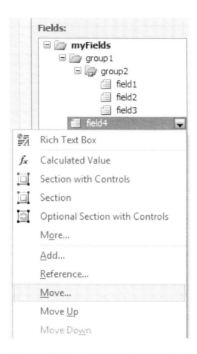

Figure 123. Move menu item on field drop-down menu.

e. On the **Move Field or Group** dialog box, expand **group1**, select
    group2 (which is bound to the repeating table), and then click **OK**.
    field4 is then moved to a location under **group2** on the **Fields** task
    pane.

Figure 124. Field4 moved to a location under group2.

f. If you hover over the rich text box on the form template, you will see the
    message "Control cannot store data correctly" appear. This is because
    the rich text box should now be moved to a column inside of the
    repeating table. So delete the rich text box control from the view (not
    from the Main data source via the **Fields** task pane).

g. Delete one of the text boxes that InfoPath automatically adds to the
    repeating table, and then drag-and-drop **field4** from the **Fields** task pane

to the empty column within the repeating table. InfoPath should automatically create a rich text box for **field4** when you drop it.

Discussion

All of the methods described above make use of the same principle, that is, that you must first have a field of type **Rich Text (XHTML)** in the repeating table, and then you can bind this field to a **Rich Text Box** control on the InfoPath form.

The four methods described above can be used to add any type of control to a repeating table. The only thing you must be aware of is that you must select the right data type and/or create the right structure for a field to be able to bind it to the control you desire.

The easiest method out of the four methods described above to add any type of control to a repeating table is probably the first method.

Exercise

Try using one of the four methods to add a **Multiple-Selection List Box** control to a column of the repeating table.

84. Create a repeating table with a fixed number of rows

Problem

You have a repeating table on an InfoPath form to which you want to assign a fixed number of rows and from which you want to prevent users from adding or deleting any rows.

Solution

You can add default rows to a repeating table and remove the ability for users to add or delete rows from it to create a repeating table that has a fixed amount of rows.

To create a repeating table that has 5 fixed rows:

1. In InfoPath, create a new **Blank Form** template.
2. Add a **Repeating Table** control to the form template.
3. Click **Data ➤ Form Data ➤ Default Values**.
4. On the **Edit Default Values** dialog box, expand **group1**.

5. On the **Edit Default Values** dialog box, right-click **group2** (or click the down arrow at the right-hand side of **group2**), and then select **Add another group2 below** from the drop-down menu that appears.

Figure 125. Edit Default Values dialog box in InfoPath 2010.

6. Repeat the previous step until you have 5 **group2** elements under **group1**, and then click **OK**.

Figure 126. Groups representing a repeating table with 5 fixed rows.

7. Right-click the repeating table and select **Repeating Table Properties** from the context menu that appears.

8. On the **Repeating Table Properties** dialog box on the **Data** tab, deselect the **Allow users to insert and delete rows** check box, and click **OK**. Selecting this option will prevent users from adding or deleting rows.

9. Preview the form.

When the form opens, the repeating table should have 5 rows and you should not be able to add or delete any rows, so the amount of rows is effectively fixed at 5.

Discussion

The **Edit Default Values** dialog box not only allows you to pre-add an amount of rows to a repeating table, but you could also specify default values for the fields in the rows you add.

To add default values to the fields in rows of a repeating table:

1. On the **Edit Default Values** dialog box, expand a **group2** node.

2. Click **field1** under the **group2** node to select it, and then in the **Default Value** text box, enter the text you want as the default value for the field.

3. Repeat steps 1 and 2 for any other field in any other row for which you want set a default value.

85. Add a sum field to a repeating table

Problem

You have a repeating table on an InfoPath form that contains a field with a number, for example, an amount for lunch bought this week. You want to add a field to the repeating table that sums up all of the money you spent on lunch this week.

Solution

You can use the **sum** function to create a grand total field in a repeating table.

To add a sum field to a repeating table:

1. In InfoPath, create a new **Blank Form** template.

2. Add a **Repeating Table** control with one column to the form template.

3. Open the **Properties** dialog box for the text box bound to **field1**, change the **Field name** to **lunchMoney**, change the **Data type** from **Text (string)** to **Decimal (double),** and click **Format**.

4. On the **Decimal Format** dialog box under the **Format** section, select **Number**, and then under the **Other options** section, select **2** from the **Decimal places** drop-down list box, and click **OK**. This will display numbers with 2 digits after the decimal point. Note: You can also set the data type on the field itself, but you will not be able to apply a format to it. Remember that controls are the visual elements that expose data stored in fields. Formatting a number to have 2 digits after the decimal point is a visual thing. Fields themselves cannot be seen without controls, so any visual display must be set on the control, not on the field.

5. Click **OK** to close the **Text Box Properties** dialog box.

6. Open the **Repeating Table Properties** dialog box.

7. On the **Repeating Table Properties** dialog box, click the **Display** tab, select the **Include footer** check box, and click **OK**. An extra row is added at the bottom of the repeating table.

8. Click in the bottom row of the repeating table to place the cursor, and then add a **Text Box** control to it. Change the data type for this text box to **Decimal (double)**, and format the number to contain 2 decimal places.

9. Set the **Default Value** of the text box in the footer of the repeating table to the following formula:

   ```
   sum(lunchMoney)
   ```

   or

   ```
   sum(../my:group1/my:group2/my:lunchMoney)
   ```

   if you have the **Edit XPath (advanced)** check box selected. Ensure that the **Refresh value when formula is recalculated** check box is selected when you set the default value, so that every time when you add a row to the repeating table or change the value of **lunchMoney**, the sum is recalculated.

10. Preview the form

When the form opens, add a few rows with amounts to the repeating table. Every time you add a row with an amount, the sum should be recalculated.

Discussion

The **sum** function returns the sum of all fields in a field or group. Each field is first converted to a number value.

In the recipe above, **lunchMoney** repeats in the repeating table, so **sum** will return the sum of all **lunchMoney** fields in the repeating table.

Exercise

The same way you added a sum field, try replacing it with a field that calculates the average of a list of numbers. Hint: You can use the **avg** function for this.

86. Count the number of rows in a repeating table – method 1

Problem

You have a repeating table on an InfoPath form and want to know how many rows are contained within the repeating table.

Solution

You can use the **count** function in a formula to determine how many rows a repeating table contains.

To count the number of rows in a repeating table from outside of the repeating table:

1. In InfoPath, create a new **Blank Form** template.

2. Add a **Repeating Table** control with 5 default rows to the form template (see *84 Create a repeating table with a fixed number of rows*).

3. Add a **Text Box** control to the form template and name it **totalCount**. This text box should be located outside of the repeating table.

4. Set the **Default Value** of the **totalCount** text box to the following formula:

   ```
   count(group2)
   ```

   where **group2** is the repeating group bound to the repeating table and represents rows in the repeating table.

5. Preview the form.

When the form opens, 5 should be shown in the text box, because the repeating table starts up with 5 rows. Insert another row. The value of the text box should increase to 6. Remove a row. The number in the text box should decrease by 1.

Discussion

The **count** function in InfoPath is a function that takes a field or group as its argument and counts the number of instances of that field or group.

In the recipe above, **group2** is the repeating group that is bound to the repeating table, so represents a row in the repeating table. If you want to count the number of rows in the repeating table, you must count the number of instances of **group2** in the repeating table, which the recipe does by using the formula:

```
count(group2)
```

Note that to count the rows in a repeating table you must make use of a field that is located outside of the repeating table and not inside of the repeating table. If you want to count rows from inside of the repeating table, you must use a technique that makes use of an XPath expression that navigates to the parent repeating **group2** node of the current node, and then counts its sibling **group2** nodes (see *87 Count the number of rows in a repeating table – method 2*).

87. Count the number of rows in a repeating table – method 2

Problem

You have a repeating table on an InfoPath form and want to know how many rows are contained within the repeating table.

Solution

You can use the **count** function together with the **preceding-sibling** and **following-sibling** XPath axes in a formula to determine how many rows a repeating table contains.

To count the number of rows in a repeating table from inside of the repeating table:

1. In InfoPath, create a new **Blank Form** template.

2. Add a **Repeating Table** control with 2 columns to the form template.

3. Set the **Default Value** of **field2** to the following formula:

   ```
   count(../preceding-sibling::*) + count(../following-sibling::*) + 1
   ```

   What this formula does is:

   a. Start at the context node, which is **field2**. This is the node on which you are currently setting the default value.

   b. Move to its parent (..), which is a **group2** node.

   c. Get all of the preceding-siblings of the **group2** node (**../preceding-sibling::***), so get all of the **group2** nodes that lie before the **group2** node of the context node.

   d. Count all of the **group2** nodes that lie before the **group2** node of the context node (**count(../preceding-sibling::*)**).

e. Count all of the **group2** nodes that lie after the **group2** node of the context node (**count(../following-sibling::*)**).

f. Add a **1** to the total because the **group2** node of the context node is omitted by both the **preceding-sibling** and **following-sibling** XPath axes, so you must include it to complete the total count. This gives the final formula of: **count(../preceding-sibling::*) + count(../following-sibling::*) + 1**.

4. Preview the form.

When the form opens, a **1** should be displayed in the text box bound to **field2**. Click **Insert item** to insert another row. The number in the **field2** text box should now display a **2**. Insert and then remove rows to see how the count changes.

Discussion

An XPath axis defines a node-set (set of nodes) relative to the current node. The **preceding-sibling** axis selects all siblings before the current node, while the **following-sibling** axis selects all siblings after the current node.

In the recipe above,

```
count(../preceding-sibling::*)
```

counts all of the **group2** nodes that are located before the **group2** node above the current field (**field2**), while

```
count(../following-sibling::*)
```

counts all of the **group2** nodes that are located after the **group2** node above the current field (**field2**). And because the **group2** node of the current field (**field2**) is excluded by the XPath axes, you must add a 1 to the total sum, which gives you the final formula:

```
count(../preceding-sibling::*) + count(../following-sibling::*) + 1
```

that counts the amount of rows in a repeating table from a field located within the repeating table.

The following figure visually explains how the XPath navigation of the recipe above works:

1. The navigation starts at the context node, which is **field2**.

2. The parent of the context node is retrieved. This is the **group2** node of the **field2** node.

3. Starting from the **group2** node of the **field2** node, all of the **group2** nodes preceding the current **group2** node are retrieved.

4. Starting from the **group2** node of the **field2** node, all of the **group2** nodes following the current **group2** node are retrieved.

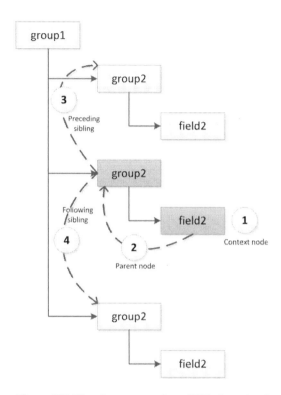

Figure 127. Visual representation of XPath navigation using axes.

Other useful XPath axes you could use in InfoPath formulas include:

- Ancestor – selects all ancestors (parent, grandparent, etc.) of the current node

- Ancestor-or-self – selects all ancestors (parent, grandparent, etc.) of the current node and the current node itself

- Child – selects all children of the current node.

- Descendant – selects all descendants (children, grandchildren, etc.) of the current node.

- Descendant-or-self - selects all descendants (children, grandchildren, etc.) of the current node and the current node itself

235

- Parent – selects the parent of the current node.
- Self – selects the current node

88. Automatically number repeating table rows

Problem

You have a repeating table on an InfoPath form and want the first column of the repeating table to contain a number that is automatically calculated whenever you add a row to or remove a row from the repeating table.

Solution

You can use the **preceding-sibling** XPath axis to automatically number rows in a repeating table.

To automatically number repeating table rows:

1. In InfoPath, create a new **Blank Form** template.
2. Add a **Repeating Table** control to the form template.
3. Right-click the text box in the first column of the repeating table and select **Change Control ➤ Calculated Value** from the context menu that appears.
4. With the first field (**field1**) still selected, click **Properties ➤ Properties ➤ Default Value**.
5. On the **Field or Group Properties** dialog box on the **Data** tab under the **Default Value** section, click the formula button behind the **Value** text box.
6. On the **Insert Formula** dialog box, select the **Edit XPath (advanced)** check box.
7. On the **Insert Formula** dialog box, type the follow formula in the **Formula** text box:

   ```
   count(../preceding-sibling::*) + 1
   ```

   What this formula does is:

   a. Start at the context node, which is **field1**. This is the node on which you are currently setting the default value.

   b. Move to its parent (..), which is a **group2** node.

   c. Get all of the preceding-siblings of the **group2** node (**../preceding-sibling::***), so get all of the **group2** nodes that lie before the **group2** node of the context node.

d. Count all of the **group2** nodes that lie before the **group2** node of the context node (**count(../preceding-sibling::*)**) and add a 1 to it (**count(../preceding-sibling::*) + 1**), because if the context node's parent is the first **group2** node in the repeating table, the amount will be zero (**0**), while you want the number to be **1**.

8. On the **Insert Formula** dialog box, click **Verify Formula** to ensure that the formula does not contain any errors. Click **OK** to close the message box that says whether the formula contains or does not contain errors. Correct any errors if necessary.

9. On the **Insert Formula** dialog box, click **OK**.

10. On the **Field or Group Properties** dialog box, ensure that the **Refresh value when formula is recalculated** check box is selected, and then click **OK**. This will ensure that whenever you add or delete a row from the repeating table, all of the **field1** field values in the repeating table will be recalculated.

11. Preview the form.

When the form opens, add a couple of rows to the repeating table and see how the rows are sequentially numbered. Then remove any row and see how the numbers are recalculated.

89. Copy data from the previous row to a new row

Problem

You have a repeating table on an InfoPath form and whenever you enter values into a row and then click insert item to insert a new row, you want the values from the previous row to be copied over to the new row.

Solution

You can use the **preceding-sibling** XPath axis to retrieve all previous rows of the context row and then apply a filter to return only the first previous row for the context row.

To copy data from a previous row in a repeating table to a new row:

1. In InfoPath, create a new **Blank Form** template.

2. Add a **Repeating Table** control to the form template.

3. Set the **Default Value** of each field in the repeating table to the following formula:

```
../preceding-sibling::my:group2[1]/my:field1
```

The formula above has been set on the first field (**field1**) in the repeating table. You will have to change the last part of this formula for each field you add the formula to (for example, **field2**, **field3**, etc.).

Deselect the **Refresh value when formula is recalculated** check box after you have set the default value. This is to prevent all fields from being changed (recalculated) if you go back and edit data in an existing row.

4. Preview the form.

When the form opens, enter data into the first row of the repeating table, and then click **Insert item** to add a new row. The text string(s) from the first row should be copied over to the second row. Now change some text in the second row and click **Insert item** to add a third row. The text from the second row should now be copied over to the third row.

Go back to the first row and change some text. If you deselected the **Refresh value when formula is recalculated** check box (as specified in step 3 of the recipe) for the default value, the data in the subsequent rows (2 and 3) should not change when you add a new row. Had you left the **Refresh value when formula is recalculated** check box selected, the data in the same field in all of the rows after the first row would have changed to what you typed into the field in the first row when you added a new row.

Go back to an existing row, click on the blue icon with an arrow, and select **Insert group2 after** from the drop-down menu that appears. A new row should be inserted after the row you are currently on and the values from the current row should be copied to the new row.

Discussion

The formula used in this recipe can be constructed as follows (also see the figure below):

1. The context node is the node you are setting the default value on; **field1** in this case.

2. You want to set the value of **field1** to the value of the **field1** in the preceding row, so you must navigate to the preceding row. And to do this, you must find the **group2** node that is the preceding sibling of the **group2** node that is the parent of the **field1** context node. So first you must use **..** to navigate to the parent of **field1**. This gives you **..** as the formula.

3. Then you must find all of the preceding siblings of the **group2** node of the context node, so you must use **preceding-sibling::my:group2**. This gives you **../preceding-sibling::my:group2** as the formula.

4. Once you have all of the preceding **group2** nodes, you only want the first preceding one, so must add a filter (**[1]**) that returns only the first preceding **group2** node. This gives you **../preceding-sibling::my:group2[1]** as the formula.

5. And once you have the first preceding **group2** node, you can navigate down to find the **field1** under that **group2** node. This results in the final formula: **../preceding-sibling::my:group2[1]/my:field1**.

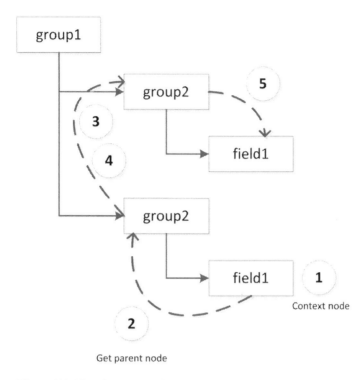

Figure 128. Flow for getting the value of a field in the previous row.

90. Auto-populate a repeating table with week periods

Problem

You have a repeating table on an InfoPath form and want to automatically populate two date picker controls in the first and second columns with week periods, where you fill in the first date in the repeating table and then have all the other date picker controls automatically populate.

Solution

You can expand on the technique described in *89 Copy data from the previous row to a new row* to automatically calculate dates and date periods in a repeating table.

To automatically populate a repeating table with week periods:

1. In InfoPath, create a new **Blank Form** template.

2. Add a **Repeating Table** control with 3 columns to the form template.

3. Change the text boxes in the repeating table into **Date Picker** controls. Name the first date picker control **startDate** and the second date picker control **endDate**. Leave the third text box a text box, but change its name to **previousDate** and delete the column for the text box and the text box itself from the repeating table, but not from the Main data source (by doing this you will be making it a hidden field; see *10 Add a hidden field*). You will be using **previousDate** as a field to help perform calculations in the repeating table.

4. To create a week period, you must first add 6 days to **startDate**. This means that the value of **endDate** should be set to a formula that adds 6 days to **startDate**. So set the **Default Value** of **endDate** to the following formula:

    ```
    addDays(startDate, 6)
    ```

    and ensure that the **Refresh value when formula is recalculated** check box is selected.

5. Once you have calculated **endDate** for a week period, you want the next **startDate** to start one day after the last **endDate**. So here you have to apply the technique from *89 Copy data from the previous row to a new row* to lookup the **endDate** in the previous row of the repeating table, and then use the **addDays** function in a formula to add 1 day to it. But because the **addDays** function only accepts a date as its first argument (and not an XPath axis), you must use a workaround by first retrieving **endDate** in the previous row by using an XPath expression with the **preceding-sibling** axis, and set **previousDate** to this value, and then use the **addDays** function to add 1 day to **previousDate** and set the result to be the value of **startDate**.

    First set the **Default Value** of **previousDate** to the following formula:

    ```
    ../preceding-sibling::my:group2[1]/my:endDate
    ```

    and then set the **Default Value** of **startDate** to the following formula:

    ```
    addDays(previousDate, 1)
    ```

    Ensure that the **Refresh value when formula is recalculated** check box is selected on both default values. Note: To set the default value on a hidden field (**previousDate**), you must open the **Field or Group Properties** dialog box for that field by double-clicking on the field on the **Fields** task pane, and then set its **Default Value** property.

6. Preview the form.

When the form opens, enter a date in the first date picker (start date). The end date should automatically be calculated and populated in the second date picker. Then click on **Insert item** to add a new row to the repeating table. Both date pickers should be automatically populated with dates for the following week period. Continue adding rows to the repeating table and see how each row is populated with a week period.

91. Count the number of occurrences of a word in a repeating table

Problem

You have a repeating table on an InfoPath form and want to know in how many rows the word "Apple" appears in the first column of the repeating table.

Solution

You can use the **count** and **contains** functions to search for and count the number of a particular text string in a field in a repeating table.

To count the number of occurrences of the word "Apple" in a field in a repeating table:

1. In InfoPath, create a new **Blank Form** template.

2. Add a **Repeating Table** and a **Text Box** control to the form template.

3. Add 5 default rows to the repeating table and fill the first field (**field1**) in each row with random words, of which 2 of them should contain the word "Apple" (also see *84 Create a repeating table with a fixed number of rows*).

4. Set the following formula as the **Default Value** for the text box:

   ```
   count(../my:group1/my:group2/my:field1[contains(., "Apple")])
   ```

   You can construct this formula as follows:

   a. Open the **Properties** dialog box for the text box and click the button behind the **Default Value** text box.

   b. On the **Insert Formula** dialog box, click **Insert Function**.

   c. On the **Insert Function** dialog box, select **Field** in the **Categories** list, select **count** in the **Functions** list, and click **OK**.

   d. On the **Insert Formula** dialog box, double-click the text that says "double click to insert field".

   e. On the **Select a Field or Group** dialog box, expand the **group1** node, expand the **group2** node, select **field1**, and click **Filter Data**. Field1 contains the text strings you want to search in, but because you only want to return **field1** instances that contain the word "Apple", you must add a filter that makes use of the **contains** function.

f. On the **Filter Data** dialog box, click **Add**.

g. On the **Specify Filter Conditions** dialog box, select **field1** from the first drop-down list box, select **contains** from the second drop-down list box, select **Type text** from the third drop-down list box, type **Apple**, and click **OK**. Note: You could have also used the **Use a formula** option in the third drop-down list box to select a field that has a value you want to use as the word to search for.

h. Click **OK** when closing all open dialog boxes.

5. Preview the form.

When the form opens, the text box should display a 2 as an indication that the word "Apple" appears in two rows in the first column of the repeating table.

Discussion

The **contains** function in InfoPath takes two arguments: A field or text string to search within, and a field or text string to search for. The **contains** function returns true if the first field or text string contains the second field or text string. Otherwise, it returns false.

As you may have noticed by looking at the formula, filter expressions are put between square brackets in the XPath expression for fields. In the following formula, **[contains(., "Apple")]** is the filter expression in the formula:

```
count(../my:group1/my:group2/my:field1[contains(., "Apple")])
```

What the formula above says when you read it from right to left is: Return all of the **field1** fields under **my:group2** under **my:group1** that contain the word "Apple", and then count how many of these **field1** fields were returned. In essence, you are counting the number of **field1** fields that contain the word "Apple".

You may have noticed that if column one contains an instance of the word "apple", so a word that has all lowercase characters, the **contains** function does not find such instances. This is because the **contains** function is looking for an exact match for the word.

To make the **contains** function look for any match, you must first convert the word you are searching for to either uppercase or lowercase, and then perform a search on either "APPLE" or "apple".

You can use the **translate** function (also see *17 Capitalize text in a text box*) to convert a word to uppercase by using

```
translate("My Word", " abcdefghijklmnopqrstuvwxyz", "ABCDEFGHIJKLMNOPQRSTUVWXYZ
")
```

or to lowercase by using

```
translate("My Word", "ABCDEFGHIJKLMNOPQRSTUVWXYZ", "abcdefghijklmnopqrstuvwxyz")
```

In the recipe above, you can replace the formula with the following formula to be able to perform a non-case-sensitive search.

```
count(../my:group1/my:group2/my:field1[contains(translate(.,
"ABCDEFGHIJKLMNOPQRSTUVWXYZ", "abcdefghijklmnopqrstuvwxyz"), "apple")])
```

This formula uses the **translate** function within the **contains** function to convert **field1** instances to lowercase before comparing them to the word "apple".

92. Highlight the last row of a repeating table

Problem

You have a repeating table on an InfoPath form and you want the last row of the repeating table to be continuously shown as highlighted with a distinguishable background color.

Solution

You can use conditional formatting on rows of a repeating table to highlight the last row of a repeating table.

To highlight the last row of a repeating table:

1. In InfoPath, create a new **Blank Form** template.

2. Add a **Repeating Table** control to the form template.

3. Select the repeating table and then click **Home ➤ Rules ➤ Manage Rules**.

4. On the **Rules** task pane, ensure that **group2** is listed below the title bar (if it is not, click the text "Repeating Table" on the repeating table to select it; do not click a field inside of the repeating table). You want to add conditional formatting to the repeating group (so to rows in the table), not to an individual field within the repeating group.

5. On the **Rules** task pane, click **New ➤ Formatting**.

6. On the **Rules** task pane, change the background color to a color of your choice.

7. On the **Rules** task pane under **Condition**, click the text **None**.

8. On the **Condition** dialog box, select **The expression** from the first drop-down list box, and then type the following expression into the text box:

```
count(following-sibling::*) = 0
```

9. On the **Condition** dialog box, click **OK**.

10. Preview the form.

When the form opens, the last row of the repeating table should be shown as highlighted and should remain highlighted as you add and remove rows from the repeating table.

Discussion

What the expression **count(following-sibling::*) = 0** does is count the amount of rows (**group2** repeating group nodes) that follow any row while going through all of the rows of the repeating table. Remember that you added the formatting rule on a row (and all rows) of the repeating table, so the condition will be applied to all rows of the repeating table.

Because there are zero rows that follow the last row, the expression for the condition will evaluate to true for that row, so that row will be highlighted.

You may have noticed that the fields within the last row of the repeating table were not highlighted. This is because you applied formatting to the rows in the repeating table and not to the fields.

If you also want the fields to be highlighted, you can copy the rule you created earlier and apply it to each field within the repeating table as follows:

1. Click the repeating table to select it, and then click **Home ➤ Rules ➤ Manage Rules**.

2. On the **Rules** task pane, click on the drop-down arrow on the right-hand side of the rule you created earlier, and select **Copy Rule** from the drop-down menu that appears. Note: You can also use the **Copy Rule** button at the top of the task pane under the title bar.

3. Click on a field inside of the repeating table to select it, and then on the **Rules** task pane, click on the **Paste Rule** button at the top of the task pane under the title bar.

Figure 129. Paste Rule button enabled on the Rules task pane after copying an existing rule.

4. Repeat the previous step for each field that you want to highlight within the repeating table.

93. Highlight alternating rows in a repeating table

Problem

You have a repeating table on an InfoPath form and you want every second row of the repeating table to have a different background color compared to the other rows.

Solution

You can use conditional formatting on rows of a repeating table to highlight alternating rows in a repeating table.

To highlight alternating rows in a repeating table:

1. In InfoPath, create a new **Blank Form** template.

2. Add a **Repeating Table** control to the form template.

3. Select the repeating table and click **Home ➤ Rules ➤ Manage Rules**.

4. On the **Rules** task pane, ensure that **group2** is listed below the title bar (if it is not, click the text "Repeating Table" on the repeating table to select it; do not click a field inside of the repeating table). You want to add conditional formatting to the repeating group (so to rows in the table), not to an individual field within the repeating group.

5. On the **Rules** task pane, click **New ➤ Formatting**.

6. On the **Rules** task pane under **Formatting**, change the background color to a color of your choice.

7. On the **Rules** task pane under **Condition**, click the text **None**.

8. On the **Condition** dialog box, select **The expression** from the first drop-down list box, and then type the following expression into the text box:

```
(count(preceding-sibling::*) + 1) mod 2 = 0
```

9. On the **Condition** dialog box, click **OK**.

10. Preview the form.

When the form opens, add a few rows to the repeating table. The second row and every second row thereafter should have the background color you specified for the formatting.

If you want the highlighting to start on the first row and then on every second row thereafter, change the expression to the following:

```
count(preceding-sibling::*) mod 2 = 0
```

And if you want every third row to be highlighted, you can use

```
(count(preceding-sibling::*) + 1) mod 3 = 0
```

Discussion

What the expression **count(preceding-sibling::*) = 0** does is count the amount of rows (**group2** repeating group nodes) that lie before any row while going through all of the rows of the repeating table.

mod is a mathematical function that returns a zero if what is specified in front of **mod** divided by what's specified behind **mod** does not have a remainder

For example: 19 mod 4 = 3 because 19 divided by 4 equals 4 with a remainder of 3 (4 x 4 = 16 and 19 – 16 = 3 so the remainder is 3).

Likewise: 16 mod 4 = 0 because 16 divided by 4 equals 4 with a remainder of 0 (4 x 4 = 16 and 16 – 16 = 0 so the remainder is 0).

In the recipe above, every time the expression of the condition results in a zero, formatting is applied to a row. To be able to highlight every other row, you must first count how many rows lie before the current row (while going through all of the rows of the repeating table) and then if the count mod 2 equals zero, that row should be highlighted.

94. Change a green repeating table to red if it contains more than 3 rows

Problem

You have a repeating table on an InfoPath form that has a green background color. As soon as you add more than 3 rows to the repeating table, you want the background color to change from green to red.

Solution

You can use conditional formatting on section controls that each contains an instance of the repeating table to change the color of the repeating table based on the amount of rows in the repeating table.

To change a green repeating table to red if it contains more than 3 rows:

1. In InfoPath, create a new **Blank Form** template.

2. Add two **Section** controls (named **group1** and **group2**) to the form template and ensure that there are no empty lines between the two section controls.

3. Click inside of the first section control and add a **Repeating Table** control to it. Delete any empty lines that are located above and below the repeating table within the section control. On the **Fields** task pane, **group1** should now contain a group named **group3** that contains the repeating group (**group4**) for the repeating table.

4. Select the entire repeating table, right-click it, and select **Borders and Shading** from the context menu that appears.

5. On the **Borders and Shading** dialog box, click the **Shading** tab, select **Color**, select green from the color picker, and click **OK**.

6. On the **Fields** task pane, drag **group4** to the form template, and drop it inside of the second section control. Select **Repeating Table** from the context menu when you drop the repeating group. Delete any empty lines that are located above and below the repeating table within the section control. InfoPath should now show information icons on all of the fields in both repeating tables saying that "Control stores duplicate data". Do not worry about this, because you will be showing only one repeating table at a time depending on how many **group4** rows are present.

7. Select the entire repeating table in the second section control, right-click it, and select **Borders and Shading** from the context menu that appears.

8. On the **Borders and Shading** dialog box, click the **Shading** tab, select **Color**, select red from the color picker, and click **OK**.

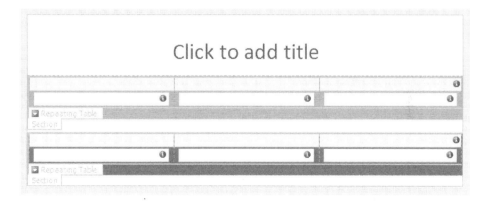

Figure 130. Two section controls containing a reference to the same repeating group.

9. Click the first section control (**group1**) to select it, and then click **Home ▶ Rules ▶ Manage Rules**.

10. On the **Rules** task pane, ensure **group1** is listed as the selected group below the title bar, and then click **New ➤ Formatting** to add a formatting rule.

11. On the **Rules** task pane under **Formatting**, select the **Hide this control** check box, and then under **Condition** click the text **None**.

12. You want to hide the first section (which contains the green repeating table) if there are more than 3 rows in the repeating table, so on the **Condition** dialog box, select **The expression** from the first drop-down list box, type the following formula in the text box:

```
count(my:group3/my:group4) > 3
```

and then click **OK**. Remember that you can use the **Use a formula** option in the third drop-down list box to construct the formula to be used as an expression on the **Condition** dialog box (also see *30 Set a maximum length on a text box* where this trick was explained for the first time).

13. Click the second section control (**group2**) to select it, and then click **Home ➤ Rules ➤ Manage Rules**.

14. On the **Rules** task pane, ensure **group2** is listed as the selected group below the title bar, and then click **New ➤ Formatting** to add a formatting rule.

15. On the **Rules** task pane under **Formatting**, select the **Hide this control** check box, and then under **Condition** click the text **None**.

16. You want to hide the second section (which contains the red repeating table) if there are 3 rows or less in the repeating table, so on the **Condition** dialog box, select **The expression** from the first drop-down list box, type the following formula in the text box:

```
count(../my:group1/my:group3/my:group4) <= 3
```

and then click **OK**. Remember that you can use the **Use a formula** option in the third drop-down list box to construct the formula to be used as an expression on the **Condition** dialog box (also see *30 Set a maximum length on a text box* where this trick was explained for the first time).

17. Preview the form.

When the form opens, the repeating table should be green. Add a couple of rows to the repeating table. As soon as you go over 3 rows, the repeating table should turn to red. Delete rows (by clicking on the down arrow icon to the left of a row and selecting **Remove group4** from the drop-down menu that appears) until you have 3 rows or less, at which point the repeating table should turn to green again.

Discussion

The trick to this recipe is having one section replace another section by placing them in such a way on the form template that there are no spaces in between them. Section controls give up their space when they are hidden and in this recipe you are making use of this fact.

Another thing to be aware of is that background colors that you set via the **Borders and Shading** dialog box cannot be accessed through rules, which is why you used section controls as containers to be able to switch colors on two controls that are bound to the same repeating group in the data source, so which display the same data in the same way, but with a different look and feel.

In the recipe above, when you wanted to delete a row from the repeating table, you selected a menu item that was called **Remove group4**. In general, this is a very bad name for a menu item and does not tell users much. You can customize these menu items on a repeating table through the **Properties** dialog box of the repeating table. For example, if you wanted to change the menu item to **Remove row** instead of **Remove group4**, you would have to do the following:

1. Open the **Repeating Table Properties** dialog box.

2. On the **Repeating Table Properties** dialog box on the **Data** tab under the **Default settings** section, click **Customize Commands**.

3. On the **Table Commands** dialog box, select **Remove** in the **Action** list, and then change the **Command name** from **Remove group4** to **Remove row**. Repeat this step to change the text for all of the menu items you would like to change, and then click **OK**. Note: You can remove menu items by deselecting the check box that is located in front of them in the **Action** list.

4. On the **Repeating Table Properties** dialog box, click **OK**.

The repeating table should now display the menu item with the new name when you use its drop-down menu to remove a row.

95. Hide the first row of a repeating table

Problem

You have a repeating table on an InfoPath form and you want to hide the first row in that repeating table.

Solution

You can use a formula together with the **preceding-sibling** XPath axis to find and hide the first row of a repeating table.

To hide the first row of a repeating table:

1. In InfoPath, create a new **Blank Form** template.

2. Add a **Repeating Table** control to the form template.

3. Select the repeating table and then click **Home ➤ Rules ➤ Manage Rules**.

4. On the **Rules** task pane, ensure that **group2** is listed below the title bar (if it is not, click the text "Repeating Table" on the repeating table to select it; do not click a field inside of the repeating table). You want to add conditional formatting to the repeating group (so to rows in the table), not to an individual field within the repeating group.

5. On the **Rules** task pane, click **New ➤ Formatting**.

6. On the **Rules** task pane under **Formatting**, select the **Hide this control** check box.

7. On the **Rules** task pane under **Condition**, click the text **None.**

8. On the **Condition** dialog box, select **The expression** from the first drop-down list box, and then type the following expression into the text box:

    ```
    count(preceding-sibling::*) = 0
    ```

9. On the **Condition** dialog box, click **OK**.

10. Preview the form.

When the form opens, the first row of the repeating table should be hidden.

Discussion

What the expression **count(preceding-sibling::*) = 0** does is count the amount of rows (**group2** repeating groups) that lie before any row (**group2** group node) while going through all of the rows of the repeating table. Remember that you added the formatting rule on a row (and all rows) of the repeating table, so the condition will be applied to all rows of the repeating table.

Because only the first row has no rows preceding it, the expression for the condition will evaluate to true for this row, so this row will be hidden.

96. Hide a row of a repeating table when a check box is selected

Problem

You have a repeating table on an InfoPath form that represents a task list. You want to be able to select a check box in any row of the repeating table and have that row become invisible.

Solution

You can use conditional formatting to hide rows of a repeating table.

To hide a row of a repeating table when a check box is selected:

1. In InfoPath, create a new **Blank Form** template.

2. Add a **Repeating Table** control with 2 columns to the form template.

3. Delete the control from the second column both on the form template and on the **Fields** task pane, and then place the cursor in the second empty cell and add a **Check Box** control to it. Name the check box control **isHidden**.

4. Select the repeating table and then click **Home ➤ Rules ➤ Manage Rules**.

5. On the **Rules** task pane, ensure that **group2** is listed below the title bar (if it is not, click the text "Repeating Table" on the repeating table to select it; do not click a field inside of the repeating table). You want to add conditional formatting to the repeating group (so to rows in the table), not to an individual field within the repeating group.

6. On the **Rules** task pane, click **New ➤ Formatting**.

7. On the **Rules** task pane under **Formatting**, select the **Hide this control** check box.

8. On the **Rules** task pane under **Condition**, click the text **None**.

9. On the **Condition** dialog box, select **isHidden** from the first drop-down list box, leave **is equal to** selected in the second drop-down list box, select **TRUE** from the third drop-down list box, and click **OK**. The following formula should now appear on the **Rules** task pane under **Condition**:

   ```
   isHidden = TRUE
   ```

   The formatting rule you just added hides any row in the repeating table if the **isHidden** check box in that row is selected.

10. Preview the form.

When the form opens, add a few rows to the repeating table and type some unique text in each row. Select a check box in any row. That row should then disappear from view.

Discussion

If you hide a few rows in a repeating table and then save or submit the form, those rows will remain hidden from view but will also remain present in the Main data source of the form. You can see this if you open the XML file of the InfoPath form in Notepad. Using conditional formatting to hide rows does not delete the rows, but just hides them from view.

Exercise

Instead of hiding a row, try setting formatting on **field1** in the repeating table to display the text in **field1** as strike-through when the check box is selected.

97. Lock rows of a repeating table using check boxes

Problem

You have a repeating table on an InfoPath form and want to disable a row so that fields in it cannot be modified when you select a check box within that row.

Solution

You can use a conditional formatting on fields in rows of a repeating table to disable them when a check box in the same row as that field is selected.

To lock rows of a repeating table using check boxes:

1. In InfoPath, create a new **Blank Form** template.

2. Add a **Repeating Table** control with 3 columns to the form template. Replace the third text box in the repeating table by a **Check Box** control, and name the check box control **isLocked**.

3. For each field in the repeating table that you want to "lock", add a **Formatting** rule to the field with a **Condition** that says:

   ```
   isLocked = TRUE
   ```

   and apply a **Formatting** of **Disable this control**.

4. Preview the form.

When the form opens, enter text in any of the fields for which you set up a formatting rule, and then select the check box in the same row as that field. The field should be locked and you should not be able to modify the text in that field. Add more rows to the repeating table and try locking fields in other rows.

Discussion

While the recipe above locks fields on an individual basis, there might be instances where you want to lock all fields in a row collectively. Because a repeating table does not support disabling a row through conditional formatting, you could choose to hide the row instead.

98. Make a repeating table read-only

Problem

You have a repeating table in InfoPath which you want to make read-only in its entirety.

Solution

You can make a repeating table read-only by making each field in the repeating table read-only by disabling the control.

To make a repeating table read-only:

1. In InfoPath, create a new **Blank Form** template.

2. Add a **Repeating Table** to the form template.

3. Click **Home ➤ Rules ➤ Manage Rules**.

4. Click one of the fields in the repeating table to select it, and then on the **Rules** task pane, click **New ➤ Formatting**.

5. On the **Rules** task pane under **Formatting**, select the **Disable this control** check box.

6. On the **Rules** task pane under **Condition**, click the text **None**.

7. On the **Condition** dialog box, select **The expression** from the first drop-down list box, type **true()** in the text box, and click **OK**.

8. On the **Rules** task pane, click the rule you just added, and select **Copy Rule** from the drop-down menu that appears.

9. Click another field in the repeating table that you want to make read-only to select it, and then on the **Rules** task pane, click the **Paste Rule** button below the title bar to paste the rule. Repeat this step for all of the other fields you want to make read-only.

10. Preview the form.

When the form opens, you should not be able to change any of the fields in the repeating table.

Discussion

By setting the expression for a condition on a rule to **true()**, the formatting rule will always run and run as soon as the form opens.

Some controls such as the text box controls have a **Read-only** property you can configure to make the control read-only, but many controls in InfoPath do not have such a property. If a control does not have a read-only property, then you must use conditional formatting to disable the control and make it read-only.

But you cannot apply conditional formatting to all controls in InfoPath either, because not all controls support it. For example, a file attachment control on a Web Browser Form and container controls do not support conditional formatting. In such cases, you would have to configure the control to disallow the user to browse, delete, and replace files (in the case of the file attachment control) or put the control on a read-only view (see *14 Add a read-only view*).

In the recipe above, you made the controls in the rows of the repeating table read-only, but users are still able to add and delete rows. If you do not want to allow users to add or delete rows, you must deselect the **Allow users to insert and delete rows** check box on the **Repeating Table Properties** dialog box. This will make the repeating table completely read-only. And if you want the repeating table to be read-only based on a condition, you can apply the same trick as explained in *94 Change a green repeating table to red if it contains more than 3 rows* to switch between a readable and a read-only version of the repeating table based on a condition.

99. Cascading drop-down list boxes in a repeating table

Problem

You have a repeating table with two drop-down list boxes in it and want to be able to select an item from the first drop-down list box and then have the second drop-down list box be populated with items related to the selected item in the first drop-down list box.

Solution

In this recipe, you will use the **RunningShoes** XML file that was used in *48 Populate a drop-down list box from an XML file*, but this time you will populate the first drop-down list box with brand names and the second drop-down list box should contain the running shoes models for the selected brand.

To create cascading drop-down list boxes in a repeating table:

1. In InfoPath, create a new **Blank Form** template.

2. Add a **Repeating Table** control with 2 columns to the form template.

3. Add a **Drop-Down List Box** control to the first column of the repeating table (see *83 4 Ways to add a rich text box to a repeating table* for how to add controls other than text boxes to a repeating table) and a second drop-down list box to the second column of the repeating table. Name the first drop-down list box **brand** and the second drop-down list box **model**.

4. Populate the first drop-down list box with data from the **RunningShoes** XML file (see *48 Populate a drop-down list box from an XML file*) by adding the XML file as a Secondary data source to the form template and then specifying it to be used as the data source for the drop-down list boxes. Use the brand **name** as the **Value** and **Display name** for the first drop-down list box.

5. Open the **Drop-Down List Box Properties** dialog box for the second drop-down list box, select the **RunningShoes** data source as the external data source the drop-down list box should get data from, and click the button behind the **Entries** text box.

6. On the **Select a Field or Group** dialog box, expand all of the nodes, select **model**, and click **Filter Data**. Because the items in the second drop-down list box should depend on the **brand** that is selected from the first drop-down list box, you must add a filter that filters **models** on **brand** but also only looks at the **brand** that is selected in the current row.

7. On the **Filter Data** dialog box, click **Add**.

8. On the **Specify Filter Conditions** dialog box, select **Select a field or group** from the first drop-down list box.

9. On the **Select a Field or Group** dialog box, ensure **RunningShoes (Secondary)** is selected in the **Data source** drop-down list box, select **name** under **brand**, and click **OK**.

10. You want the brand **name** in the **RunningShoes** Secondary data source to be the same as the brand **name** selected in the first drop-down list box which is located in the Main data source, so on the **Specify Filter Conditions** dialog box, select **Use a formula** from the third drop-down list box.

11. On the **Insert Formula** dialog box, type **current()/my:brand**. **current()** gives you a reference to the current row (**group2** group node) in the repeating table and **my:brand** is the XPath expression to the **brand** field under the **group2** group node of the current row.

12. Click **OK** when closing all dialog boxes.

13. To prevent any previously selected item from appearing in the **model** drop-down list box whenever you reselect an item from the **brand** drop-down list box, you must add a rule to the **brand** drop-down list box to clear the **model** drop-down list box. So click the **brand** drop-down list box to select it, click **Home ➤ Rules**

➤ **Manage Rules**, and then on the **Rules** task pane add an **Action** rule with the following action:

```
Set a field's value: model = ""
```

14. Preview the form.

When the form opens, verify that the second drop-down list box is empty, and then select a brand from the first drop-down list box. The second drop-down list box should be populated with shoe models for the selected brand.

Add several rows to the repeating table, and then from any row select a brand from the first drop-down list box. When you look in the second drop-down list box in the same row as the drop-down list box from which you just selected a brand, the second drop-down list box should contain the running shoe models for the brand you selected.

Discussion

If you do not know the XPath expression to a field, you can use the **Copy XPath** functionality to look it up.

In the recipe above in step 11, an assumption was made that you know that you can retrieve the value of the brand field through the **my:brand** XPath expression when your context node is a **group2** group. But if in reality you do not know that this is the case, you can click on **brand** on the **Fields** task pane in InfoPath Designer 2010, click on the down arrow on the right-hand side of **brand**, and select **Copy XPath** from the drop-down menu that appears. This will copy the following XPath expression to the Windows clipboard:

```
/my:myFields/my:group1/my:group2/my:brand
```

Because **current()** gives you a reference to the current row in a repeating table, and **my:group2** represents a row in the repeating table, you can delete everything in the XPath expression starting from **my:group2** going backwards and replace it with **current()**, which will result in the following XPath expression:

```
current()/my:brand
```

The expression above returns the value of **brand** selected in the first column of the repeating table and located in the same row of the repeating table where the second drop-down list box is currently being populated.

If you look at the **Entries** text box on the **Drop-Down List Box Properties** dialog box of the second drop-down list box, you will see the following XPath expression:

```
/ns1:brands/ns1:brand/ns1:type/ns1:model[../../@name = current()/my:brand]
```

The following figure shows how the **group2** group relates to a repeating table and where **current()** fits into the entire picture.

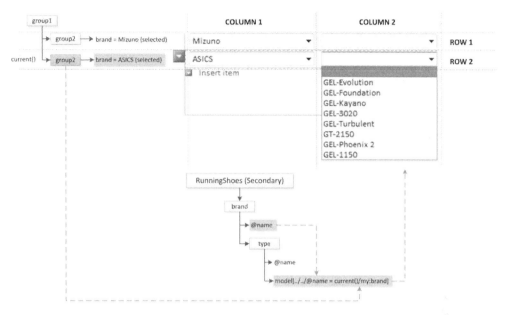

Figure 131. Relationship between repeating table, data sources, and current().

How to interpret the figure displayed above:

- The **RunningShoes** Secondary data source is used to populate the drop-down list boxes in both columns of the repeating table.

- The drop-down list box in the first column is populated with brand names (**RunningShoes ➤ brand ➤ @name**).

- Mizuno is selected as the brand in the drop-down list box in the first column and first row of the repeating table and ASICS is selected as the brand in the drop-down list box in the first column and second row of the repeating table.

- The drop-down list box in the second column is populated with models (**RunningShoes ➤ model**), but is filtered on the brand name in the Secondary data source being equal to the selected brand name in the Main data source in the first column in the same row (**RunningShoes ➤ model ➤** where **brand/@name = current()/my:brand**).

- The items in the drop-down list box in the second column and second row of the repeating table are being displayed, and because ASICS was selected in the drop-down list box in the first column and second row of the repeating table, the drop-down list box in the second column and second row of the repeating table displays ASICS running shoe models.

This recipe does not have to be restricted to looking up data in the same Secondary data source that is used to populate two drop-down list boxes. You could populate each drop-down list box with data from two different Secondary data sources and still use the technique described above to create dependent or cascading drop-down list boxes in a repeating table.

100. Export a repeating table's contents as a string

Problem

You have a repeating table that has one column containing a text box and you want all of the text entered in rows of the repeating table to be concatenated to form one long string.

Solution

You can use the **eval** function to export the contents of all of the rows in a repeating table.

To export a repeating table's contents as a string to a text box:

1. In InfoPath, create a new **Blank Form** template.

2. Add a **Repeating Table** control with one column and a **Text Box** control to the form template.

3. Set the **Default Value** of the text box outside of the repeating table to the following formula

   ```
   eval(group2, "..")
   ```

   and ensure that the **Refresh value when formula is recalculated** check box has been selected. In the formula above, **group2** represents the repeating group bound to a repeating table.

4. Preview the form.

When the form opens, type a piece of text in the text box within the repeating table. Move away from the text box by clicking elsewhere on the form. The second text box below the repeating table should be updated to contain the value from the text box within the repeating table. Add a couple of rows to the repeating table with more text and see how the text in the text box below the repeating table is updated.

Discussion

The **eval** function returns the values of a field or group, and takes two arguments. The first argument defines the field or group the **eval** function should operate on, and the second argument defines the expression to calculate for the field or group. Usually, the **eval** function is nested within a function that operates on a field or group, such as **sum** or **avg**.

The formula in the recipe above returns the value of the anonymous parent (**".."**), which is a concatenated string of all of the parent's children (**group2** nodes). The latter is a W3C standard.

If you have three rows in the repeating table with the text "a", "b", and "c", respectively, the resulting value of the formula would be "a b c".

101. Export a repeating table's contents to a text box with line breaks

Problem

You have a first name and last name column in a repeating table to capture a list of contact names. You want to be able to loop through all of the names in the rows of the repeating table and construct a list of names (first name plus last name) that can be displayed as one piece of text in a multi-line text box with line-breaks.

Solution

You can use the **eval** function to export the contents of all of the rows in a repeating table.

To generate a list of names with line-breaks from rows in a repeating table:

1. In InfoPath, create a new **Blank Form** template.

2. Add a **Repeating Table** control with 3 columns to the form template. Name the first text box in the repeating table **firstName**, the second text box **lastName**, and the third text box **lineBreak**. Make the **lineBreak** field hidden by deleting the repeating table column it is located in.

3. Add a **Text Box** control to the form template and on its **Properties** dialog box on the **Display** tab, select the **Multi-line** check box to make the text box accept line-breaks and multiple lines of text.

4. Add a data connection to an XML file (see *32 Get data from an XML file*) that has the following contents:

```
<?xml version="1.0" encoding="UTF-8" ?>
<break>&#xD;</break>
```

and name the data connection **LineBreak**.

5. Set the **Default Value** of the **lineBreak** field in the repeating table to be equal to the value of the **break** group in the **LineBreak (Secondary)** data source. Note: To set the default value on a hidden field, you can double-click the hidden field on the **Fields** task pane to access its properties and then set its default value.

6. Set the **Default Value** of the multi-line text box to the following formula:

```
eval(eval(group2, 'concat(normalize-space(concat(my:firstName, " ",
my:lastName)), my:lineBreak)'), "..")
```

Ensure that the **Refresh value when formula is recalculated** check box is selected on the **Properties** dialog box.

7. Preview the form.

When the form opens, type a first and last name into the text boxes in the repeating table. As you type and leave the text boxes, the multi-line text box should be updated. Continue adding rows to the repeating table and typing names. The multi-line text box should eventually be populated with the names from the repeating table as a list of names displayed on separate lines.

Discussion

The **eval** function returns the values of a field or group, and takes two arguments. The first argument defines the field or group the **eval** function should operate on, and the second argument defines the expression to calculate for the field or group. Usually, the **eval** function is nested within a function that operates on a field or group, such as **sum** or **avg**.

In the recipe above, you used the **eval** function twice. The first **eval** function (the inner one) was used as follows:

```
eval(group2, 'concat(normalize-space(concat(my:firstName, " ", my:lastName)),
my:lineBreak)')
```

The preceding formula takes a **group2** node of the repeating table, and returns the concatenation of the **firstName**, **lastName**, and **lineBreak** fields in that **group2** node.

The **group2** in the formula is the group the **eval** function should work on, and the second argument is the expression the **eval** function should perform on that group, so the result of the evaluation.

Let us first dissect the expression for the second argument in the **eval** function above.

First **firstName** and **lastName** are concatenated using the **concat** function. And a space is added between these two fields.

```
concat(my:firstName, " ", my:lastName)
```

Then the **normalize-space** function is used to remove unwanted empty spaces between the concatenation of the first name and the last name (see *19 Join two text strings and remove spaces if either text string is empty*)

```
normalize-space(concat(my:firstName, " ", my:lastName))
```

and then a line-break is appended to the result by using the **concat** function for a second time.

```
concat(normalize-space(concat(my:firstName, " ", my:lastName)), my:lineBreak)
```

And finally, the **eval** function is used on a **group2** node in the repeating table to return the value of the concatenations of its fields (the expression between single quotes).

```
eval(group2, 'concat(normalize-space(concat(my:firstName, " ", my:lastName)),
my:lineBreak)')
```

The second **eval** function (the outer one) is used to retrieve the contents of all of the **group2** nodes as a string. The most basic formula to get this done is the following:

```
eval(group2, "..")
```

The preceding formula returns the value of the anonymous parent ("**..**"), which is a concatenated string of the contents of all of the parent's children (**group2** nodes). The latter is a W3C standard.

In the final formula, you want to get the contents of all of the **group2** nodes, but you also want to apply the concatenation you constructed earlier for a **group2** node to all of the **group2** nodes, so that the line-break is included between the concatenated fields in each **group2** node.

So you must replace **group2** in the previous formula by the **eval** formula you constructed earlier. This results in the following final formula when you combine the two **eval** formulas:

```
eval(eval(group2, 'concat(normalize-space(concat(my:firstName, " ",
my:lastName)), my:lineBreak)'), "..")
```

Index